A GIFT TO THE NATION
From Ohio and Wayne National Forest

The 1987 Capitol Christmas Tree

By Dan Kincaid

DEDICATION

This book is dedicated to the people of Washington and Monroe counties in Ohio who helped with activities, events, publicity, fund raising, and other logistics related to cutting the 1987 Capitol Christmas Tree from the Wayne National Forest and sending it to the nation's Capitol; and a special thank you to the residents of the Frontier Local School District who took such pride in sending "their" tree to Washington, D.C.

This project showed the full potential of what all of our local communities could accomplish.

REVIEWS AND READER COMMENTS

When Dan told me of his plan to nominate the Wayne to provide the U.S. Capitol Christmas Tree for 1987, I had doubts he could pull it off. The Wayne is one of the smaller and more obscure National Forests in the country. But as time passed, with his persistence and vision, things started to fall into place and it became a reality. It became a source of pride for the local community. It was a "big deal" to them that a tree from Washington County would adorn the lawn of our nation's Capitol. Everyone wanted to be involved in the activities surrounding the event and to see that the chosen tree made its way to Washington, D.C. safely. I was glad to be part of the whole process and I still have some treasured mementoes of the occasion.
Dave Greenwood, Retired Forestry Technician, Wayne National Forest

Memories of the Capitol Christmas Tree trip make us think of happy times for so many people. It was a huge community effort from the citizens of a very small community and surrounding areas. No on one shirked, no one complained. All were proud of being a part of our great country. I hope others get to experience the joy and pride we all felt. Our thanks to you, Dan, for spearheading the project. You guided us through the process of selecting the perfect tree, "our tree", and getting it to Washington, DC and allowing the people in attendance to be a unique part of history. Never again

will our small high school band experience playing in our Capitol, nor hearing Mary Carson sing the national anthem, nor singing along with the Congressional members, nor having our handmade ornaments adorn "our" Capitol Tree. Thank you, Dan.
Gil Courtney, President, The Peoples Savings Bank, New Matamoras, OH

Tucked into the hills of southeastern Ohio is a gem, the Wayne National Forest. For 10 years Dan Kincaid wrote many newspaper articles about the environmental, economic and social values of this valuable resource. The story of how the many communities and schools came together to send the 1987 Capitol Christmas Tree to Washington D.C. is one that needs to be told and remembered. It shows the power of people working together to celebrate this great resource and the forest's value to the communities. It also inspires the readers to pursue other possibilities of how the Wayne National Forest can be a focal point to create new opportunities.
Terry Hoffman, Deputy Forest Supervisor, Wayne and Hoosier National Forests, 1987-1989

My wife, Betsy, and I had just returned to Marietta in October 1987 after bicycling around the world on our honeymoon. We quickly learned about another adventure taking place locally. Wayne National Forest Marietta Unit Supervisor Dan Kincaid was undertaking an incredible community effort, transforming a Norway spruce tree from the national forest into the U.S. Capitol Christmas Tree.

Dan always stood out for his advocacy for the Wayne National Forest Marietta Unit, as well as the surrounding Washington County and Southeastern Ohio communities. He was one of the area's biggest cheerleaders for an often forgotten part of our country.

It speaks volumes about Dan that 31 years later in 2018, the 7-by-9-inch spruce plaque made from the actual tree, thanking me for my reporting in The Marietta Times about the National Capitol Christmas Tree, stands in our living room next to a wedding photo. That is one example of how that project touched thousands and is a tribute to Dan's enthusiasm and his love for the forest and our community.

No forestry supervisor before or after Dan brought the energy and compassion he did connecting the Wayne with the Marietta area community. As another example of Dan's continuous community outreach, he distributed dwarf spruce trees to those who attended his retirement gathering in 2006. Our dwarf spruce now grows outside our kitchen window. Although Dan moved from the community years ago, his spirit and enthusiasm remain here every day.

Dan's writings about the Capitol Christmas Tree undoubtedly will bring back many good memories for thousands of people here in the Mid-Ohio Valley.

Roger G. Kalter, former journalist for The Marietta Times and Marietta City Council Representative

The day Dan Kincaid came to our office to ask my father, "R.O." Wetz, if he would be interested in hauling the Capitol Christmas Tree was one of Dad's highlights in life. Of course, there was a quick "yes" and from that day forward until it was delivered, it became R.O. Wetz Transportation's highest priority. Dan, Mack Haessly, and Dad often spoke two to three times a day about the details and plans on how to make it all happen.

Dad was able to secure an oversized trailer from East West Trailer long enough to handle the massive tree. After the tree was down and loaded on the trailer, it was transported to one of our warehouses. Our responsibility was to keep it safe before taking it on over to Washington. While under Dad's supervision, the tree was kept watered and secure under lock and key. The day prior to making the trip, it took six to eight volunteers to tarp and protect the tree during transit.

Our Dad appointed his senior driver, Robert McElfresh, and his 1986 Freightliner Cab-Over to make the final delivery to Washington, D.C. With my Dad following in a van behind the tree, they successfully delivered it to the Nation's Capitol. Many thanks to Dan and the other volunteers of this great community.
E.O. "Tag" Wetz, for the Wetz Family, and R.O. Wetz Transportation/Wetz Warehousing

When asked to join in on cutting the National Capital Christmas Tree, lots of fond memories came to mind of all the family "picnics on the hill," as we called them. The Holdrens would have one every weekend in the summer. They were held just around the bend from where the National Tree was growing. The picnics were at the home of Charles and Cora Ann Holdren, my paternal grandparents. Joseph and Ruth Holdren were my great, great, great, great Grandparents. I have a picture of their home place with a small Norway spruce tree in the yard; we now believe that tree to be the National Capital Tree.

In the days leading up to the tree cutting event many different souvenirs were sold in my shop, Oopsa Daisy Florist in Newport. There were ornaments and glass canister sets with an etching of the tree and date. I still have mine today. When the day of the cutting arrived, a large crowd gathered - TV crews, reporters and many members of the community. Frontier High School even brought busloads of students from school. Everyone was excited. We thought this was the biggest thing ever!

My cousin, Judy Holdren Beaver, and I were given the honor of making the first ceremonial cut on the 1987 National Capital Christmas Tree. With pride and honor, we ran that crosscut saw like we knew what we were doing! Many special memories were made that day.....and still remain.

Sandra Holdren Binegar, owner of Oopsa Daisy Florist, Newport, Ohio and descendant of the original settlers of the property where the 1987 Capitol Christmas Tree was located.

It was a thrilling experience to perform The Star Spangled Banner at our nation's Capitol for the Christmas tree lighting ceremony. Surrounded by my family and friends, I was honored to represent Washington County, Ohio.
Mary Anderson Carson of New Matamoras, who sang the National Anthem at the U.S. Capitol on December 9, 1987 during the Lighting Ceremony

Participating in the Lighting Ceremony for the Capitol Christmas Tree was a terrific opportunity for the members of the Frontier High School Marching Band. Due to the generous donations and bus ticket sales, we were able to travel cost-free and see the Vietnam Memorial Wall, Arlington National Cemetery, and the various monuments prior to the lighting. Cougar pride was flying high as we played Christmas carols on the plaza at the west lawn of the Capitol overlooking the Christmas Tree. During a reception after the ceremony, we were able to meet and talk with members of Congress. It was an unforgettable experience for us all.
Sarah Carson Coulter, member of the 1987 FHS Cougar Marching Band

To this day, thoughts of the 1987 Capital Christmas Tree project trigger unforgettable memories. It was a privilege to be able to assist with the cutting of the Norway spruce from a historical homestead on the Wayne National Forest. Dan Kincaid's vision brought people together and was a phenomenal achievement. The value of the enthusiasm and pride that the project generated cannot be overstated. Forest Service staff and community members came together to ensure that our tree became the People's Tree. Dan, thank you for the vision that made the project a success. It was an honor to be part of the Forest Service family that helped coordinate the activities.

Art Martin, Retired Forestry Technician, Wayne National Forest

In 1987 planning was well underway for the celebration of Marietta's 200th "Birthday," which would occur the following year. It was a time of intense enthusiasm, excitement, and planning in Marietta and all of Washington County. Hundreds of citizens were organizing year long community events, raising funds and taking great pride in marketing our, "First in Ohio," bicentennial celebration. Our history as the first organized settlement in the Northwest Territory in 1788 is a source of community pride, even in today's busy world. In 1987 Ohio's Tourism Slogan was "Ohio, the Heart of it All". In Southern Ohio we promoted: "Ohio the Heart; Marietta and Washington County the Start of it All."

So in 1987 the stage was set to begin our celebration in style with Dan Kincaid, Wayne National Forest Marietta Unit Supervisor leading the way. It was Dan's inspiration and idea that led to Washington County providing the U.S. Capital Christmas tree. Ohio had never promoted a tree for consideration, as we have predominantly hardwoods, but Dan found a Norway spruce that fit the requirements. The selection, cutting, and send off to Washington, D.C. involved a great deal of effort and hard work by local citizens.

The Capital Christmas tree was the spectacular beginning of our year-long Marietta Bicentennial celebration. The D.C. ceremony to light the tree was cold and breezy, but our tree looked majestic. A large delegation from Marietta and Washington County was in attendance. House Speaker Wright, Senator Glenn and a host of other officials were there, also. Speaker Wright flipped the switch and that magnificent Norway spruce, planted on the Holdren homestead so long ago, lit up the sky with glittering lights. Thank you, Dan, for helping to make that event possible.

Nancy Putnam Hollister, Mayor of Marietta, 1984 - 1991

TABLE OF CONTENTS

Page Listing for the Exhibits Chapter:

PREFACE

The modern history of the Capitol Christmas Tree dates back to 1964, when a live 24-foot Douglas fir was purchased from Buddies Nurseries in Birdsboro, Pennsylvania and planted on the west lawn of the United States Capitol in Washington, D.C. According to one website, the Speaker of the U.S. House of Representatives, John W. McCormack, had suggested the idea to J. George Stewart, who was Architect of the Capitol (AOC) at that time and who supervised maintenance of the Capitol Grounds. Another website indicated that Senator Carl Hayden of Arizona, President Pro Tempore of the U.S. Senate, presided over the first lighting ceremony on December 18, 1964.

From all information that I could gather, each year since the initial ceremony in 1964, the Speaker of the House has presided over the tree lighting.

It is also interesting to note that there is some mention in the records of a chorus singing and a lighting ceremony taking place for a 40-foot Norway spruce at the U.S. Capitol on Christmas Eve 1913. Records of the Architect of the Capitol also show correspondence from 1919 that indicates a Christmas tree was purchased that year. And here and there in records and various correspondence since those years, you will find mention of a Christmas tree in the Capitol during the holiday season. However, it was not until 1964 that a definite and formal procedure was initiated and a tree-lighting ceremony established.

Now, back to the 1964 tree. Each year through 1967 this live Douglas fir tree was decorated and a tree-lighting ceremony was held. Unfortunately, a combination of factors, including a severe wind storm in the spring of 1967 and root damage from various causes, led to the tree dying in 1968. It was cut and removed that same year.

The 1968 Christmas tree was put together from two white pines brought in from Finksburg, Maryland. This make-shift tree was 30 feet tall and it was not considered to be an adequate process for future Capitol trees. In 1969 a full 40-foot white pine tree was cut and brought in from Westminster, Maryland.

An idea had been floating around that it would be nice if the tree could be cut and brought in each year from one of the country's National Forests. The USDA Forest Service (USFS) agreed and since 1970 the agency has worked closely with the Capitol Architect to select and coordinate the delivery of the tree to the U.S. Capitol each year. That initial 1970 national forest tree was a 40-foot Norway spruce that came from West Virginia's Monongahela National Forest (NF).

Each year the tree is also accompanied by decorations made by local school children from the tree's home state. Many of these ornaments, as well as some permanent decorations and lights that are stored by the AOC, are used to fully decorate the tree.

A complete listing of the Capitol Christmas Trees by year, species, size, national forest, and state of origin is included as an exhibit in the back of this book. You will notice three exceptions to the tree originating from a national forest. Two of those were in 1977 and 1978, when the tree was supplied from state forests – a 52-foot white spruce from the Nemadji State Forest in Minnesota and a 60-foot Norway spruce from the Savage River State Forest in Maryland, respectively. The USDA Forest Service was still heavily involved with those two efforts, along with the state agencies and, of course, the AOC.

It is not surprising that these two trees came from state forest lands. Since the early 1900's the U.S. Forest Service has worked cooperatively with state agencies in a variety of natural resource activities, especially in firefighting efforts, forest management, and forest health projects. In fact, an entire branch of the USFS, called State & Private Forestry, is devoted to providing technical and financial assistance to states, tribes, and various other non-profits, universities, etc. So, the two state forest trees were widely seen as excellent choices, highlighting the strong federal-state forestry partnership.

In 1982 a 50-foot balsam fir was provided from the Riley Bostwick Wildlife Management Area (WMA) in

Vermont to serve as the Capitol Christmas Tree. That WMA had an interesting history. Mr. Bostwick had a 40-year record of active management of his private woodlands. He was heavily involved in Christmas tree production, as well as other forest management activities. In fact, he had provided Christmas trees for the White House in 1923 and 1967. The White House tree is commonly known as the National Christmas Tree, as distinguished from the U.S. Capitol Christmas Tree, which is often referred to as the People's Tree. The 1923 tree is thought to have been the first-ever National (White House) Christmas Tree.

When Bostwick's property became certified as part of the American Tree Farm System, it was honored as containing the one-millionth acre of certified tree farms in the country. The USFS, through its State and Private Forestry branch, works cooperatively with the states and the American Tree Farm System by serving on state advisory committees and other activities. By 1970 the Vermont Fish & Wildlife Department had acquired the Bostwick property as a gift and currently manages it as public lands for the citizens of the state. When suggested as the source for providing the 1982 Capitol Christmas Tree, it was widely agreed that the 50-foot balsam fir from the Riley Bostwick WMA would be an appropriate choice.

Back in the late 1970's and early 1980's, when I first began to think about the Capitol Christmas Tree, it was commonly assumed that the tree should come from east of the Mississippi River. It was thought that a western location would be too distant and make the transportation logistics too difficult and costly. All trees came from the east until 1986, when a Shasta red fir was provided to the Capitol from California's Klamath National Forest.

The national forest that the tree comes from is chosen a few years ahead of time, so before 1986 the Wayne NF had already been selected to provide the 1987 tree. Mind you, the exact tree is never confirmed by the Capitol's Landscape Architect until a few months prior to its cutting, selected from a pool of candidates.

Because of the public relations successes and positive publicity that the Capitol Christmas Tree had been receiving in the 1970's and early 1980's, those of us in the east began to hear that the western national forests wanted in on the "action," so to speak. But we were safe on the Wayne NF since we were already in the pipeline for the 1987 tree, provided we received final approval of a specific tree from the Capitol's Landscape Architect. More on that later in the book.

But once California got in on the action in 1986, it wasn't long until other western national forests got involved. In 1989, 1990, and 1991 the trees came from Montana, Colorado, and New Mexico. California furnished it again in 1993 and 1995, and over the next

10 years Utah, South Dakota, Colorado again, Oregon, and Idaho got involved.

For the 14 year period from 2005 to this year, 2018, the Capitol Christmas Tree has come from western national forests 12 times. Some are repeat states, but new states include Washington, Arizona, Wyoming, and even Alaska. California national forests have provided four trees, while Colorado and Montana have provided three each. Most of the country's national forests are located in the western states and most of the high level decision makers for the agency are either from the west or have extensive experience working in the west.

So, it will be a minor miracle if the Wayne NF ever provides the Capitol Tree again. Many, many things would have to fall into place and, as they say, the stars would have to align. But, in any case, the local residents in the area surrounding the Marietta Unit of the Wayne National Forest will always remember 1987 fondly – the year that "their tree" served as the U.S. Capitol Christmas Tree.

As far as the "eastern" National Forests go, five trees have come from the state of Michigan, four each from Minnesota and Vermont, and three from Wisconsin.

NOTE – You will see the tree referred to as the Capitol Christmas Tree, the National Capitol Christmas Tree, or the U.S. Capitol Christmas Tree. The last title is probably preferred. Sometimes a tree for a state Capitol may be called their Capitol Christmas Tree, which can cause confusion. And the tree at the White House is usually referred to as the National Christmas Tree, which can also be confused with the National Capitol Christmas Tree.

INTRODUCTION

As early as 1981, I first began thinking about the possibility of a Capitol Christmas Tree coming from the Wayne National Forest in Ohio. I had several reasons in my mind as to why this would be a great idea and those will be discussed further in this book. In fact, I mentioned the possibility in a newspaper article I wrote for the local newspapers in Marietta and Woodsfield in December of 1981. The eventual outcome was that the Marietta Unit of the Wayne National Forest did indeed furnish the 1987 Capitol Christmas Tree. There were many things involved in getting selected and then, of course, there were the logistics of the whole project. These items are all covered in this book.

Between 1981 and 1990, I wrote 469 weekly columns for the local newspapers about a variety of national forest and natural resource topics. About 38 of those weekly columns either mentioned the Capitol Christmas Tree or were entirely devoted to the subject; of course, the majority of those columns were written in 1987 and 1988, the year of the actual cutting and the following year.

These 38 columns or portions of these columns are included in an addendum near the end of this book. They also appear in their entireties in my three previous books entitled, **Your.....Wayne National Forest, Volumes I, II, and III.** Volume I included columns written in 1981 and 1982; Volume II covered the years

1983- 1986; and Volume III contained columns written from 1987 - 1990.

As you can imagine, when I first suggested that the Wayne National Forest provide the Capitol Christmas Tree, the skeptics were many. I got a lot of quizzical looks, grins, head shaking, and snickers. Plus, there were comments like:

- We don't have suitable large Christmas trees on the Wayne National Forest.
- The Capitol tree is usually a spruce or fir from northern states.
- What would ours be? A Virginia pine?
- All we have here are oaks, hickories, maples, and other hardwood trees.
- Maybe we could send them a yellow-poplar or an Ohio buckeye.
- And on and on.

But in the end, we did receive approval. The Wayne National Forest provided the Capitol Christmas Tree in 1987 – a majestic and historical Norway spruce. The project proved to be a huge success. The local community leaders and citizens got on board in an amazing way and provided the fantastic support necessary to make a project of this size possible. And a significant number of Forest Service employees also got involved to ensure the success of the effort.

The only things I take credit for are:

- Coming up with the original idea;
- Being hard-headed enough to stick with the idea, despite the initial naysayers, until we received final approval;
- Insisting that the tree come from the Marietta Unit and not from Athens or Ironton, as some Forest Service people initially thought would be okay (more on the reason why the Marietta Unit of the Wayne National Forest <u>had to be</u> the chosen location is explained in the book);
- Recruiting volunteers and assistance from the local community (although this turned out to be fairly easy once everyone understood the significance and the scope of the project);
- And coordinating the project at the local level to keep it all organized, under control, and headed in the right direction.

But as far as the whole project goes, it could not possibly have occurred at the level of success we enjoyed without the help and support of many, many, many people. Too many to mention probably. But I will try to cover it all to the best of my ability in the following chapters.

I apologize up front if I have forgotten to mention anyone, any company, school, or organization that was involved in the 1987 project. There were so many. I feel like I have covered things accurately and as fully as my memory and notes make possible. Also, this book is written primarily from our local viewpoint, which, of course, is where the action was taking place. It is also written with the primary purpose of capturing the entirety of this historical event, while I am still able and before too many more of the principal players pass away. I hope that future generations can use this book as a historical basis to help recall what happened in the area regarding 1987's Capitol Christmas Tree event.

Read on to find out how a small national forest, located in the hardwood country of southeastern Ohio, mobilized a dedicated cadre of local citizens, community leaders, and Forest Service employees to provide the 1987 U.S. Capitol Christmas Tree.

Even today, over 30 years later, if you mention this project in Monroe or Washington counties; in Marietta, Newport, and New Matamoras; or anywhere in the Frontier Local School District; you get an immediate smile and the nodding of heads: Memories return ......
and then the stories begin.

Chapter 1

My Early Thoughts about the Capitol Christmas Tree - Through December 1983

I don't remember hearing anything about the U.S. Capitol Christmas Tree until after I began working for the U.S. Forest Service (USFS) in 1974. I worked on the Monongahela National Forest (NF) in Bartow, WV in 1974 and 1975. During my time there and at various meetings in Elkins, I heard it mentioned that the Monongahela NF had provided the tree for the nation's Capitol in 1970. Other than that, I didn't really think too much else about it. I later learned that 1970 was the first year that the tree had come from one of the National Forests.

Over the next few years I worked at Ironton, Ohio on the Wayne NF; Ely, Minnesota on the Superior NF; and Blairsville, Georgia on the Chattahoochee NF. Again, at various meetings and through Forest Service newsletters, I would occasionally hear and read about the Capitol Christmas Tree. From what I read and heard, it seemed to be a pretty big deal for the locations that were chosen to provide the tree each year. I remember reading that the Monongahela NF had provided the Capitol Christmas Tree, for a second time, in 1976. That tree, as I recall, came from the Richwood, WV area.

While working in Georgia, I began writing a weekly newspaper column for newspapers in Union and Towns counties. (Note: Those columns have been captured in my book, **Your....Chattahoochee National Forest**.) The topics for the columns varied, but were generally about Forest Service activities or other outdoor and natural resource subjects.

My December 20, 1979 column for the Georgia newspapers was on the topic of the Capitol Christmas Tree. That column is provided in its entirety in the Exhibits section of this book. I had begun to take closer notice of the annual event and this column detailed the selection process and some of the history as I knew it at the time. The 1979 tree was a 52-foot white spruce from the Nicolet NF in Wisconsin.

In my 12/20/79 column, I noted that *"local communities have even held going-away ceremonies for 'their' tree and the townspeople then accompanied it by caravan to the Capitol."*

The public relations aspect of this annual event had begun to capture my attention. By that point in my forestry career, I had begun to realize that while foresters were very good at managing forests, as a profession we were not very good at public relations. I won't spend much more time on that specific topic, but suffice it to say that for the remainder of my forestry career I placed a high emphasis on community relations, media outreach, conservation education, and other similar efforts.

I concluded that 1979 column by writing that *"the U.S. Forest Service is very proud to help coordinate the Capitol Christmas Tree program. Perhaps someday the Chattahoochee National Forest will furnish our nation's Christmas tree."*

A year later, I found myself working at the Marietta Unit of the Wayne National Forest along the Ohio River in southeastern Ohio. The office was located in Reno, OH just a few miles upstream from Marietta. By January 19, 1981 I had once again begun to write a weekly forestry and outdoor column.

(Note: Those columns continued until September 10, 1990 and were titled **Your....Wayne National Forest**. The columns were regular features in three newspapers – The Marietta Times; The Monroe County Beacon; and The Spirit of Democracy. The Logan Daily News ran many of the columns, too, and from time to time they would appear in The Athens Messenger and a couple of West Virginia newspapers.

By September 10, 1990, when I wrote my last article, 469 columns had been written. Fittingly, that last column mentioned the Capitol Christmas Tree. Those 469 columns have been captured in three separate books, **Your.... Wayne National Forest, Volumes I, II, and III.**)

The first time I mentioned the Capitol Christmas Tree in my Ohio columns was on December 14, 1981. It was essentially a re-write of the 1979 column I had written in Georgia with the additional mention that the 1980 tree had been a white spruce from Vermont's Green Mountain National Forest; and that the 1981 tree, a 65-year old, 52-foot white spruce, would come from the Hiawatha NF in the Upper Peninsula of Michigan.

Once again, I ended the column with…. *"Perhaps someday the Wayne National Forest will furnish our nation's Christmas tree."*

That possibility was never far from my mind. By then, I fully realized how big an event it was for the National Forests and the local communities to get involved with furnishing the Capitol Christmas Tree.

When I had transferred from Georgia in July 1980 to the Wayne National Forest in Marietta, Ohio, my supervisor, Athens District Ranger Bob Joens, and the Forest Supervisor, Doug Bird, had an early meeting with me to outline their expectations.

Since I was located in Marietta, an hour from the main District Office in Athens, they wanted me to operate in a more independent manner than the typical Assistant Ranger. And one primary goal they wanted me to focus on was to work toward better community relations with local residents and to generate a better understanding locally of what the national forest was all about.

That was a primary reason for me to begin writing the weekly newspaper columns. Of course, I had written weekly columns for a couple of years in Georgia before moving to Ohio, so it was not that big a deal for me to continue that aspect of my job.

By the time I had written that 12/14/81 column about the Capitol Christmas Trees, I was beginning to explore possibilities of making that happen in Ohio. I knew it would be an uphill battle and would face many obstacles, but I thought it would be a wonderful thing for both the Wayne National Forest and the local communities.

Within a few months after I had begun my duties on the Wayne National Forest in July 1980, Forest Supervisor Doug Bird transferred to a position back out West, where he had previously worked. Fortunately, Harold Godlevske, who had been serving as the Deputy Forest Supervisor, was named the new Forest Supervisor. Harold, who served in this new position from 1980 – 1987, was extremely supportive of public relations activities and he continued to encourage all of my community outreach efforts in the Marietta area.

It was in 1981 when I first mentioned to Harold Godlevske and Bob Joens the idea of the Marietta Unit of the Wayne NF furnishing the U.S. Capitol Christmas Tree. To their credit, they didn't laugh me out of the room, but they were a little skeptical that this could be done.

As mentioned in the Introduction of this book, the Wayne NF is primarily a hardwood forest, with a predominance of oaks, maples, yellow poplar and various other deciduous trees – definitely not Christmas tree material. The primary evergreen tree growing naturally on the Wayne NF is the Virginia pine, also not very good Christmas tree material.

From 1970 – 1981 the U.S. Capitol Christmas tree had been either a fir or a spruce species. Those were balsam or Fraser fir; and Norway, red, black, or white spruce. No red oaks or sugar maples on that list!

But I had done a little preliminary on-the-ground-research around the Marietta Unit and by late 1981, I was convinced that we could provide a suitable Norway spruce to be the Capitol Tree. You see, the process of "building" the Wayne NF meant purchasing land from willing sellers to add to the national forest land base. Much of the purchased land had included old home sites. A number of the old home sites had featured Norway spruce trees, many of which had become very tall and very shapely over the years. And they sure looked like Christmas trees to me.

I continued to mention this to Harold and Bob any time I had a chance. By mid-1982 Harold seemed convinced that I was serious about being able to pull this off. I assured him that we had many potential trees from which to choose, probably 50 or more, and that any of them would fit the criteria for selection by the Capitol's

Landscape Architect. Years later, I had to admit that probably only five or six of the trees were truly suitable, but that didn't seem to me to be an insurmountable problem in 1982. After all, they only needed one tree! I also assured Harold that we could definitely get enough local supporters and volunteers to carry out the many responsibilities that the project would require.

Let me digress for just a moment to mention that my 12/13/82 newspaper column was written about the Capitol Tree that year, a 50-foot balsam fir, coming from the Green Mountain National Forest near Rochester, Vermont. And who should be there for the cutting of that tree? None other than our Wayne NF geologist, Lynn Kantner.

Lynn, who was stationed at our Marietta Office, periodically provided geologic advice and expertise to National Forests in Vermont, New Hampshire, Missouri, Illinois, and Indiana, in addition to her work for the Wayne NF. She had been in Vermont on a work assignment and was able to watch the cutting ceremony, along with the other Green Mountain National Forest personnel.

These ceremonies are quite impressive and Lynn explained to me that the Governor of Vermont had helped cut the tree; and that there were also short messages by Vermont's Fish and Game Commissioner, as well as the Green Mountain National Forest Supervisor. Practically the entire town of Rochester had turned out for the send-off ceremony, and local citizens, schools, and organizations provided hundreds of hand-made decorations to accompany the tree. This got me even more excited about what kinds of local possibilities there would be for a tree coming from Ohio.

I once again mentioned in my article that..... *"wouldn't it be nice if the Wayne National Forest could one day provide the Capitol Christmas tree?"*

Years later I learned that the 1982 tree had not actually come from the Green Mountain NF. It came from the Riley Bostwick Wildlife Management Area, which was managed by the Vermont Department of Fish and Wildlife, even though the USDA Forest Service was the federal agency coordinating the cutting of the tree. The reasons for this are explained in the Preface of this book, as well as in a note after my 12/13/82 newspaper column in the Exhibits section of this book.

One other problem needed to be resolved if the Wayne NF was to provide a Capitol Tree. The list of which national forest would supply the U.S. Capitol Christmas Tree each year was put together several years in advance. That allowed the appropriate national forest plenty of time to scout out potential trees and to begin preliminary planning. And the year that I wanted the Wayne NF to supply the tree – 1987 - was already promised to the Chippewa NF in Minnesota. (I'll explain why 1987 <u>had</u> to be <u>our</u> year a little later.)

During a field trip by Harold Godlevske to visit the Marietta Unit of the Wayne National Forest in the spring of 1983, I took him to see a Norway spruce that I suggested could be used as the Capitol Christmas tree. He was definitely warming up to the idea. Of course, as opportunities allowed throughout the rest of 1983, without getting too pushy, I continued to remind Harold about the tree we had looked at on-the-ground earlier that year.

On January 13, 1984 I wrote an official letter to the Forest Supervisor (Harold Godlevske) proposing that the Wayne NF's Marietta Unit furnish the Capitol Christmas Tree in 1987. I laid out all the reasoning and background for the idea and provided two photos of potential trees. I also included the Regional Office's tentative list of Capitol Trees and which national forests they would come from between 1984 and 1995. Most of this had been previously mentioned to Harold, but this put our proposal in writing and asked that it be presented to the Regional Office. (**Note** – A copy of this 1/13/84 letter is included in the Exhibits section of this book.)

Now, I'm not sure what Harold Godlevske told our Regional Office; nor am I sure what he discussed with the Forest Supervisor of the Chippewa NF. But I do know that by mid-1984, the Wayne NF had replaced the Chippewa on the internal Forest Service list of national forests supplying future Capitol Trees. And we were listed for 1987! Things were beginning to shape up. The Chippewa NF was moved forward five years and did supply the Capitol Tree in 1992.

Also, I want to mention that in late 1982 Gary Coleman had come in to replace Bob Joens as District Ranger at Athens and he remained in that role for two years, until about November of 1984. Gary continued his support for the Marietta Unit supplying the 1987 Capitol Tree. Since Gary was my immediate supervisor, this support was very important to the further planning of the project.

My 12/19/83 newspaper column told of the Chequamegon National Forest in northern Wisconsin supplying a 52-foot tall white spruce for that year's Capitol Christmas Tree. It had been grown on the site of a former CCC (Civilian Conservation Corps) camp and was selected to help both the Chequamegon and the CCC celebrate their 50th anniversaries.

I concluded my column by writing that…… *"there are some possible candidates for a Capitol Christmas Tree on the Wayne National Forest, too. Maybe within the next few years Ohio can furnish a tree and go down in history with other states as a contributor to this annual program. I'm working on some ideas to make that happen. Wish me luck."*

This was the first time that I had felt confident enough to let the reading public know, via my newspaper column, that something was in the works for the Wayne NF to hopefully supply a future U.S. Capitol Christmas Tree.

Now, on to 1984 and beyond!

Chapter 2

The Official Announcement in 1984 Through Early 1987

As mentioned in the previous chapter, by mid-1984 the Wayne NF had replaced the Chippewa NF on the internal Forest Service list of forests supplying future Capitol Trees. And we were listed for 1987. All of our preliminary work up to that point was paying off.

I saw a copy of that list sometime in the summer of 1984 and by December our Forest Supervisor's Office had put out an official news release stating that the Wayne National Forest had been selected to provide the Capitol Christmas Tree in 1987.

In my 12/10/84 newspaper column, I stated that..... *"I've been dying to let everyone know, but I was told to wait for the "official" news release to come out. For now, all we can say is that we will furnish the tree. There will likely be no more specifics announced for a couple of years."*

And true to my word, I didn't say much publicly about the project for the next two years. I wrote one column in December of 1985 and one in November of 1986 about our efforts, and that was all until 1987.

But the hard work began from that point in 1984 forward because we now had to fulfill all the promises and assurances we had been making over the previous three years. There were still a lot of things that had to occur to ensure that the project would be successful.

In the December 1984 column, I explained a little bit of what had gone on behind the scenes for the previous few years and why 1987 was the year that we wanted the Wayne NF to furnish the Capitol Tree. Here's part of what I wrote in 1984:

..... *"I pushed hard for us to supply the tree and for the 1987 date because it will tie in to the 200th anniversary of the signing of the Northwest Ordinance. That date will also serve as a lead-in to Marietta's 1988 bicentennial celebration, which from early indications will be a year full of festivities, celebrations, and other activities. The Christmas tree will be cut in late November or early December of 1987, transported to Washington, D.C., erected, lights installed about two weeks before Christmas, and left standing on into January of 1988. So you see, the entire process will be quite a kick-off to Marietta's 1988 festivities."*

I then went on to explain further about the significance of the Northwest Ordinance and the establishment of Marietta:

"For those of you who aren't history buffs, the Northwest Ordinance opened up for settlement all the lands north and west of the Ohio River that now

comprise Ohio, Indiana, Michigan, Illinois, Wisconsin, and part of Minnesota. It was an act of immense historic significance in the development of the United States. And, of course, Marietta was the first permanent settlement established in the Northwest Territory under the terms of the 1787 Ordinance. The first settlers left New England in December of 1787 and arrived at what is now Marietta in April of 1788.

We know that by furnishing the 1987 Capitol Christmas Tree, the Wayne National Forest can contribute to the overall efforts of the bicentennial celebrations."

One other thing I mentioned was that some of our Forest Service personnel at our other offices didn't see why the Capitol Tree couldn't come from our Ironton or Athens units. After all, they reasoned that they were part of the Wayne National Forest, too. They were actually searching their areas for possible Capitol Tree candidates.

They didn't fully understand that the tree <u>had</u> to come from the Marietta Unit because that was where the story of the Northwest Territory, the Northwest Ordinance, and basically the state of Ohio began – in Marietta in 1787 and 1788. Anyway, I continued to point that out and to work hard to make sure that the 1987 Capitol Christmas Tree did come from the Marietta Unit of the Wayne National Forest. Eventually, once all of our employees saw the support we were garnering in the Marietta and Washington County area, I believe everyone came around and helped to make the project a huge success.

Although I didn't write any more about the Capitol Tree until 12/16/85, there were a lot of things going on in terms of planning for the big event. After all, we still had to get final approval of the exact tree, as well as do preliminary planning for the cutting, transporting, and community activities.

I contacted a couple of the National Forests that had supplied previous trees to learn as much as I could about what would be expected of us. The more I learned about the project, the more I realized we would need a dedicated group of Forest Service employees and local citizens to pull off a quality event.

I called the Capitol's Landscape Architect to gather information, too. I learned from him that he would not come for a site visit to inspect our candidate tree and give final approval until the spring of 1987. That kind of put a little fear into me because I knew we couldn't wait until six months before the cutting was to take place to begin our plans.

But before we hung up, he assured me not to worry and that he had always been able to give final approval for a tree on his site visits. I'll paraphrase a little bit here, but essentially he said, "Dan, don't worry. Between you and me, I could take a telephone pole, get some branches, drill holes to put them in, and make a suitable Capitol Christmas Tree. As long as you have some trees to choose from that are green, the right height, and you can get to them with felling equipment, then we'll make it work."

With those parting comments I began to feel much better about the final "approval" process.

Much of 1986 was spent putting together an action plan and timeline, as well as lists of people to contact for help and support. And I must say that no one turned us down. It was amazing. I could see that this was going to be a special event in the history of Marietta, Washington County, and the Wayne National Forest.

After my December 1985 column, although we were busy with planning for the event, the next time I wrote a newspaper column about the Capitol Tree project was on 11/10/86.

That was the first time, I believe, that I had mentioned officially that the tree would be a Norway spruce. I discussed the difference between the Capitol Christmas Tree and the White House Tree and, once again, explained the tie-in to the bicentennial celebrations of the Northwest Ordinance and the founding of Marietta.

In the column I wrote that..... *"we're looking at such activities as a cutting ceremony; a caravan around Ohio possibly climaxing with a send off ceremony from Columbus; local artists providing a sketch for the official Christmas cards which will commemorate the event; local firms to help cut, lower, wrap, and ship the tree; school groups and organizations to prepare posters, ornaments, and cards to accompany the tree to Washington, D.C.; magazine articles; and groups to furnish and sponsor the approximately 20 additional, smaller trees which must be sent to D.C. also. The smaller trees, ranging in height from eight to about 30 feet, go in such places as the Capitol rotunda, the Supreme Court, and the Department of Agriculture."*

Those were just some of our early thoughts and, of course, things changed and evolved as we got closer to the November 1987 cutting date.

And in this column I mentioned several of the key people who had been involved with the project up to this point in time: Forest Supervisor Harold Godlevske; District Ranger Chuck Myers; former District Rangers Bob Joens and Gary Coleman; other Forest Service employees Teena Sechler, Dave Kissell, Art Martin, Dave Greenwood, John Kerr, and Gloria Eighmey; Ohio Department of Natural Resources botanist Marilyn Ortt; Marietta Mayor Nancy Hollister; Bicentennial Commission President Barbara Lovely; and Tourist and Convention Bureau (TCB) Director Phyllis Richerson.

These last four people were absolutely key in helping plan and elevate the project to one that was recognized as being important to the entire state of Ohio. In a short while other individuals would begin to play important roles in the project, including Gil Courtney, President of the Peoples Savings Bank in New Matamoras; Calvin Martin, Instructor at Frontier High School; and Washington County Commissioner Sandy Matthews. And soon others became important players, also. They will be mentioned in the next chapter.

Now, prior to the November 1986 column (I believe it was in October), the Landscape Architect for the U.S. Capitol, Paul Pincus, gave us final approval for our tree in an on-site visit. I had been getting a little nervous about the final approval process because, as mentioned earlier, we really only had five or six trees that I felt were truly suitable; not five or six thousand, or more, like some of the northern forests had to choose from.

So, I called Paul Pincus again and asked if he could come sooner to approve our tree, instead of the spring of 1987 that he had told me previously. He didn't really see the need, but sensing my nervousness, he somewhat reluctantly agreed to come take a look that fall.

Working in our favor was the fact that Pincus' boss, the Architect of the Capitol George White, was an Ohio native. White had been told earlier that the 1987 tree was coming from Ohio and he was very excited about that fact. I'm sure Pincus wanted to please his boss.

During Pincus' site visit, we showed him four or five trees. He actually chose the one that I had favored all along, a very nice Norway spruce sitting close to the banks of the Ohio River just north of Frontier High School. We also set up Pincus to have lunch with Mayor Hollister, TCB Director Richerson, and Bicentennial Commission President Lovely. When he heard the outstanding presentations of support from those three ladies, we pretty much had the battle won. They explained how the Capitol Tree event would fit into the Bicentennial celebrations and make it even bigger than might otherwise be possible.

My January 12, 1987 column listed the key projects that the Wayne National Forest would be working on during the coming year and, of course, one item listed was the Capitol Christmas Tree Project.

After this, I didn't mention the tree in print again until April 6, 1987, although there was a lot going on toward planning a top notch project. (Then between September 14 and December 28, 1987 there were 14 columns devoted to the topic.)

Here's what I covered in the April 6, 1987 column:

In addition to the Wayne National Forest furnishing the Capitol Christmas Tree for 1987, southeastern Ohio will also provide the following trees:

** a 24-foot tree for the U.S. Botanical Gardens*

** a 24-foot tree for the Supreme Court*

** an 18-foot tree for the U.S. Department of
Agriculture patio*

** an 18-foot tree for the Senate Private Dining Room*

** a 12-foot tree for the House Public Dining Room*

** a 12-foot tree for the Senate Public Dining Room*

*"Early plans are for the trees to come from a state
forest, the City of Marietta, an Ohio tree farm, the City
of Athens, the City of Ironton, and one other source. A
few smaller 8-foot trees have to be sent to Washington,
D.C., also. These will be provided by the Ohio
Christmas Tree Growers Association.*

*Members of the Marietta Tree Commission have begun
their search for a presentable 18-foot tree from within
the city limits. It should be a well-formed, symmetrical
tree -- a Norway spruce, if at all possible. If anyone
knows of such a tree, or would be interested in
donating a tree for this purpose, please contact a
member of the Marietta City Tree Commission."*

Chapter 3

From Early 1987 into November– A Busy and Productive Time

I want to mention at the beginning of this chapter that all kinds of activities had been in progress since the Capitol's Landscape Architect gave final approval in late 1986 of our selected Capitol Christmas Tree. My January 12 and April 6, 1987 columns discussed what was happening during that time period. And then, starting with my 9/14/87 column, readers got a heavy dose, almost every week for the rest of the year, of items related to this once-in-a-lifetime event.

This chapter will give the details of everything related to the Capitol Christmas Tree up through the first part of November 1987. Chapter 4 will be devoted to more specifics of the actual Cutting Ceremony on November 20 and the Send-Off Ceremony on November 21, while Chapter 5 will give details of delivering the tree and the lighting ceremony in D.C., which took place on December 9, 1987.

I want readers to understand that there were many, many, many things happening; and they were not necessarily in chronological order.

Some days there was so much going on that it was difficult to keep track of it all. And if we were working on, say, 100 separate items to make the event special and memorable, it was not like let's do number one, then number two, then number three, and so on. It was almost always working on three things at the same time on one day; then the next day doing numbers forty-one, six, and eighty-three; then the next day starting some new items, as well as going back to change or fine tune something that had been worked on three weeks previous.

It wasn't exactly like organized chaos, but I'm sure it seemed that way to some outsiders. Of course, we had a number of people who would work on certain aspects of the planning and then get back to me or the committee with the status at certain key times. I pretty much had to keep track of all the on-the-ground and local activities to ensure that everything would fit into the final plans.

And before I get into the meat of this chapter, I want to give thanks to Teena Sechler, Public Information Officer in our Supervisor's Office in Bedford, Indiana. While I was trying to direct or keep tabs on all of the local activities, Teena kept the Forest Supervisor and the Regional Office in Milwaukee in the loop. I kept Teena informed and she, in turn, let me know of anything that the Supervisor's Office or the Regional Office needed an update on.

Teena attended several of our local planning committee meetings, too, which was very helpful. She then began to get involved directly with certain tasks that will be discussed later in this book. Plus, as things neared the time for scheduling the delivery of the tree to the U.S. Capitol, she was able to coordinate most of that with our National Office in Washington, D.C.

I'll use my weekly columns beginning with 9/14/87 to kind of guide my thoughts on this chapter, but I'll fill in from memory or from other notes or sources whenever possible.

Weekly Column, Your.....Wayne National Forest – September 14, 1987:

I wrote 14 columns during the next 16 weeks pertaining to the Capitol Christmas Tree and everything going on surrounding the event. This week's column told readers that the actual cutting of the tree would take place on November 20 and that a send-off ceremony would be held the following day; and I quickly recapped highlights of the previous few years leading up to this point.

I mentioned the souvenir jars that we were selling as one of our fundraising projects. There were three different sized jars or canisters per set and they were produced for us by the famous glass plant that was located just across the Ohio River from Marietta – Fenton Art Glass of Williamstown, WV. These jars were sold as one of our fundraising projects.

We were not allowed to pay for things associated with this event out of Forest Service funds. The only thing covered by Forest Service spending was the cost of employee salaries and their vehicle use. Everything else had to either be donated or covered by our fundraising efforts. And although most things related to the event were donated to us, we did have to buy certain items and pay for some services.

Back to the jars. They were clear glass with lids and were to be used, I suppose, as candy jars or something similar. There was a small, medium, and large jar, standing about six, eight, and ten inches tall, respectively. On the front of each jar was a milky, white etching of the U.S. Capitol with a Christmas tree standing in front. Below this was printed *"1987 Capitol Christmas Tree – Wayne National Forest."* They were collector's items for sure.

The first three sets of jars were purchased by Washington County Commissioner, Glenn Miller; Marietta Mayor, Nancy Hollister; and local resident and businessman, Calvin Mendenhall. We advertised the availability of the jars primarily by word of mouth, but the newspapers also mentioned them. We placed them in all of the Forest Service offices; most of the area's state, city, and county government offices; and many local businesses. And they sold like hotcakes! The cost was $20 per set, but you could purchase them individually - $8.50 for a large canister; $8.00 for the mid-sized one; and $7.50 for a small jar.

I can't remember how much profit we made on each jar and I'm not sure how many we ordered from Fenton's, but it was several hundred of each size. By October 12, there were fewer than 100 jars left to sell.

I mentioned in the September 14 column that members of our Planning Committee included employees of both the U.S. Forest Service and the Ohio Department of Natural Resources (ODNR), as well as, initially, seven key local community members. Committee members would come and go from time to time, depending upon what particular effort we were involved with at any point. But these seven were instrumental in getting us started out on the right footing. And some of them were heavily involved throughout the entire process. Those seven were Gil Courtney, Marilyn Ortt, Barb Hamilton, Iwana Simon, Marty Kitchen, Harry Cogswell, and Wayne Schafer.

Gil was President of Peoples Savings Bank in New Matamoras and throughout this entire process, and even afterward, he was probably the most enthusiastic and involved person for everything we did, especially those things involving Frontier Local School District. After all, the tree was located near Frontier High School, not far from New Matamoras, and the residents of Frontier District were elated to have the tree come from their area. Gil donated time and money to the project; recruited many volunteers for us; arranged publicity efforts; helped arrange logistics for transporting the tree to D.C.; coordinated (and I think helped pay for, along with the Matamoras Area Business and Community Organization) several bus loads of Frontier District residents to attend the eventual lighting ceremony in the nation's Capitol on December 9; and probably many more things that I was unaware of. He was like a whirling dervish set in motion to help make this historical event something that would never be forgotten in the area. And yes, he accompanied us to D.C. when we delivered the tree to the west lawn of the U.S. Capitol. If something was going on, it seemed like Gil was involved. We became good friends and remain so to this day.

Marilyn Ortt was a local resident and a premier botanist. She was employed by the ODNR and was a big supporter of the Wayne National Forest. This project captured her interest and she was willing to do anything and everything we asked of her to support our efforts. Marilyn loved the outdoors and she loved the local area. She served on the Marietta City Tree Commission and was involved in just about everything locally that had to do with nature, the outdoors, and the environment. She was invaluable to the success of the Capitol Christmas Tree project.

Barb Hamilton was a member of the Marietta City Council. Along with her friend, Iwana Simon, they volunteered to coordinate the efforts of involving local schools and students in this project. Both ladies, as I recall, were former teachers or had involvement with local education efforts. They visited many schools to publicize our event and to involve students with making ornaments, having poster displays, designing cards, putting on skits and plays, writing reports, and to work with teachers and principals to make this something that the students would never forget. They ensured that the two primary themes – the Capitol Christmas Tree and the Bicentennial celebrations were the focus of their efforts. They had various types of contests set up for the students and presented awards to the winners at the send-off ceremony for the tree on November 21 in front of the Hermann Fine Arts Center at Marietta College.

Barb and Iwana collected ornaments made by students from a several-county area and these were transported in boxes along with the tree to D.C. Many of the ornaments were presented to Ohio Congressional members on our tree delivery trip in November, while those ornaments that were weather resistant were actually used to help decorate the main tree on the Capitol lawn. I especially remember the pleased reactions of Senator John Glenn and U.S. Representatives Douglas Applegate, Clarence Miller, and Michael Dewine when we delivered some of the ornaments to their offices.

Hamilton did much more, too. She helped arrange for the Marietta High School band to play during the send-off ceremony. She helped make arrangements at the college and with the city. And on two separate Monday mornings she met me bright and early at Peoples Bank on Second and Putnam streets in downtown Marietta to help set up window displays about the Wayne National Forest, the Capitol Christmas Tree, and the Marietta Bicentennial.

Let me digress for just a moment. I was born and raised in West Virginia. From an early age I learned to love sports and to love the WVU Mountaineer teams. I later graduated from WVU with my degree in Forest Resource Management. I especially loved Mountaineer basketball and, of course, I knew about the All-American players such as Jerry West, Hot Rod Hundley, Ron "Fritz" Williams, Rod Thorn, Mark Workman, Leland Byrd, and Fred Schaus. All were from West Virginia, except Schaus, who was from Newark, Ohio.

Then there was WVU's first All-American basketball star, West Virginia native Scotty Hamilton, who led WVU to the national championship at the time, the NIT in Madison Square Garden, in 1942. And yes, as you might be guessing, Barb Hamilton was Scotty's wife. This impressed me greatly, as you might imagine. I can't remember how that first came to my attention, but it may have been when I stopped by Barb's house one morning to pick up some items related to the Capitol Christmas Tree and I saw a picture of Scotty. She was always pleased when I asked about her husband's All-American basketball days at West Virginia University. She was quite a sports fan and never seemed to tire of my questions. That made her even more special to me.

After serving in the military and dabbling in professional basketball for a few years, Scotty Hamilton became a high school coach and then the head coach at Washington and Lee College in Virginia. Eventually, he and Barb came to Marietta, Ohio where Scotty served as the long-time athletic director at Marietta High School. He had passed away in 1976. Barb was to later pass away in 1989 and I devoted a March 1989 newspaper column to her memory. It is included in the Exhibits section of this book.

Marty Kitchen was the Director of the Recreation Department for the City of Marietta. I had known Marty for a number of years since I played basketball and softball in the city leagues. She even hired me to referee some of the league basketball games for several years in the evenings at the Marietta Armory. Once on our planning committee, Marty immediately began to work on ways to publicize the Capitol Christmas Tree. She had a lot of contacts locally and helped us recruit volunteers and receive donations. She sold commemorative jars, ornaments, and Christmas cards for us through her office and helped place those same items in a number of stores and businesses around Marietta.

Wayne Schafer was a long-time County Commissioner for Washington County and there may have been one or two people in the county that he didn't know, but I doubt it. Soon after arriving in Marietta for my new job at the Wayne National Forest in 1980, I got to know Wayne and we became friends. He was always very level headed and gave great advice. I used to kid him that the Wayne National Forest was named after him.

Community relations must never have been a high priority with the Forest Service in that area in previous years because there was a lot of misunderstanding and resentment from local residents about the Wayne National Forest. The main gripe was that the Forest Service had purchased a lot of private land over the years to help form the national forest. Anything that was going bad in the eastern part of the county, where the national forest was located, was blamed on the Wayne NF by many people – whether it was a bad economy, lack of tax base, bad roads, or you name it, probably even the weather. Over my tenure there, from 1980 to 1990 I worked hard to dispel rumors, communicate with local citizens, and generally work to make the Wayne NF a good neighbor. I believe we were largely successful and the Capitol Christmas Tree event was seen as a huge positive project by everyone in the area. I was very pleased with that.

Wayne Schafer had been born and raised in the heart of the Wayne National Forest and he knew the problems and the feelings of local people as well as anyone. Serving as County Commissioner and now living down in Marietta, he came to understand the pros and cons of the national forest; he separated fact from fiction; and he gave great advice to all concerned about the relationship between the national forest and the local area. He certainly was a proponent of trying to capture the positive value of having a national forest nearby.

Well, when we began our planning meetings there wasn't anything that came up that Wayne didn't have a positive suggestion for; as I have said, he literally knew everyone, and he was able to make contacts for volunteer assistance and financial contributions that were amazing. He had retired as County Commissioner by the time the Capitol Christmas Tree was to be cut, but his knowledge of the local area and local people was invaluable to our planning efforts. Also, I might add that Wayne's successor as County Commissioner, Sandy Matthews, was a resident of Frontier Local School District; was a supporter of the national forest; and also became a key player in making the Capitol Christmas Tree project a success. She will be mentioned more later in this book.

Harry Cogswell ran Apex Feed and Supply in Marietta. It was your typical farm supply store and over the years we frequently purchased items there for Wayne National Forest projects – hay, rope, seed, hardware or tools of various types, and so on. Harry agreed to serve on our initial planning committee and had great suggestions for just about anything that involved tools, supplies, or equipment. His company donated lots of materials for the project and occasionally, when something needed to be paid for, that came out of the proceeds of our fundraising efforts or contributions from various sources. As I recall, Harry also sold sets of the commemorative jars at his business.

We had so many different places selling jars, cards, and ornaments that I don't know how we ever kept up with it. But we did, and that job fell upon our local Forest Service secretary, Connie Morris. She did an unbelievable job of tracking everything, collecting the money, and keeping a ledger of expenditures and finances for our committee to view as they deemed necessary.

I had talked with national forest employees in California, Michigan, and Minnesota, where the three previous Capitol Christmas Trees had come from, and by the summer of 1987 I had a pretty good idea of what types of equipment would be necessary to accomplish the cutting and transporting of our tree. Soon, I would confirm this and make necessary adjustments in our planning after conferring with Casimier Wojakowski, a retired lumberjack from the Upper Peninsula of Michigan, who would be coming to supervise the cutting, wrapping, and loading of our tree. More on Casimier later.

But by September, with help from two of our local Forest Service employees, John Kerr and Dave Greenwood, as well as some of our planning committee members, I had lined up the two trucks that would transport the main tree and the "companion" trees to D.C., as well as other heavy equipment, trucks, and trailers that would be necessary for the project. Greenwood and Kerr were instrumental in just about every phase of the Capitol Christmas Tree project. Another Forest Service employee at our Marietta Unit office, Gloria Eighmey, also provided valuable help in several phases of our project. It would not have gone as well as it did without these three key individuals.

In the September 14 column I mentioned that supplies and equipment were coming from Wetz Transportation – Marietta; Kenmack Lumber – Newport; Busch Construction - Vienna, WV; Black's Tree Service - - Marietta; B.F. Goodrich - Oak Grove; and Apex Feed - Marietta.

 The main tree was to be loaded onto a flatbed trailer and hauled to D.C. by a Wetz Transportation truck. Roy Wetz was extremely helpful in volunteering a truck and trailer for this. When Roy, or R.O. as most people called him, wasn't around, we coordinated things with one of his two sons, Tag or Chip. Spare branches and companion trees (more about these later) were hauled by a truck and trailer owned by Kenmack Lumber of Newport. Gil Courtney actually helped us arrange this, as he was a good friend of both Mack and Kenny Haessly.

I listed Busch Construction in this column, but actually I think the correct name was Busch Crane Rental. They were located a few miles away in Vienna, WV, a suburb of Parkersburg. They provided the large crane that was used to gently lower the tree to the ground once it was cut. Black's Tree Service of Marietta helped on the day of the cutting by using their bucket truck to fasten various cables to the tree, as well as to trim several of the lower branches off the tree before it was felled. Those branches were saved and accompanied the trees to D.C. on the Kenmack Lumber trailer. And Apex Feed & Supply and B.F. Goodrich of the Marietta suburb of Oak Grove provided various supplies, smaller trucks, and trailers to haul necessary items to and from the cutting site.

I also mentioned, without going into specifics at that time: that we were getting help from Frontier High School, Marietta College, Marietta High School and Elizabeth Cottle; that River Press was printing Christmas cards and Casto Glass Company was making souvenir Christmas tree ornaments, both items meant to commemorate the historic event; and that several smaller trees would also be sent to use at various locations in D.C. More on that later. And I told readers that the souvenir jars were going like hot cakes and if they wanted a set, they had better get one soon. At that time there were just a few left at our Wayne National Forest offices in Athens and Reno; and the Marietta Tourist and Convention Bureau on 3rd Street had three sets left, too.

I concluded that 9/14/87 column by telling readers that *"I know I've missed someone or some group. I do apologize, but I promise to go into more detail as we lead up to the November 20 cutting date."*

Weekly Column, Your.....Wayne National Forest – September 21, 1987:
I listed the following as providing cash donations toward the project and thanked them: Paul Warren and the folks at Warren Drilling; Sam Cook at Broughton Foods; the Marietta Kiwanis Club; Tony Popp and Marietta Savings; and Jim Meagle and the crew at Dime Bank.

Since this entire project was supposed to function through contributions and donations, the above monetary donations were very helpful. Most companies and individuals totally contributed their time and equipment costs, but not all were able to do so for various reasons. Many of them did, however, reduce their costs and charges to us. We used the cash donations to cover those expenses.

I also thanked Mr. and Mrs. Jess Latimer of Marietta and Mr. and Mrs. Luke Arnold of Oak Grove. They would furnish smaller trees from their properties, which would go to the U.S. House of Representatives and the U.S. Department of Agriculture Patio, respectively.

I mentioned Frontier High School, which helped in so many ways. Bob Forbes, the principal, and his people were extremely helpful and I promised to provide a more detailed account on all of Frontier's efforts at a future date.

I updated where commemorative jars could be purchased by listing additional locations: Sugden's Book Store, Harpers Landing, Wallahalla Gallery, and Huck's Farm Market, all in Marietta; and Hole in the Wall Gift Shop operated by the Mendenhall's on County Road 9 (Eightmile Road) east of Marietta.

Weekly Column, Your.....Wayne National Forest – October 12, 1987:
It was three weeks before I wrote another column about the Capitol Christmas Tree on 10/12/87, but we were still busy with planning things, of course. After all, the cutting ceremony was to occur in just a little over five weeks. The main gist of the October 12 column was to announce the availability of the Christmas cards that we produced to highlight the event.

River Press of Marietta printed 5,000 Christmas cards for us. It was customary for the national forest supplying that particular year's Capitol Christmas Tree to send 1,000 cards to our national office in Washington,

D.C. for their use. They sent them to various dignitaries and officials throughout the country. Then, 1,000 cards each were sent to our Forest Service offices in Athens, Ironton, and Bedford, Indiana, for them to sell. That left us with just 1,000 cards to sell at the Marietta (Reno) office. And by the time this newspaper column appeared, we had already sold 200.

I announced to local readers that..... *"You'll definitely want to buy some cards, either to send out for Christmas or just to save as souvenirs. They come wrapped 10 to a package and they sell for only $3.00 per package. At that price I don't expect the cards to last very long, so if you want some, just come to one of our offices--Marietta, Athens, or Ironton."*

The front of the Christmas card featured the U.S. Capitol with a Christmas tree standing in front of the building. In the lower middle portion of the card was an outline of a Christmas tree bulb with a scene depicting how the tree might have looked as it stood in the front yard of a pioneer home in the area 100 years previous. To the right was the Ohio River with a sternwheeler heading downstream.

It was a very nice design and was provided by Lynn Murel, a wildlife biologist in our Athens office, and a friend of hers, Tim McKenzie. The front of the card also read "*Wayne National Forest, Capitol Christmas Tree-1987.*" A photo of the card is included in the Exhibits section.

The inside of the card provided room to write a holiday message on the left side and on the right side was the following greeting, which was written by Teena Sechler of our Supervisor's Office:

**"In honor of the bicentennial of the Northwest Ordinance,
the people of Ohio present to the nation---
a Norway Spruce from the Wayne National Forest.**

**The tree's history is tied to the story of a young salesman,
who gave out seedling spruce trees as he traveled through Ohio.**

It was planted in the river country on a farm near Marietta, the first settlement in the Northwest Territory.

The 1987 Capitol tree is a special legacy of the pioneers who settled this country 200 years ago.

**From Ohio,
the heart of it all,
with best wishes to the nation...
HAPPY HOLIDAYS.**

It was a fitting message that perfectly summed up the event that was about to unfold in our area. The cards were such a hit that we eventually had to have a few thousand more printed in order to meet the demand.

As I concluded that week's column, I let readers know that the souvenir jars were selling very fast and that we had fewer than 100 sets left. So, if they wanted to purchase these souvenir items, they had better act soon. I also reminded them to mark November 21 on their calendars for the big Send-Off Ceremony to be held in the parking lot of the Hermann Fine Arts building at Marietta College at 2:00 p.m.

I wrote...... *"There will be several dignitaries, speakers, bands, and so forth present. Let's all join in making this an event that will long be remembered in our area."*

Weekly Column, Your.....Wayne National Forest – October 20, 1987:
Back in the 1980s we didn't have all of the electronic and social media available like we do today. There was no Twitter or Facebook or such things. To reach large numbers of the public in that area, we had to rely primarily on newspaper coverage, and some radio. We did do a few radio interviews on the local talk shows and news segments, in addition to the newspaper coverage. The nearest TV station was about 15 miles away in Parkersburg, WV and they didn't do any coverage of our event that I can remember until the day of the cutting. But we did send out some news releases to radio and TV stations, as well as newspapers.

So, in my October 20 column, I once again reminded folks that the Cutting Ceremony would occur on Friday, November 20 and the Send-off Ceremony on Saturday, November 21 - the first event was to be held in the Wayne National Forest at the actual tree cutting site;

and the second ceremony was to be held in the parking lot of the Hermann Fine Arts Center at Marietta College. I reminded the public that everyone was welcome to attend either, or both, of these ceremonies. After all, we wanted as many people to attend as possible.

I told readers that..... *"We certainly do encourage you to attend because this is undoubtedly a once-in-a-lifetime happening for our area. If the U.S. Capitol Tree ever comes from southeastern Ohio again, it will sure surprise me. And if, by chance, it does, then I'm sure we'll all be six feet underground by then. As we get closer to the November 20-21 dates, you can read more of the specifics, times, etc. in this column and in other newspaper, radio, and TV announcements. If all else fails, give us a call at 373-9055 for more details."*

I also mentioned that the list of people and companies that were donating time, money, equipment, or supplies for the Capitol Christmas Tree project continued to grow. It was becoming a real community effort to get the main tree and several smaller trees to Washington, D.C. And it was becoming a real effort on my part to keep track of all those contributing, so that I could give proper public recognition and thanks to them.

In that week's column I thanked:

<u>Carlton Oil Corporation,</u> Newport – For pledging to donate manpower and the use of a truck with a heavy duty winch the day of the cutting.

<u>Newport Lumber Company,</u> Newport – For donating plywood to make four signs which were attached to the side of the trailers that hauled the trees to D.C., as well as another sign that was used locally, and which was painted by Frontier High School.

<u>Blauvelt Sign Company,</u> Marietta – For donating paint for the signs.

<u>Jean Pickering, Sign Painter,</u> Lowell -- Jean did the actual painting and lettering of four signs.

<u>Gil Courtney of the Peoples Savings Bank,</u> New Matamoras and the <u>Matamoras Area Business and Civic Organization</u> (MABCO) -- Gil had already donated considerable time and effort in helping plan for our festivities. He was also helping to make arrangements to have equipment furnished for our use and was coordinating the job of New Matamoras' supplying a smaller tree to be sent to Washington. This smaller tree went to the Senate Public Dining Room and was displayed during the Christmas season. MABCO contributed money for the overall project, as well as individual members of the organization to help with various tasks.

<u>Frontier High School</u> – We had tremendous cooperation and assistance from John Hoff - District Superintendent, Bob Forbes - Principal, and Calvin Martin - Instructor. The Capitol Christmas Tree, of course, came from within Frontier School District, not

far from the high school, and these individuals wanted to make the event one that would be long-remembered in their area. Calvin's FFA group assisted with several items leading up to and during the cutting ceremony. Frontier High School was heavily involved in the Nov. 20 activities, including such things as the band, choir, transportation, parking, handing out programs, and a number of other things.

<u>Washington County Career Center</u> -- Dave Barrett, Dave Rose, and Terry Schafer offered any assistance that we needed; in particular, the forestry class on the day of the cutting; and the welding class to make a brace to hold the heavy butt and trunk of the tree in place during shipment to D.C.

Weekly Column, Your.....Wayne National Forest – October 26, 1987:

The Capitol Christmas Tree project continued to roll along. I announced that we had received cash donations from the Marietta Rotary Club and the Citizens Bank of Beverly to help cover expenses for this once-in-a-lifetime event.

McDonald's on Pike Street in Marietta and Newport IGA also volunteered to furnish food for the workers who would be cutting down the tree and working around that site on November 20.

Pete Suerken, John Eaton, and Dave Schatz -- all with the Ohio Division of Forestry (ODOF) – pledged to assist us with gathering and storing the approximately

20 additional trees which we had to send to Washington, D.C., along with the main tree. These trees were stored until the day of shipping at the ODOF Nursery in Reno, which was managed by Eaton. Of course, the trees had to be kept cool and to be watered for several days until the day of shipping, which was a job in itself.

These smaller trees went to various Congressional offices, the Senate, House of Representatives, Supreme Court, Department of Agriculture, and a few other places, such as the U.S. Botanical Gardens and the Smithsonian Institution. Without the help of the state ODOF employees, we'd have had a difficult time completing the entire Christmas tree project.

On the day that we delivered the main tree to the west lawn of the U.S. Capitol, November 30, 1987 (more on that later), we also delivered the companion trees. The Capitol's Landscape Architect secured these trees and had them taken by his crews to the various offices the next day, where we were waiting to make the formal presentations, along with delivering the ornaments made by Ohio school students

I also announced that we had sold out of Christmas cards within the first few days of their availability and that River Press was going to print 3,000 more to help meet the local demand. We hadn't expected this much demand for the cards. From my discussions with other national forests, where previous Capitol trees had come from and based upon recommendations from the Forest Service national office, the initial 5,000 seemed like plenty. It was more work for our local staff, but we were pleased that the cards had proven to be such a big hit.

I advised people to call our office to make sure we had cards available before they drove to buy them and that if they waited too long, we would probably sell out once again. I thanked readers for their support through purchasing these cards, which will *"serve as souvenirs and keepsakes for many years to come."*

Weekly Column, Your.....Wayne National Forest – November 2, 1987:
I tried to mention in my newspaper columns everyone and every organization or company that helped with this event, to publicly recognize them for their contributions. In this book I am trying to do the same, so as to record and capture for history's sake everyone that was involved in this project.

Around the end of October Stowe's Truck and Equipment Company of Reno called to offer time and equipment to help with our project. A day or two later Jim Mitchell called with a similar offer from his company, American Petroel, Inc., which was a local oil and gas producer. By that time I knew we were going to have plenty of heavy equipment and trained operators available to do everything necessary at the site to cut and load the Christmas tree.

We had also been told by the Capitol Landscape Architect Paul Pincus that we needed to locate and cut an additional Norway spruce tree of similar size to the selected tree. He said we should use 30-40 branches from that second tree for "cushioning" the main tree during transport, as well as to cushion the companion trees that were to be shipped on the second trailer. Pincus said that he would also use these branches, as needed, once the tree arrived at the Capitol to replace any limbs on the main tree that got damaged during transport.

We did locate another acceptable tree on Wayne National Forest land about a mile down the road, not far off of Rt. 7, for this purpose. And since we had plenty of equipment promised to help us, it became no problem to cut down this tree, too. We actually went down to that site after the crowd had dispersed the morning of the Cutting Ceremony to accomplish that task. It went off without a hitch.

This did make me remember the conversation that I had with Pincus a couple of years previous, when he told me that he could probably make a presentable Christmas tree from a telephone pole. He had an augur at the Capitol maintenance facility that he had evidently used in previous years to replace limbs or fill in empty spaces in trees. He also told me that several years previous to our event, a selected tree from one of the national forests up in the Lake States had "dropped" the last 20 or 30 feet to the ground as it was being lowered, damaging or breaking off a number of limbs on one side. But in that case, since there were literally thousands of similar trees in the forest to choose from, they just went down the road and cut another tree. We wouldn't have that luxury in Ohio, so it was one more little thing that I worried about in the back of my mind.

I took one last opportunity in the early November newspaper column to fill in readers on the status of our commemorative jars and Christmas cards. Those two items had been our primary fundraising activities and both of them promised to be collector's items. I didn't want anyone to miss the chance of buying them, if they waited too long and we sold out. We had actually sold all of the sets of jars that we had at our local office, so we called back the ones that had been at our Forest Service offices in other towns, so that we could meet the demand locally.

I did find out that a few jars were still available at Huck's Farm Market, Apex Feed and Supply, Birdwatcher's Digest, Harper's Landing, and the Marietta Tourist and Convention Bureau, as well as with Marty Kitchen at the Marietta City Recreation Department. In New Matamoras there were a few jars still available at the Par-Mar #4 Station; some at Oopsa Daisy Florist in Newport; and Marge Rinard still had jars for sale in Monroe County at the Park District Office in the Courthouse at Woodsfield.

As far as the Christmas cards go, we were just about out of them, also. And I wasn't sure if we had time to order more from River Press. I hoped that everyone who wanted cards and jars could get them, but I didn't want to get stuck with a bunch of them later on either. It was kind of a tricky balancing act. I found out, and let readers know, that there were still a few packs of cards left at Sugden's Book Store, the Marietta Tourist & Convention Bureau, Oopsa Daisy Florist, and from Marty Kitchen and Marge Rinard.

I'm not sure how Connie Morris, our secretary, kept track of where all of the jars and cards were located, but she did with the able assistance of Lois Severin, who worked for us under the Senior Community Service Employment Program (SCSEP). They made final collections, kept records, used available money to purchase and pay for needed items, kept receipts, and made a full accounting to our Planning Committee.

I also announced that 72 Christmas tree ornaments were scheduled to arrive any day at our office. As mentioned earlier, these glass ornaments were produced by Casto Glass. Casto was located across the Ohio River in Ellenboro, WV, only about 10 or 12 miles due south as the crow flies from where the Capitol Christmas Tree was to be cut. The ornaments were flat, crystal disks, some square and some round, with the "1987 Capitol Christmas Tree" logo on them. We sold them for $5.00 apiece and by that time we already had about 30 of them promised. Well, we did sell out and I would go on to order another 100 ornaments because of the demand and we sold them all, too.

I mentioned in that early November column that we had sent out written invitations to several elected officials, organization presidents, chairmen, superintendents, principals, and so forth. That had been a tradition for the Forest Service to do over the years. The invitations were to the Tree Cutting Ceremony on November 20 and the Send-Off Ceremony on November 21. Naturally, when you send out something like this, you are going to forget someone; or someone is going to think they should have received one, too. I apologized in my column to those who hadn't received an invitation, but assured them that it was not intentional. I reiterated that EVERYONE in the general public was invited to both ceremonies.

Chapter 4

The Cutting Ceremony and the Send-Off Ceremony

Well, the time for the cutting was almost here: Friday, November 20, 1987 at 9:00 a.m. It had been fun and interesting over the previous few years to plan for this event. And to see the level of participation, cooperation, and volunteerism from the local community was particularly gratifying. But I was certainly going to be relieved when we got that big tree on the ground, wrapped, and ready to go to D.C.

Once again, as I get into this chapter, I apologize if I leave someone out, misspell a name, or get the timing of things a little out of order. It has gotten somewhat tedious (and discombobulating, as they say), as I have reviewed my old newspaper columns, videos, and photographs from over 30 years ago. We kept some records at the time, but we were all so busy that the taking of formal notes just didn't happen.

Still, I think you'll be pleasantly surprised at how much detail is covered in this book. And that is my primary purpose: to capture, for historical purposes, as much as possible about this event. It will certainly give future local historians a good place to start when writing about the 1987 Capitol Christmas Tree in future publications. That is why there are so many names mentioned on these pages. But I may miss listing someone; I sincerely hope not.

Up until just a few weeks prior to the scheduled cutting, we had been able to keep the actual location of the tree a secret. Of course, we later learned that, since there were not a lot of potential Capitol Christmas Trees in our area, quite a few people had a strong hunch about which tree it was going to be. And also, as it got closer to the time of the cutting, we had to let several key people know about the exact location. We swore everyone to secrecy, but you know how that goes.

We also had to go in and clear the area around the tree in order to make the felling operation safe; and we couldn't wait until the day before to do this. There were briars, brush, a few small trees, and one large, partially dead silver maple that had to be removed. One of its limbs was actually growing into the side of the Norway spruce. Once we completed those clearing tasks and brought in a few of loads of gravel for the short access road, it was pretty evident that this was going to be the site.

Almost everyone in the area was so proud of what was going to take place that we didn't really consider that vandalism might occur. But we began to hear from some sources that a few "yay-hoos" (as one of my friends called them) had bragged that they ought to go in and cut the tree down or damage it in some way. So we began to do patrols of the area about the first of

November. Those patrols included Forest Service personnel, as well as the Washington County Sheriff's office and the State Highway Patrol. Deputies and officers even parked on the site a few nights, off and on, to let people know that it was being watched.

The closer we got to November 20, the more worried I became. Once we got to within a week or so of the cutting ceremony, I decided that we needed to go into overdrive to watch the site. We had come too far to let something happen at that point. I talked with Washington County Sheriff Dick Ellis and Lt. Herman at the local Ohio Highway Patrol office again. They both agreed to pay even closer attention to the site with extra patrols.

Gil Courtney stepped up, once more, and volunteered to bring his travel trailer to the site, so that people guarding the tree could stay there overnight in a warm, dry place. After all, it was mid-November and the nights were getting very cool. Forest Service personnel or volunteers who stayed at the site overnight to provide extra security included: Dave Kantner, John Beugel, Mike Pethtel, Marilyn Ortt, Gil Courtney, Greg Danver, Matt Farnsworth, Donnie Allen, Rick Taylor, John Kerr, Dave Greenwood, Lynn Kantner, Bill Engle, Art Nicholson, Gloria Eighmey, Anne Davey, and Regina Martin. I even stayed one night.

A big thank you also went out to Southeastern Security and Investigations. They donated five days of surveillance at the tree site on Sheets Run just prior to the cutting. This was a tremendous help to us - ensuring that nothing happened to the tree prior to November 20. So, with all of this extra security assistance, I began to worry less about vandalism to the tree. That was good because there were enough other things to worry about.

In my last newspaper column that appeared prior to November 20, I reminded folks that "everyone and anyone" was invited to the ceremonies. "These events will be long-remembered in the history of our area and you'll certainly want to be there if at all possible."

I then proceeded to provide directions to the tree cutting site:

"If you do want to attend the Cutting Ceremony on 11/20/87, here's how to get there: Go to Frontier High School between 8:00 a.m. and 8:30 a.m. and park in the lot on the east side of the school beside their maintenance garage. As you face the high school with State Route 7 to your back, the lot is on the left. There will be shuttle buses which will take you to the actual tree site in the woods. Please arrive at Frontier early, so we can get everyone to the tree by 9:00 a.m. Frontier High School is located right on State Route 7, about 20 miles northeast of Marietta. Following the ceremony the buses will take you back to the high school. Don't linger or you'll have a long walk back."

I told readers that the ceremonies both days would include welcomes, short speeches by dignitaries, singing, band music, and other related goings-on; and that bad weather was predicted - chilly, with possible rain or even snow. So, the actual programs would be short, hopefully lasting only about one-half hour each.

I also gave folks a little heads-up on some things, so they knew what to expect and perhaps would not be disappointed. First, the tree itself would not be completely cut down during the Friday ceremony, although there would be some small ceremonial cuts made by certain dignitaries using a cross-cut saw. For safety reasons everyone but the workers had to be off the site by 10:00 a.m., when the final felling operation would begin. The reason? We would be using a crane, a truck and trailer, a skidder, a pick-up with a winch, and a tree-service bucket, among other things. The site would become a small construction-type area, under the direction of Mr. Casimier Wojakowski from Escanaba, Michigan, and for safety reasons we couldn't allow onlookers to get too close while the tree was coming down.

Second, I reminded people that if things went well on Friday, then the next day the tree would be wrapped, loaded, and lying on a flatbed trailer at the send-off ceremony in Marietta; but that it would not be set upright, and that no one would be allowed to touch it. We certainly didn't want folks snipping off small branches or pieces of the tree for souvenirs before we shipped it to D.C. I later found out that some of this had happened anyway.

In that last column before the two ceremonies, I caught up on giving thanks to: the Frontier Lions Club, Central Trust Company, and the Matamoras Area Business and Civic Organization for cash donations; Dave Padgitt of the Ohio Division of Forestry for use of equipment; Peoples Banking and Trust in Marietta for use of their display window; all Washington County schools for their involvement in class projects related to the Capitol Christmas Tree; and Elainea Delatore, Tonya Ice and Brenda Bowersock, students at Frontier High School, for their volunteer help; also all the teachers at Frontier High School, especially Calvin Martin and Randi Buckton, as well as Barbara Benson at Newport Elementary School.

I told readers that we had been getting calls from TV, radio, and newspapers from all over Ohio -- Cincinnati, Akron, Cleveland, Columbus, P.M. Magazine -- you name it. Once again, our area was doing something special that all Ohioans wanted to know about.

My final thoughts to the readers were: *"When this Capitol Tree project first began in our minds about 5 years ago, we weren't sure it would ever actually happen. Then in 1986 when we finally became certain that it would happen, it seemed as though 11/20/87 would never get here. Well, folks, like a big snowball gathering steam and size as it rolls to the bottom of the hill, the time is now here -- with all the momentum a truly historic event always brings. Many of you have helped make it possible. Please come join us on 11/20 or 11/21 to become part of this truly historic event."*

I also told them that many related columns would follow in weeks to come -- thank-you's, a description of the lighting ceremony in Washington, D.C. on 12/9/87, and a final perspective on the whole event.

Well, we had a few days to go before the cutting of the tree and lots of last minute details to attend to. Casimier Wojakowski (and his wife) came in a couple of days early to get his bearings, look at the site, visit with me to go over what materials and equipment we had lined up; and to let me know if there was anything else he would need in order to make sure we got the tree on the ground, wrapped, and loaded properly. Phyllis Richerson, of the Marietta Tourist and Convention Bureau, had arranged donated lodging and meals for the Wojakowski's and we covered their travel expenses from Escanaba, MI and back - out of money gained through our fundraising efforts.

From my notes of over 30 years ago, I know that lodging for the Wojakowski's was provided by Knight's Inn; and that food was provided by Bonanza, Rax, Burger King, First Settlement, Broughton's, Domino's Pizza, Bob Evans Restaurant, and Hardees. There may have been others and, if so, I apologize if I have forgotten.

Casimier was an outstanding person and we came to be good friends. For many years afterward we stayed in touch and exchanged Christmas cards each Holiday Season. He was always interested in how things were going on the Wayne National Forest and in the local area. When future national forests would call me inquiring about how we handled certain items for our event, I always recommended that they also get in touch with Casimier. He was definitely a pro at directing the felling of our tree. Casimier had done this for some previous national forests, as well as for a couple of state agencies that provided trees for their state capitols. He also told me that he had provided several trees for corporate entities that were cut in his area of Michigan and over in Wisconsin, and then delivered to Chicago, Milwaukee, and other cities.

Casimier was pleased with the equipment we had lined up and we decided which pieces should be located on site the day before the cutting and which ones could be delivered later that day on 11/20. We made sure we had backups for everything, except the crane, of course. Casimier made a list of a few additional items that we should have on hand November 20 and we purchased those locally or got them donated.

Since the R.O. Wetz flat bed trailer was going to haul the tree to D.C., we had it brought in to the site ahead of time and used it as our speakers platform the day of the cutting. After the crowd dispersed on November 20, we moved the trailer way off to one side out of the way before moving it back in to position it for the loading of the wrapped tree.

We made final contacts with all of the equipment operators; dignitaries who would be speaking; the bands, choirs, scouts, and color guard for their roles; Frontier High School for the parking, buses and other things; the Sheriff and Highway Patrol for crowd and traffic control; returned phone calls from a number of media outlets; and any last minute details that we needed to confirm.

The morning of the cutting we had a final meeting early in our office (I think it was at 7:00 a.m.) of all Forest Service employees, as well as several members of our Planning Committee, who had roles that day.

We then proceeded to the site of the cutting, where many of those involved had been getting things organized. John Kerr and Dave Greenwood, along with Wojakowski, directed where things would be located. For example, we had to reserve an area for the high school band, the choir, and the honor guard. There were other considerations, too.

Frontier High School officials had also been arranging the parking lot and buses for those wishing to attend the cutting ceremony. In addition, they brought in portable bleachers from their football field for spectators to sit on, although there were more people standing than sitting that morning.

There were porta-johns and we had to pre-position some of the equipment; and Lynn Kantner, Gloria Eighmey, Lois Severin, Regina Martin, and Connie Morris set up a registration table near the entrance to the site. We weren't necessarily going to sign everyone in, but I did want to know which dignitaries and media were there. We also answered questions from visitors, many of whom began arriving at the site around 8:00 a.m.

Connie and Lynn later gave me an estimate of at least 750 people in attendance. It could have been even more; but in any case, it was extremely crowded, young and old alike. People wanted to be there, if at all possible, to witness this historical event. The cutting took place on a Friday, a school day and a work day, so that probably kept the attendance down a little. Thank goodness! I'm not sure the site would have held very many more people.

The next day in Marietta, a Saturday, there were more people in attendance, probably over 1,000 (although initial estimates had been 500). But we had much more room with the streets blocked off in front of Marietta College's Hermann Fine Arts Center. Thinking back, I believe we planned it this way so as not to interfere with college classes during the week. Barb Hamilton and

Marty Kitchen had made arrangements with Marietta College and Mayor Nancy Hollister arranged for the road blockings and security with her police and street departments.

Oh, yes, we did bring along Smokey Bear for the Friday cutting ceremony, primarily because we knew there would be young children present that morning. Many parents in the Frontier Local School District wanted their kids to be there to witness history. And, as usual, Smokey was a hit with the kids. Every time I looked over that way, someone was taking a photo of their kid with Smokey.

Art Martin and Dale Newell of our Wayne National Forest office in Athens were also there to help. Dale took photos that day and Art was in charge of the crosscut saw, which was loaned to us from Hocking Technical College in Nelsonville, and would be used for ceremonial cuts of the tree before the final felling of the giant spruce.

The formal ceremony was to begin at 9:00 a.m. and Casimier had told us we needed to have the public off the site no later than 10:00 a.m., so that he would have time to get everything done before dark – cut and lower the tree, wrap it, and load it on the trailer.

Before going further, let me mention that there were hundreds of people taking photos and shooting video, not even counting the media. So, I have no way of knowing what all photos and tapes exist from the events. Of course, we had several Forest Service people also taking photos - like Dale Newell, who I mentioned earlier, and Lynn Kantner, who seemed to be everywhere. In addition, many people later sent photos to me.

And Lynn Kantner's son, Ray Beach, shot video of both ceremonies for the Forest Service. Ray was studying movie production at Ohio University in Athens. His brother, Cullen Beach, assisted him. I do have a copy of that tape and have reviewed it to refresh my memory and to get as much information from those two days as possible for this book. The tape was high quality, very well done, and the script for the tape was written by Lynn. They asked me to narrate the script for later dubbing into the videotape. A copy of the script is included in the Exhibits section of this book.

Also, Dean Beaver, of Newport, and Brian Brooks, President of the FFA Chapter at the Washington County Career Center, gave me copies of videos that they took and I have reviewed those, too.

The two 4-foot by 8-foot signs made by Frontier High School were placed on sturdy tripods in front of the Kenmack trailer so that people could see them and take pictures. Shorty Martin from the Frontier High School FFA Chapter stood guard by the signs. The signs were colorful and had Christmas Trees painted on them.

One of the signs read: **"1987 Capitol Christmas Tree – In Honor of the Bicentennial of the Northwest Ordinance: From Ohio, the Heart of it All."** And it listed those who had contributed to the sign: **Frontier Local School District; Frontier FFA; Haessly Lumber Company; Newport Lumber; and the Teachers & Students of Frontier High School.**

The other sign read: **"1987 Capitol Christmas Tree from Ohio – The Buckeye State."** Below that it read: **"Norway Spruce Tree From Ohio, The Heart Of It All."** And below that – **"Season's Greetings from Ohio."** In one corner was written: **"Provided By: Wayne National Forest; Washington County, Ohio; and Frontier Local School District."**

These two signs, along with others painted by Jean Pickering, were later attached to the two trailers that transported trees to the U.S. Capitol. They were seen by thousands of people during the trip to D.C. and were brought back after the trees were delivered.

Standing on the Speakers Platform just prior to the start of the ceremony, I looked out upon the crowd and was amazed at the turnout. The Frontier band and choir stood out because they were dressed in their light blue school color uniforms. Many of their parents and relatives were there, too. I remember seeing Gil Courtney in the crowd, as well as R.O. Wetz, Wayne

Schafer, Frank Voytas, Ron Cornell, and Jack Haessly. Of course, I looked over to where my wife was standing and she gave me a thumbs-up and a smile. I also remember seeing Gale Eddy, Jack Clift, and George Joy.

There were hundreds of others, but I still remember seeing those mentioned above. Now, it was time to begin. We had asked Sandy Matthews, Washington County Commissioner and resident of Frontier District, to be the morning's emcee and she readily agreed.

Sandy took the stage shortly after 9:00 a.m. and welcomed the crowd by saying: "On behalf of the Capitol Christmas Tree Committee, I want to welcome you to this historic occasion." And she completed her welcome by reminding everyone that "this is a once in a lifetime event and we here today will be a part of history."

Sandy then introduced the New Matamoras American Legion Post 378 Flag and Honor Guard; the Frontier High School band, directed by Lynn Johnson, which would play the National Anthem; and following that, the Frontier FFA students, who would lead everyone in the Pledge of Allegiance. She called on Reverend Dwight Umbel of the New Matamoras Church of the Nazarene to provide the Invocation.

Sandy then turned it over to me to introduce special guests. Our committee had decided to publicly recognize as many people in attendance as possible – to give everyone a sense of the widespread support we had enjoyed, as well as to provide a historical record of their presence that day. I knew this would be no easy chore. I had to get through this as quickly as possible because of our time constraints. I read from a list and from some scribbled notes. I was certain that I would miss someone or that I would get a name or organization wrong. (Since we didn't keep a written record of that day, I have had to reconstruct, as best I could from old videos, those mentioned that morning).

So that there is a little better flow in this chapter, those that I introduced at the Cutting Ceremony, including the equipment operators, are included in a separate document in the Exhibits section at the back of this book.

I also recognized Terry Hoffman, Deputy Supervisor for the Wayne and Hoosier National Forests; and Frank Voytas, Supervisor for the Wayne and Hoosier National Forests. Frank had recently assumed this position from Harold Godlevske, who had retired. Frank would go on to serve in his position from 1987 – 1993. I asked Frank to come forward and give some remarks. He kept it short, thanking those who had come to the ceremony; remarking that he was very impressed with the turnout and the level of cooperation and coordination; and he told them he was looking forward to working with the local residents in the future.

I reminded the crowd that the tree we were cutting today was probably set out on the banks of this Ohio River property around the turn of the century by Joseph and Mary Holdren. Several of their descendants were in the crowd that day.

I asked Jim Apgar, who was our Acting District Ranger, to come forward to make a few comments and he introduced Roland Schaar, the first District Ranger on the Athens District of the Wayne NF from 1935-1940. Roland was over 80 years old by that time and had flown to Ohio from his home in Madison, Wisconsin to be present at this event. He briefly reminisced about first arriving to work in this area over 50 years previous.

I then turned things back over to Sandy Matthews, who introduced the Frontier High School Chorus, under the direction of Bill Bigger. The chorus sang two numbers. Sandy also introduced the Frontier High School Band and Majorettes. They played several short numbers, under the direction of Johnson.

Sandy then asked Reverend Kurt Landerholm of the Newport United Methodist Church to provide the Benediction. After that, much of the crowd dispersed. Those that remained either watched or participated in several ceremonial cuts of the tree with a crosscut saw provided by Hocking Technical College. Art Martin of the Wayne National Forest's Athens Office was caretaker of the saw and provided instruction and assistance to those who were unfamiliar with the tool.

Teena Sechler introduced the following saw teams:

- Sandra Binegar and Judy Holdren Beaver
- Roland Schaar and Wayne Schafer
- Dan Kincaid and Ed Johnson (of the Agri-Country TV show in Columbus)

I then took over to introduce additional "sawyers":

- Dick Young and Sandy Matthews
- Frank Voytas and Terry Hoffman
- Gil Courtney and Donna Knowlton
- Teena Sechler and Carolyn Phipps
- Jack Haessly and Ron Cornell
- Mack Haessly and his wife
- Kenny Haessly and his wife
- Art Martin and Jim Apgar
- Donnie and Sandra Binegar
- Terry Schafer and Brian Brooks

I mentioned to the crowd that the tree would be cut down with a Poulan chainsaw. It had been a tradition for several years for that company to donate the saw for cutting the Capitol Christmas Tree.

Casimier Wojakowski seemed to be getting a little nervous, as it was around 10:00 a.m. by that time; so, we cleared the site and began the operation for the day's primary objective: cutting the Capitol Christmas Tree and getting it to the ground in one piece!

Casimier took control. The crane was already on-site, but it had to be positioned just right. Then there was also moving the other vehicles and equipment to their assigned spots and bringing in the Black's Tree Service bucket truck for two things: 1) attaching the various cables, chains, and guide ropes, in the proper locations up on the tree; and 2) cutting off branches from the bottom 20-25 feet of the tree. These branches would be saved to serve as a "bed" for the main tree to lie on during transport.

I had talked with Paul Pincus and we decided that the tree we brought over would be about 55-feet tall. Since the tree in the woods was approximately 80-feet tall, that was the reason we had to cut off the bottom section before we took it to D.C.

Casimier went up in the bucket with Greg Black to decide where to place the chains, ropes, and cables in final locations; Casimier then came back down and Greg re-ascended to make the final attachments; after which Greg cut off all of the lower branches. Next, Casimier and Mack Haessly decided where to make the "notch" cut and the back cut on the tree in order for it to go where it could be gently laid on the ground for wrapping the branches. The branch spread of the tree was about 35-feet and those branches had to be brought in and tied tightly for a final width of about 10-feet prior to transport on the roads.

Danny Thompson, John Kerr, Art Martin, and Dale Newell seemed to be all over the place helping connect and position things on the ground. Dale had put on his work coveralls after serving as a photographer earlier during the ceremony. I stayed close by Casimier to watch him and serve as his "gopher" for anything he needed. Watching him direct the operations was kind of like watching a conductor direct an orchestra. He certainly knew what he was doing.

As Mack made his final cut and the tree began its slow "fall," Casimier directed the crane and other equipment operators so as to lay it gently on the ground. The Carlton Oil crew placed the brace under the butt of the tree, located so that Mack would then have room to cut off the bottom log.

It wasn't long before the Carlton Oil crew and Forest Service personnel began the slow process of pulling in the branches. They tied them off to the main trunk of the tree with heavy nylon rope, bringing them in to a final total width of 10-feet once the wrapping was complete. The wrapping process took four hours; Casimier was planning on six hours. And he told me that one time in the Lake States that entire phase of the operation had taken nearly two eight-hour days. So, our crew was very efficient during this phase.

Fittingly, it had begun to snow during this part of the operation, lending a very "Christmassy" feel to things. Once the tree was wrapped, the crane's cable was re-attached to lift it onto the Wetz trailer. Danny Thompson even got aboard the tree and "rode" it on to the trailer, directing the crane operator to position it properly.

Before our Forest Service people had to leave that day, we took a group photo. It included: Jim Apgar, Roland Schaar, Dan Kincaid, Terry Hoffman, Gloria Eighmey, Art Martin, Dale Newell, Dave Greenwood, Frank Voytas, Connie Morris, and Lynn Kantner. I think Teena Sechler and Lois Severin had gone back to Marietta to go over plans for the following day's Send-Off Ceremony; and John Kerr, Bill Engle, and Bob Florence were down at the nearby site of the "companion" tree that we had to cut in order to gather the "extra" branches that the Capitol Landscape Architect had directed us to provide. These branches were then brought up to our location and used as packing and cushioning around the main tree. Once everything was in D.C. a week or so later, the architect used the extra branches to fill-in any sparse spots on the main tree or to replace any limbs that had been damaged during transport.

When we finally finished all of our work, it was dusk, and the R.O. Wetz truck and trailer pulled off the site with the tree. It was stored overnight at their facility and they brought it to the Send-Off Ceremony the next day. As we headed back toward Marietta, we were looking into a beautiful sunset. We all felt a sense of relief that this "tricky" part of the process was finished and had gone off without a hitch – no injuries or accidents, no equipment problems, and no damage to the tree.

Now, we had to prepare for the next day's ceremony. We knew there would be a lot of folks present for that ceremony, media included, and we wanted to make sure it was done to a high standard, also.

Our Forest Service employees gathered in the office the next day, Saturday morning, to go over final plans, while other members of our Planning Committee, Marietta City officials, local police, and Marietta College employees were preparing things at the ceremony site – in front of the Hermann Fine Arts Center at the college.

Prior to leaving our office, we took one more group Forest Service photo for our records. This photo included: Lois Severin, Gloria Eighmey, Connie Morris, Lynn Kantner, Teena Sechler, Bill Engle, Art Nicholson, Bob Florence, Dan Kincaid, and Dave Greenwood. We all had specific jobs to do that day. Lois didn't get to see much of the ceremony because she was stationed in the lobby of the Hermann Center, where we provided punch and cookies for those in attendance. She also brought with her several sets of the commemorative jars. We had been asked to do that because many people had inquired as to whether we had any left to sell. We only had a few left.

The Send-Off Ceremony began at 2:00 p.m. with Marietta Mayor Nancy Hollister as the emcee. She welcomed everyone and reminded the crowd of the significance of this event. She then asked VFW Post 5108 to present the colors and for the Marietta High School Band (known as the "Wall of Sound"), under the direction of Marshall Kimball, to play the National Anthem. Following that, Butch Hawkins and Marietta Boy Scout Troop 203 led the crowd in the Pledge of Allegiance. The Mayor then asked Pastor Don Shuler of the First Baptist Church in Marietta to provide the Invocation.

Nancy asked me to come forward and thank a few key people, including Ohio Division of Forestry employees Pete Suerken, Dave Padgitt, Floyd Stine, John Eaton, Rich Jones, and Nolan Danner. More on their specific contributions a little later. I also recognized ODNR employees from Columbus: Dave Bergman, Lynn Malowney, John Piehowicz, Anne Wickham, and Bernice Wilson, who participated on the Planning Committee in the early stages. Wickham, a native of Marietta and former classmate of both Mayor Hollister and Commissioner Matthews, came forward to give a few remarks from the ODNR perspective.

I thanked Ray and Cullen Beach for filming the events of the past two days and I asked Casimier Wojakowski to come forward. We presented him with one of the official Capitol Christmas Tree ornaments and a Forest Service cap. Casimier praised the planning committee and the community, saying that he had never seen so much involvement and spirit in any of his previous cutting assignments. He also said the ornament would go to his wife.

I thanked Marietta College for the use of their facilities, and also Howard Korn the head of the college Security Staff, Sheriff Ellis, Lt. Herman of the Ohio Highway Patrol, and the Marietta City Police for security during this day.

I told the crowd about Teena Sechler's story, "A Drummer's Gift," which had appeared in the most recent edition of Redbook Magazine. Many in the crowd had read that story. It concerned a young "drummer" or peddler who traveled the Ohio country in the late 1800s and who gave a gift of a spruce tree seedling to the wives who would come out and look at his wares. It was surmised that this was how our Capitol Christmas Tree had come to be planted nearby, along the banks of the Ohio River. Teena's story is included in the Exhibits section of this book.

Teena then came forward on behalf of the Planning Committee and introduced each of us. She presented a bouquet of flowers to both Connie Morris and Lois Severin for their assistance to the committee. She asked Frank Voytas, Jim Apgar, and Roland Schaar to give short remarks and also asked Barbara Lovely to come forward to talk about the two Bicentennials (the Northwest Ordinance and the City of Marietta.)

The following flags were then presented to Forest Supervisor Frank Voytas, who promised that they would accompany the tree to DC:

- The U.S. Flag and the Ohio Flag, both presented by Bernard Cleveland, Jr. of the VFW Post 5108
- The Marietta City Flag presented by Mayor Hollister
- The Washington County Flag presented by Commissioner Matthews
- The Bicentennial Flag presented by Barbara Lovely

Teena had Iwana Simon come forward to present awards to all of the students from Washington County schools, who had won contests for various categories of art, writing, skits, and other projects and talents related to this event. It was quite amazing to see the students from all over the county who had participated and won contests.

Mayor Hollister then introduced the Marietta High School Band to play and sing a few numbers, finishing their medley with "O Christmas Tree."

Tim Wallace, Minister from the Reno Christian Church, gave the Benediction and the Send-Off ceremony was over. Of course, many people stayed and mingled, had cookies and punch, and talked for the next hour. After that, the Capitol Christmas Tree was off to a local storage facility for several days until we delivered it to Washington, D.C.

Chapter 5

Delivering the Tree and the Lighting Ceremony

Following the Cutting Ceremony and the Send-Off Ceremony, I began my next week's newspaper column this way:

"Whew! The big day has finally come and gone. The nation's Capitol Christmas Tree is safely on the ground -- wrapped and loaded and just about ready for its trip to Washington, D.C. That's right. We've had it stored in a local warehouse for the past few days while we finished gathering the other 25 odd-sized smaller trees that go to various offices and buildings in the District of Columbia."

So, that's what was going on. We didn't head straight to D.C. following the Send-Off. Roy Wetz stored the Capitol Tree, keeping it cool and watered down, at his warehouse just south of town. Meanwhile, we were gathering up the "other" trees that we had been instructed by the Capitol Architect to provide.

Some of those other trees were shipped in to us from various parts of Ohio, contributed by members of the Ohio Christmas Tree Growers Association. These trees were what you would call a normal Christmas tree size and were slated to go in the individual offices of the Ohio Congressional delegation. The tree species varied,

89

but were mostly Douglas fir, Scotch pine, and Norway spruce. There may have been a couple of white pines and Fraser firs in there, too. Those were stored in a cool warehouse at the Ohio Division of Forestry Nursery in Reno. Nursery Superintendent, John Eaton, was very willing to assist us with this part of the overall project.

Also stored there, as we cut them locally, were the other odd size trees ranging anywhere from 12 to 24 feet in height, that went to various places such as the Smithsonian Institution; the Supreme Court; the U.S. Forest Service Office; the U.S. Botanical Gardens; the USDA lobby and the USDA Patio; and both the House and Senate Dining Rooms. At the final tally, I think we ended up taking 29 smaller trees with us, in addition to the Capitol Tree. All of the smaller trees were transported on the Kenmack Lumber trailer.

Every day for a week, Dave Greenwood of our office coordinated the caretaking of this "smaller" group of trees. Since the state nursery was right across the road from our office in Reno, it was fairly easy for him to do. Dave, Gloria Eighmey, Bill Engle, Art Nicholson, and Bob Florence watered those trees daily and even packed sphagnum moss around some of the trunks. John Kerr and Lois Severin from our office helped on some days, as did Marilyn Ortt from our Planning Committee.

In the last chapter I mentioned several ODOF employees, in addition to John Eaton at the nursery. They helped us gather the 12 to 24-foot trees. Some of those trees had been located with the help of the Marietta Tree Commission, the Matamoras Area Business and Civic Organization, the Ohio Tree Farm program, and a couple were donated to us by homeowners after reading one of my newspaper columns. After being located and approved, primarily by Pete Suerken of the ODOF and Marilyn Ortt, we still had the chore of cutting them down, wrapping them, and transporting them to the state nursery.

Here's where the rest of the ODOF assistance came in. Rich Jones and Nolan Danner brought over a log loader from Hocking State Forest and, I'll tell you, without that piece of equipment, we'd have been in big trouble. Then there was Dave Padgitt, from ODOF's Fire Control Office in Barlow. He had his long, tilt-bed truck with him and we used his winch to help load and unload the two larger trees. Floyd Stine from Suerken's crew helped wrap the trees, along with Forest Service employees Dave Greenwood, Gloria Eighmey, John Kerr and Bill Engle. It was a real team effort and we couldn't have accomplished it without everyone's help. It took the better part of a week to get this all done.

So, that's what was going on during the week following the two ceremonies. We also had to gather all of the ornaments made by school children from all over eastern, southern, and southeastern Ohio. We had requested those to be delivered to our Marietta (Reno) Office, and most were. But we had to pick up some of them, too. And those from quite a distance away, such as from Lawrence County, Muskingum County, Coshocton County, Hocking County, and other locations.......those were brought to us by either a local ODOF forester from those counties, or by our Forest Service employees in Athens and Ironton. Some of these ornaments were used to help decorate the Capitol tree, if they were weather resistant, while others were going to be delivered by us on December 1 to individual Congressional offices.

I finished that week's newspaper column by thanking several folks once again. Many had been mentioned in previous columns, but they all seemed to appreciate any recognition we could give them. And we certainly appreciated their assistance:

"Others who have donated time, money, or equipment: Haessly Hardwood Lumber Company -- materials for signs painted by Frontier High School; Gil Courtney -- use of a camper for several days preceding the cutting ceremony (parked on-site for security personnel); Harry Cogswell, Apex Feed -- rope used to tie the main tree; Matamoras Area Business and Civic Organization for three Christmas trees, two of which they got from the Mr. and Mrs. Norman Johnson farm in Monroe County; Marge Rinard of the Monroe County Park District in Woodsfield, who helped with publicity and fundraising sales of jars, cards, and ornaments; Dave Archer with Pioneer Pipe and Ray

Johnson of Apache Tank -- furnished time and materials for constructing a brace to help support the tree on the back of the trailer during its trip to D.C.; the Washington County Career Center welding class put the finishing touches on the brace; Howard Edgar Contractor, Incorporated -- dozer work on the tree site; Mike Pethtel, Eric Wagner, Cindi Hier, Elainea Delatore and other Frontier High School students -- painting of two beautiful signs for the events; Dave Kantner, John Beugel, Mike Pethtel, Marilyn Ortt, Gil Courtney, Greg Danver, Matt Farnsworth, Donnie Allen, Rick Taylor, John Kerr, Dave Greenwood, Lynn Kantner, Bill Engle, Art Nicholson, Gloria Eighmey, Anne Davey, and Regina Martin -- overnight security work. It took a lot of people to pull this off. Most have been mentioned previously.

Thanks to each and every one of you from your..........Wayne National Forest.

**I'd also like to give special thanks to the secretary at our Marietta Office – Connie Morris. She was involved in almost all facets of this event. She served on the planning committee; coordinated ordering and selling of the ornaments, cards, and commemorative jars; helped with logistics for both the cutting event and the send-off ceremony; served as our official record keeper for all things connected to this event; answered tons of questions on the phone and with walk-in visitors; and typed all of my newspaper columns, which I scratched* *out, sometimes in almost, I'm sure, unintelligible scribbles. And her able assistant, Lois Severin, who worked closely with Connie, helping out with whatever came up. Both of these ladies staffed our on-site information table at the cutting ceremony, along with Lynn Kantner. A big thank you to all of them!"*

We loaded most of the 29 smaller trees on November 27 and it was a big job. We put them on a Kenmack Lumber trailer and spent most of the day doing it. We used John Eaton's forklift to help load the two 24-foot and two 18-foot trees. Without that forklift I'm not sure how we would have loaded those four trees. We had a good crew there that day as Bob Florence and Marilyn Ortt helped the Kenmack crew -- Mack Haessly, Jr., Roger Taylor, and Tony Lauer.

Well, by Saturday, November 28, 1987 we had all of the trees loaded on to the Kenmack trailer; the trailer was covered; and the Capitol Tree signs were attached to the side of the trailer. We loaded the ornaments and other paraphernalia into vans and cars; and we were ready to head toward Washington, D.C.

Early the next morning, November 29, 1987, we all gathered at Roy Wetz' business location in Marietta and were ready for the long 300-mile trip to Washington, D.C. Bob McElfresh drove the Wetz truck with R.O. Wetz riding shotgun part of the time; Mack and Kenny Haessly took turns driving the Kenmack rig; Lynn Kantner and I were in a Forest Service vehicle; and Gil

Courtney, Randy Carletti of East-West Trailer Company, and Dave Edwards of Ravens Trailer followed in Gil's van and one other car.

We got on Interstate 77 south in Marietta, took it to U.S. Rt. 50 east in Parkersburg, WV and followed that road until we hit I-79 north in Clarksburg, WV. From there we drove to Morgantown, WV, where we connected with I-68 east.

We stopped for lunch at a truck stop and restaurant just off of I-68 near Bruceton Mills, WV before we crossed the state line into Maryland. It was at this restaurant that Gil Courtney ordered a slice of coconut crème pie. He loved it! Best he had ever eaten, he said. And he talked about it until we made it back to Marietta a few days later. In fact, on the return trip we had to stop at that restaurant for Gil to buy two whole coconut crème pies to take home with him. As you can imagine, he took a lot of kidding from our group about that.

Well, soon we were back on the road heading east on I-68 through western Maryland. Part of the stretch between Cumberland and Hancock was not yet completed, so we were on U.S. Rt. 40 for awhile. And wouldn't you know it, we got tangled up in a 3-hour, 38-mile traffic jam. We received lots of honks and waves from cars and trucks – people could read the words on the signs, which had been attached to the sides of the two trailers. They knew what we were hauling.

Lynn Kantner had traded places with Roy Wetz after lunch and she rode in the big truck with Bob McElfresh. She spent a lot of time on the CB radio. Her "handle" was Snowflake, while Bob's was Snowball. Lynn and Bob helped us keep our sanity during that traffic jam. What an experience that was!

McElfresh told many of his trucker friends on the CB radio that *"today I'm driving the only truck in the country that is hauling the U.S. Capitol Christmas Tree."*

Well, we finally hit I-70 east in Hancock, MD and then on to Frederick, MD, where we took I-270 toward D.C. Our plan all along was to stop in Rockville, Maryland, where we would stay overnight in a motel, with the trees securely locked in the fenced city police compound. I had made those arrangements with the Rockville City Police Department after talking with both Paul Pincus, the Capitol Landscape Architect, and my counterpart from the Ottawa National Forest in Michigan, who had coordinated the 1985 tree delivery. They had stored their tree at that location in Rockville in 1985, prior to heading into the Capitol the following morning, and they highly recommended that we do it. It worked out well.

Teena Sechler arrived separately and met us at our motel in Rockville. She had been busy the previous week finalizing arrangements for the delivery of the tree to the Capitol lawn, as well as setting up appointments to deliver ornaments to many of the offices of the Ohio Congressional delegation. And she was coordinating this with officials from our Forest Service Washington Office. We all met to go over final details of what would happen the next day – Monday, November 30, 1987.

Well, early the next morning the U.S. Capitol Police met us at the Rockville Police Station and gave us a formal escort the rest of the way, 25 miles or so – sirens, flashing lights and all. It was great. We didn't have to stop at another light and drove all the way right on to the Capitol Lawn!

There were a number of local spectators and a few newspaper reporters and photographers waiting there for us. They had known of the approximate arrival time. In addition there was a contingent of Forest Service and USDA officials, as well as Ohio Congressmen Applegate, Miller, Dewine, and Regula. And Capitol Landscape Architect Paul Pincus. The tree was now his! Our primary job was finished. We had gotten the Capitol Christmas Tree to D.C. in one piece.

There was more for us to do there over the next couple of days, as well as to return for the Lighting Ceremony on December 9, but what had begun as a farfetched idea in 1981 was now pretty much completed. I was proud of what we had accomplished, of course, but considering all the things that could have gone wrong over the past several years, I also felt a sense of relief.

In my local newspaper column that week, I caught up
on a few odds and ends:

- I mentioned that Casimier Wojakowski told me
  that the ground crew at the cutting operation was
  the best he had ever worked with. I had told him
  that it was because of his expert leadership, but
  being the humble person that he was, he said, *"a
  band leader is only as good as his band."*
- I apologized if I had been short or abrupt with
  anyone during the two ceremonies (I don't think
  I was, but who knows), but that there had been
  so much happening that I was on system
  overload for a couple of days. As my wife said
  later, "At times, I acted like I was in a tizzy." But
  now it's better. I'm back to my same old jovial self.
- I wrote: *"How about a hand for that Carlton Oil
  crew led by Danny Thompson? They, along with
  Jeff Edgar, jumped right in and had that tree
  tied up in no time flat. The Carlton crew
  included Roger Strickler, Jack Strickler, Danny
  Thompson, Jr., Harold Edgar, and Frank
  Edgar."*
- I also said to readers: *"Want one of those Capitol
  Tree T-shirts or sweatshirts? They're done very
  nicely and will be excellent keepsakes. Contact
  Bill Creighton at Creighton Sports Center in
  New Matamoras. He can have them done to say
  New Matamoras; Bicentennial of the Northwest*

> *Ordinance; Wayne National Forest; or whatever you want."*

- And for readers who had not been at the cutting ceremony, I wrote that: *"It was great to have Sandra Binegar, Carolyn Phipps, and Judy Beaver, all descendants of the Holdren family -- on hand for the festivities. The Holdren's had originally owned the property where the Capitol Christmas Tree was cut.......before it became part of Wayne National Forest. It made a good tie-in with the historical aspect of the whole Capitol Christmas Tree event."*

After delivering the tree on November 30, we were invited into the House Dining Room for lunch. That was quite a treat for all of us. For the next two days, Teena, Lynn, and I delivered ornaments and made courtesy calls to the Ohio Congressional delegation, as well as to the USDA and Forest Service offices. Paul Pincus had his crew take all of the 29 smaller Christmas trees to their respective locations, so that when we arrived with the ornaments, the trees were there also.

Teena had worked with our Forest Service Washington Office staff to set up as many visits as possible with the Ohio delegation. Some members were not available on those days for various reasons, but as I recall, we made it to many of them. I especially remember visiting with Senator Glenn and Congressmen Dewine and Stokes. They were each highly pleased with our efforts and with all of the ornaments that we took to them that had been made by Ohio school children.

While we were delivering the ornaments, our trucking contingent, along with Gil Courtney, had been doing a little sightseeing and also were treated to a tour and lunch by Congressman Applegate, followed by a meeting in his office to discuss things that were important to them in his District of southeastern Ohio.

When we all returned home a couple of days later, we were very relieved that we had accomplished our main objective – getting the trees to the Capitol in one piece. But there were still some logistics to work on, as far as returning for the lighting ceremony on December 9.

And Gil Courtney went to work on lining up buses to take as many people as possible from Monroe and Washington counties (mostly from Frontier School District) to that event. He also made sure that the Frontier High School band was included and that their way was completely paid for. There ended up being five bus loads of people from that area attending the lighting ceremony. In addition, Phyllis Richerson was lining up a couple of buses to do the same from Marietta with the help of Larry and Janet Steinel from Uniglobe Travel in Marietta.

Gil worked tirelessly behind the scenes with Congressman Applegate and with George White, Architect of the Capitol (AOC), to get approval for the

Frontier Band to perform during the Lighting Ceremony. George was to serve as emcee for the ceremony and he had a lot of control over the agenda.

Gil was working on something else, too. He wanted to get approval for New Matamoras' Mary Carson to sing the National Anthem on December 9. It hadn't been common in previous years for a local high school band or a local singer to be part of the formal Lighting Ceremony. I'm told that Gil made many assurances and promises in getting both of those performances approved. I believe he also had to submit a tape recording for George White to listen to before final approval was given. And in the end, during the December 9 ceremony, the performances by Mary Carson and by the Frontier band were outstanding. They were proud to have participated in the ceremony and all of us from "back home" were extremely proud of them, also.

Before I forget it, let me mention that Capitol Landscape Architect Paul Pincus, who coordinated the annual Capitol Christmas tree event in those days, remarked to me that he had never seen such widespread local interest in the festivities. I took that as a huge compliment directed toward all of Washington County and surrounding areas.

In my last newspaper column before the Lighting Ceremony, I mentioned that Casimier Wojakowski told me, that in addition to the outstanding local community support he had observed for our project, there was more media coverage at our cutting ceremony than all the others he had ever participated in combined. That covered several states and 20-some years of experience. Quite a compliment!

I figured that Casimier was right, too. We had TV and newspaper coverage from Marietta, Parkersburg, Columbus, Cleveland, Akron, Cincinnati, Dayton, Wheeling, Pittsburgh, Huntington, Charleston, Clarksburg, and several others for the cutting and send-off. And then, Cable News Network and several of the metro DC papers and TV stations also gave us good coverage for the lighting ceremony.

In my column I also told readers – *"Don't forget to watch "Agricountry" with Ed Johnson on Channel 10-TV, Columbus at 7:30 a.m. on Saturday, December 19. That's the Christmas show which will feature a several minute segment on our Capitol Tree cutting. Ed and his crew were down here on November 20 for quite awhile to film and interview people. Check your local listings to make sure of the time, but 12/19/87 is the right date. The exact time does vary in some towns, however, but it is always early on Saturday morning."*

(I have a clip of that Agricountry segment that Ed sent to me afterward. On the segment, he interviewed both me and Judy Holdren Beaver.)

In that column I also tried to get caught up on publicly thanking folks for donations toward the project: Swan Lumber Do-It-Center, Marietta -- lumber; fuel for the R.O. Wetz Transportation and Kenmack Lumber trucks from Bill Hollister at Par Mar Oil and Chuck Pannier at Englefield (Duke Oil Co.); and the following Washington County financial institutions which helped cover meal and lodging costs for the truckers who took the trees to Washington -- Bartlett Farmers Bank, Peoples Savings Bank of New Matamoras, Lower Salem Commercial Bank, Waterford Commercial & Savings Bank, and Peoples Banking & Trust Company of Marietta.

Finally, it was Wednesday, December 9, 1987 and we were back in Washington, D.C. for the 5:00 p.m. Lighting Ceremony. Earlier that morning the Frontier High School Future Farmers of America participated in two exciting ceremonies. They made U.S. Representatives Doug Applegate and Clarence Miller honorary Frontier Chapter members and presented each congressman with an FFA jacket.

The students, under the direction of advisor Calvin Martin, had prepared a formal ceremony complete with remarks and participation by seven FFA members. They did a fine job and each Congressman seemed very pleased with the honor. The students were Matt Farnsworth, Greg Danver, Mike Pethtel, Shorty Martin, John Buegel, Mike Berentz, and Bruce Becker.

Superintendent John Hoff and Principal Bob Forbes accompanied the FFA group, as did Fred Yonda who took videos of the ceremonies. Calvin had also invited me to attend and I tagged along to take some black and white photos for the group to use in future school newsletters, in their High School Annual Yearbook, and other publications.

My wife Vicki, son Brent, and daughter Shannon were with me on this trip. Our oldest son, Jeff, was a freshman at Glenville State College and he was tied up with final exams, so he couldn't come with us. In the early afternoon we were able to visit the USDA and Forest Service Headquarters and meet the Secretary of Agriculture, the Forest Service Chief, and others.

We also spent 15 minutes in the office of Assistant Secretary of Agriculture, Wilmer Mizell. We didn't talk agriculture or forestry, either. We talked baseball. Some will remember him as "Vinegar Bend" Mizell, who pitched for the Cardinals and Pirates in the late 1950's and early '60's.

This meeting had been arranged before we got to D.C., so I had brought along a 1957 Topps baseball card. Vinegar Bend autographed it for me and apologized for the grief he caused me in 1960 when his Pirates beat my beloved New York Yankees in the World Series. Somehow, after that, Bill Mazeroski's fluke home run in Game 7 seemed easier to take.

That meeting had been set up by Al Wolter, Assistant Director of the U.S. Forest Service Office of Information (OI). I had known Al for many years. In fact, I worked for him when he was the District Ranger at Ironton on the Wayne NF back in the mid-1970s. He was very proud that the Wayne NF furnished the 1987 Capitol Christmas Tree. By the way, Al had worked for Don Girton, the Director of OI, until about 1985. Don had also served as Forest Supervisor of the Wayne and Hoosier National Forests in the 1970s. Small world!

Soon, it was nearing time for the Lighting Ceremony, so we went back up to the outdoor patio at the U.S. Capitol, facing west toward the Washington Monument, where the tree was standing on the lawn waiting to be lit. The Navy Band was sitting off to one side playing "Joy to the World" and other seasonal Christmas music prior to the ceremony beginning.

George White (AOC) was the emcee for the evening and he delayed things for just a few minutes so that as many of the Ohio Congressional Delegation as possible could make it down to the ceremony. They had been in session that day and had been voting on various items.

 We were told that some of them had been in meetings to discuss various aspects of the talks that were currently occurring down at the White House between President Reagan and Russian General Secretary Gorbachev. That was referred to as the Washington Summit and took place from December 8 – 10, 1987.

The two had agreed on reducing the size of their nations' respective nuclear arsenals and were working on a "missile treaty." Looking back, it was an exciting time for us to be there with the tree, but it was also an important and historic time for the country.

White finally kicked off things by welcoming everyone in attendance, including the approximately 500 people from Washington County, Ohio. Some say it was really only about 400, but in any case there were a lot of Ohioans there that evening. White also thanked those Forest Service officials that were present for their support of this annual event. I'm not sure of all those Forest Service officials who were present, but I do know that the Chief, Dale Robertson was there, as well as the Deputy Chief, George Leonard. Others present were Associate Chiefs Jeff Sirmon and Al West; Director of Public Affairs Ed Vandermillen; Regional Forester Floyd Marita from Milwaukee, WI; Wayne-Hoosier NFs Supervisor Frank Voytas; Deputy Supervisor Terry Hoffman; Wayne-Hoosier Public Information Officer Teena Sechler; and Acting District Ranger Jim Apgar.

White gave a short history of the Capitol Christmas Tree, dating back to the first official tree in 1964. (I wrote about that history in the Preface of this book.) He also mentioned the difference between the White House Tree, which he called the national tree, and the Capitol Tree, which he called "the people's tree."

White asked Mary Carson to come forward and sing the National Anthem. I must say that she did an outstanding job, which was recognized in subsequent remarks by White and several other speakers.

George then introduced the Speaker of the House, Representative Jim Wright of Texas, who was known for his eloquent and 'silver-tongued' linguistics. He didn't disappoint that day either, as he gave a powerful and skillful speech filled with patriotic and scriptural references about Christmas.

When Speaker Wright was finished talking, he walked over to the balcony and flipped the switch to light up "our" Christmas tree. And it was beautiful. "Magnificent," as Mayor Nancy Hollister would say a few minutes later. Depending upon who you were talking with, "our" tree was from Wayne National Forest; or it was from Washington County or Frontier School District; or it was from Newport, New Matamoras, or even Marietta; and to most of the others, it was simply from Ohio.

Mayor Hollister was next to give remarks and she did a great job, referring to the Bicentennial of the Northwest Ordinance, the *"beautiful City of Marietta, Wayne National Forest, the State of Ohio, Washington County, New Matamoras, Newport and the tree – our queen of the forest and our gift to the nation."*

She was followed by Ohio Governor, Richard Celeste, who also gave fine remarks on behalf of the state. He said that the *"tree symbolizes our hopes and prayers as the two world leaders meet."* Celeste recognized George Patton, who came with him, and represented the handicapped workers at Belco Crafts in St. Clairsville, OH. They had brought along some handmade ornaments for the Ohio delegation. Celeste concluded by presenting George White a Christmas wreath made in Ohio. Most of the speakers that evening knew that White was a native Ohioan and made reference to that during their presentations.

Senator John Glenn came forward and said that this evening, with the tree from Ohio in the background, *"We are standing in one of the most beautiful spots in the world. This is one of the most beautifully decorated trees I have ever seen anywhere."*

White then introduced Lynn Johnson and the Frontier High School band, which played a medley of Christmas music, including: Deck the Halls; Angels We Have Heard on High; Hark the Herald Angels Sing; Joy to the World; and O' Come All Ye Faithful. When they were finished, White thanked them for doing such a great job.

Congressman Regula then spoke followed by a number from the Navy Band – "Oh, Christmas Tree." Five more members of the Ohio delegation then made brief remarks before the ceremony ended. Those were:

Congressman Applegate, Congresswoman Oakar, Senator Metzenbaum, Congressman Miller, and Congressman Eckart.

Congressman Applegate, whose District the tree came from, gave a shout out *to "Gil Courtney; Kenny and Mack Haessly; Mary Carson; and Dan Kincaid of Wayne National Forest."* Wow! I hadn't expected that. He also called Gil Courtney *"the Cecil B. DeMille of Washington County."* Thinking back on it, I'll bet Gil gave my name to the Congressman.

There were too many people present to recognize everyone, but it was great to have all three Washington County Commissioners there -- Sandy Matthews, Glenn Miller, and Dick Young. We certainly appreciated their support and involvement in the activities.

After the ceremony, Senator Glenn invited several Forest Service people to his officc for eggnog and cookies. That was quite a treat being able to talk with him in a less formal setting. He and his wife were very friendly, down-to-earth people. I guess that's not too surprising since they hailed from a small Ohio town – New Concord - just up the road from Marietta.

Senator Glenn and I talked about New Concord's other famous son, the Ohio State basketball star, Jay Burson. My wife Vicki, son Brent, and daughter Shannon were there, too, enjoying the conversation. Believe me, we took plenty of photos. Unfortunately, our oldest son Jeff was unable to be there because he was away at college, studying for semester exams. He would have enjoyed meeting Senator Glenn, I'm sure. Senator Glenn promised to send autographed astronaut photos of himself to our three kids – and he did!

Vicki and Senator Glenn also had a long chat about his boyhood friends in New Concord, the Cooper family, one of whom was the father of Marietta physician, Dr. Warren Cooper. Vicki was a registered nurse, working for Drs. Cooper and White at Marietta Ob-Gyn Associates.

George Merkel, Director of Alumni Affairs at Marietta College, also put on a very nice reception at the Master Hosts Inn in D.C. following the ceremony. He had quite a nice set-up with cookies, sandwiches, and all the fixin's. We went over for a short while and it was enjoyable talking with George and his wife, Joan, about Marietta College and everything else as the evening progressed.

Governor Celeste and Mayor Hollister also hosted a reception for dignitaries and the many Ohioans who had traveled to D.C. for the lighting ceremony.

As everything related to the Lighting Ceremony wrapped up that evening, there was a mixture of emotions -- some of us were relieved that it was over; others were sad to see it end; some had been in awe of the tremendously beautiful setting and the ceremony itself; and everyone was proud, extremely proud, that the Wayne National Forest and all of Washington County were able to participate in such an event.

We were sure that for many, many years to come, when the Christmas season approached and we read about Capitol Christmas trees, that we would all fondly recall the time when "our" tree was sent to Washington, D.C.

Chapter 6

Wrapping Up Things

After the Lighting Ceremony we returned home and finally had a chance to catch our breath. However, there were still quite a few newspaper columns that I wrote for the next several weeks that pertained to follow-up items related to the entire Capitol Christmas Tree event. These were things that the reading public needed to know about.

One of the best ways for me to fully remember what all occurred during that time period is to review my newspaper columns. In my last column of 1987 I covered some odds and ends related to the Capitol Christmas Tree. Here are a few things I wrote in that article:

I've been asked if there were any "special" little things which happened during the Capitol Christmas tree hoopla which I'll never forget. Sure there were - many of them.

Standing above all else has to be the many friendships we made and the great cooperative efforts of hundreds of local people who made the entire operation such a huge success. I'll certainly never forget that.

Neither will I forget the many cards, calls, and thank you's we've received. We really feel honored to have been part of an event which focused such a large amount of positive publicity on our area. And you know what? We had fun doing it! Thanks to all of you.

Some of the other things which stand out:

*I'll never forget running all those red lights on the morning of November 30, either, as we received our police escort, taking the tree from Rockville, Maryland to the U.S. Capitol. It was great! All those lights and we didn't even have to stop. If only I could do that when I'm in Columbus.

*And R.O. Wetz' fender bender. Pardon me, Roy, for mentioning it, but heck, it wasn't your fault anyway. DC drivers during the morning rush can be real maniacs and this guy was no exception. He tried to squeeze his size 4 car into a size 3 space and it just wouldn't fit. The big, burly dude appeared ready for an argument with Roy, but when Mack Haessly, Bob McElfresh, Gil Courtney, Kenny Haessly, and I joined Roy, the fellow mysteriously calmed down.

*Linda Roderick and Phil Straw of Congressman Miller's office, Jim Hart of Congressman Applegate's office, and Martha DiSario of Senator Glenn's office were all extra nice to us -- being rookies in D.C. as we were. Thanks go out to all of them!

*It was a real pleasure to meet and talk with the Chief and Associate Chief of the Forest Service -- Dale Robertson and George Leonard -- and also the

Secretary of Agriculture, Richard Lyng, and his Deputy, Peter Myers.

**R.O. Wetz said he wasn't sure whether that was Gil Courtney with us or not. He couldn't get a good look at him because he always had either a video camera or a CB mike in front of his face. What a crew! Seriously, though, we had a great time and Gil got a lot of good film footage. We even ate a couple of coconut pies. Right, Gil?*

**North Hills School in Marietta recently planted a Norway spruce to commemorate the Capitol Tree and the bicentennial of the Northwest Ordinance. Each Christmas, many folks will remember the tree, when it was planted, and why. What a great project for grade school kids to be involved with."*

TV moments that we were made aware of:

- Someone sent me a news clip from TV Channel 9 Eyewitness News in D.C. They compared the White House and Capitol Trees, and interviewed several people who unanimously said that the Capitol Tree was the prettiest. The newscaster stated that there were 5,000 lights on the Capitol Tree. I don't know where they got that figure, but probably from Paul Pincus or George White. There was also an item on TV Channel 5 in D.C.
- I also received a clip from TV Channel 4 in Columbus, OH that showed the tree being

> delivered to the Capitol. They must have gotten
> that from a sister station in D.C. In that clip they
> also dubbed in on-site interviews with me and
> Gil Courtney, taken the day of the cutting.
> - WTAP-TV in Parkersburg, WV had a pretty
>   lengthy segment about the cutting and send-off,
>   in which they interviewed me, Casimier
>   Wojakowski, Sandra Binegar, and Judy Holdren
>   Beaver.

I'd like to give special thanks to The Marietta Times and the Parkersburg News/Marietta A.M. newspapers. Their reporters covered all of the Capitol Christmas Tree festivities for their readers from beginning to end; and they didn't miss much; they were everywhere. A couple of reporters even rode on the buses to D.C.

<u>Note</u>: In the Exhibits section at the end of this book, I will provide a list of all of the local newspaper coverage from writers other than myself that I have been able to re-capture, plus some stories and information that was sent to me from non-local sources. I'm sure I don't have everything, but this will give you an idea of the wide coverage we received.

I also want to mention that Robert Conrad, Chief of the U.S. Forest Service's National Media Office, sent a note to Teena Sechler in late December 1987 congratulating us on all of the publicity we had received for our tree. He told Teena that he had been in his position for 12 years and that he had never seen so much media attention devoted to the Capitol Christmas Tree. *"Best job, by far,"* he told her.

With the primary events related to the Capitol Christmas Tree now behind us, I had other Forest Service items to mention in my columns.

My first column to appear in 1988 announced that the Wayne National Forest Land Management Plan would be released in a few days. That was the culmination of several years' worth of work, including large amounts of public input.

I invited the public to "join with us in implementing the plan and in helping us monitor its progress -- sort of keeping tabs on how things are working out. We believe that fostering a good working partnership with the public is one of the ways we can make the Wayne the best National Forest in the country." And, of course, one of our best ever partnership activities had been the Capitol Christmas Tree project.

But there were still a few tree-related things to mention in that week's column, too. That continued off and on for a few months, and from time to time in 1989.

In that first 1988 column, I also mentioned that:

- I had received copies from several people of a recent Washington Post newspaper article, which gave detailed descriptions of many of the Christmas trees in and around the Washington, D.C. area. The author's conclusion was that the U.S. Capitol tree, furnished by Wayne National Forest, was by far the prettiest one. He felt that the White House tree was not "in the same league" with the Capitol tree and he went on to call our Norway spruce "spectacular." But we knew that already, didn't we? One more thing to remind us all that we were involved in a truly special event this past Christmas season.

-     Paul Pincus, the Landscape Architect for the U.S. Capitol, who coordinated the Christmas tree festivities on the D.C. end, also dropped me a note about the Washington Post article. He had been involved in the Capitol Tree program since it started 24 years previous and he said that this was the first time the Washington Post had ever bothered to do an article about it. Another first for our Washington County tree!

-     We also received personal thank you's for the Christmas tree effort from Senator Glenn and Representatives Applegate, Miller, and Stokes, among others. We definitely got the feeling that the entire Ohio Congressional delegation was extremely proud of the fact that the Buckeye State furnished the 1987 tree.

-     I announced that we had received one last order of 100 Christmas tree ornaments. We had sold out of two previous orders and had not anticipated ordering any more. But there were just too many people who were disappointed that they didn't get one. So, we called Casto Glass and they whipped us out one more batch. I told readers that, *"They're first-come, first-serve and will no doubt go fast. No orders or reservations please. Call to see if we have any left and then pick them up at our Reno office. Once again, thank all of you for your interest in and support of the 1987 Capitol Christmas Tree project."*

During the next two weeks I mentioned a number of items in my columns related to the Capitol Christmas Tree.

Transport Topics, a national trucking magazine, had recently featured a color cover photo of the Capitol Tree being unloaded on November 30 in D.C. There was also a short story inside the magazine about the tree, mentioning R.O. Wetz Transportation and Kenmack Lumber, Inc.

Ohio Woodlands, the quarterly magazine put out by the Ohio Forestry Association, announced that its next issue would include photos and a story about the Capitol Tree. And the best thing? The magazine cover was going to be a color photo that I had taken of the tree back in early November before the cutting. Lynn Kantner was sitting on a tree stump in the foreground pointing up to the tree. We were especially excited because Ohio Woodlands was always sent to every high school library in the state.

Also, it was now official! The Capitol Tree, at least part of it, would be returning to Washington County, Ohio.

We planned to use the tree in conjunction with 2 or 3 local high school shop classes -- Frontier High and Washington County Vocational School, in particular. Gil Courtney was primarily responsible for getting permission to bring the tree back. He worked closely with Congressman Douglas Applegate, Capitol Architect George White, and Landscape Architect Paul Pincus to make it happen. I wrote, "Way to go, Gil!" and promised more details at a later date.

I told readers that I had received a nice note from Casimier Wojakowski, who had traveled to Ohio from Michigan in November to help us cut the Capitol Christmas Tree. A couple of weeks earlier I had sent Casimier some newspaper clippings, and so had a few other people, which mentioned what he had done to help us. He really enjoyed them and said that he and his wife held a warm spot in their hearts for all of their Washington County friends. They had really enjoyed their three-day stay here.

Casimier had also been in touch with R.O. Wetz and he wrote that he and his wife had watched the December 9 tree lighting ceremony on Cable News Network. His local newspaper, The Escanaba (Michigan) Daily Press, had featured several articles on Casimier and our tree. He wrote that he had received more press "than Gary Hart" in his area. He said he told the Daily Press editor that they had made him famous, but he'd rather they make him rich.

What a fine fellow. It was certainly a pleasure meeting and working with him on the Capitol Tree project.

Danny Thompson, of Carlton Oil Corporation, had some beautiful Christmas cards made which showed his crew standing in front of the Capitol Tree before it was cut. They took a group photo right after a snowfall that we had in early November, and it was quite a shot. Employees standing in front of the tree were: Linda Boron, Frank Edgar, Harold Edgar, Art Edgar, Jack Strickler, and Roger Strickler. The cards read, in part, *"Carlton Oil Corporation is proud to have assisted in cutting and preparation for shipment of the tree to the Capitol. Best Wishes for the Holidays and Health and Happiness throughout a Prosperous New Year."* Cards were sent to various customers and friends of Carlton Oil, and they proved to be very nice keepsakes. The cards were signed by Warren Kimber, Jr., Martin Heller, and Dan Thompson.

Harold Mueller of Marietta sent me a clipping from Stars and Stripes, the newspaper published for U.S. servicemen in Europe. It was an article about none other than our Capitol Christmas Tree, which was getting not only local, state, and national coverage, but now worldwide coverage as well! Harold's son was serving with the U.S. Army in Germany and had sent the article home.

I asked anyone who had photos (color or black and white), slides, or videos of anything related to the

Capitol Tree event to contact us at 373-9055. We wanted to have as much pictorial documentation as possible of the events. I told readers that, "We can have copies made of your slides and negatives if you'd just let us borrow them for a short while. Thanks for your help with this."

Carolyn Phipps, one of the granddaughters of Joseph and Mary Holdren, had loaned us a couple of old turn-of-the-century photos from which we had copies made. They showed the Holdren family and we planned to display them in a prominent place in our Reno office. The Holdren's, of course, were the likely planters of the Norway spruce which had been selected as the 1987 Capitol Christmas tree. The land at the mouth of Sheets Run, where the tree had grown, was now part of the Wayne National Forest and had been since 1969. But the land had been in the Holdren family for many, many years throughout the 1800's and the early part of the 1900's. The Capitol Tree was probably planted sometime around 1900 or soon thereafter.

About half of the column that I wrote on March 21, 1988 contained further information about what was happening with the butt sections of the Capitol Christmas Tree. But I opened the column with a tribute to Hugh Patterson, who had recently passed away. I had become friends with Hugh over the previous several years. He lived near Sitka, out on State Route 26 northeast of Marietta, near Wayne National Forest land. Hugh was quite a fellow and one of the most interesting outdoorsmen I had ever known. We were all saddened with his passing.

As for the tree trunk, many people were aware that R.O. Wetz Transportation of Marietta was able to swing by the U.S. Capitol in mid-January and bring back two 19-foot sections of the tree trunk. These were then unloaded and stored for a few days by the Forestry Class at the Washington County Career Center, where the logs were sawed down to shorter lengths.

Then the logs were divided up amongst the Washington County Career Center, Frontier High School Band Boosters, Swiss Hills Vocational School in Monroe County, and the Frontier Future Farmers of America. These groups planned to use the wood to make souvenirs for fund raising events, and so on.

From the original 25-foot butt section of the Capitol tree (remember, we shortened it from 80 to 55-feet prior to shipping to D.C.), which had been stored by Kenmack Lumber of Newport, we were also able to saw out a few hundred board feet of lumber. Kenmack Lumber did the sawing in February of 1988 and Haessly Hardwood Lumber Company of Newport Pike dry kilned the boards for us. Haessly Hardwood also ran the boards through their planer and we picked them up in late February.

We then began the long process of edging the lumber in our shop, culling out the bad stuff, and cutting out and finishing the many, many, many plaques, which we presented to those who had helped us throughout the entire project. Those people ended up with an actual "piece of the tree."

Zide's Sport Shop agreed to donate metal tag plates for the plaques, so we attached those and before long we distributed those mementos. A photo in the Exhibits section at the end of this book shows what the plaques looked like. The tags read:
"Thanks For Your Help With The 1987 Capitol Christmas Tree Project – Wayne National Forest." Art Nicholson routed the edges of the plaques in our shop; branded outlines of two spruce trees on them; and put a coat of shellac on each plaque. About half of the plaques were designed horizontally and half vertically. Each one was about 7 x 9 inches in size. I can't remember how many plaques we made and presented, but it was well over 100.

I thanked all of those who had helped in this "follow-up" portion of the Capitol Christmas Tree project and wrote that *"bringing things to a successful and memorable close is every bit as important as the earlier work."*

In my April 4, 1988 column, I mentioned that Pat Murphy recently pointed out in one of her "Birds I View" columns for The Marietta Times that the proper name for our local geese was Canada goose, not Canadian goose.

It immediately reminded me of something which had been bugging me and had been on my mind for quite awhile. The proper name for the tree species which had served as the 1987 Capitol Christmas Tree was Norway spruce, not Norwegian spruce.

Many of my news releases and columns over the previous year had been incorrectly edited to read "Norwegian spruce;" and several broadcasts by various media from around the state ended up with the incorrect name, Norwegian spruce, too.

So I told readers to *"remember, not only are the birds Canada geese, but the trees are Norway spruce."*

In my April 18, 1988 column I told readers that Phyllis Richerson would soon be leaving our area. She was Director of the Marietta Tourist and Convention Bureau and had been one of the key members of our Capitol Christmas Tree Planning Committee. Phyllis had been instrumental in several phases of the project, including assistance with selling souvenir cards and jars; getting the ball rolling for the two tour buses which went from Marietta to Washington, D.C. for the lighting ceremony; and helping host lunch for Paul Pincus, the Capitol Landscape Architect, when he made his trip to Washington County in September 1986 to give final approval for our Norway spruce tree.

I recalled that at first Pincus wasn't totally positive about our tree, but after Phyllis and a couple of others (Barbara Lovely and Nancy Hollister) gave him the hard sell, he became convinced. They pointed out the connection to the bicentennial celebrations and the expected high level of local enthusiasm and before long Pincus was sold on approving our tree. I told readers that Phyllis would be sorely missed and wished her the best. I concluded by sincerely thanking her for all she did during the 1987 Capitol Christmas Tree project.

On April 25, 1988 I wrote about a Review Team of Forest Service officials, primarily from our Regional Office in Milwaukee, Wisconsin, which was looking at projects and activities on the Wayne National Forest. They spent time at all three Wayne NF locations – Ironton, Athens, and Marietta. On the first afternoon of their Marietta visit, we took the Team to the Capitol Christmas Tree site and discussed plans for a picnic area to be built there. We were joined by Gil Courtney of New Matamoras, who gave special insight into the Capitol Tree project and also suggested how we might build toward some cooperative recreation projects in the Frontier School District.

Just a week later, I announced that the memory of the Capitol Christmas Tree project would live on in yet another way: We had finished building a picnic area on the site near Sheets Run. Actually, it was not completely finished yet, but it was certainly usable.

We had installed two picnic tables, fire rings, benches, and seats, as well as placing new signs on State Route 7 directing people to the area. There were some minor additions to be made in the near future, but most things were in place.

We had received advice and assistance on the project from Pete Edgar, Jeff Edgar, Gil Courtney, Marilyn Ortt, Lewis Grimes, Calvin Martin, and several Frontier High School students. The Frontier FFA Club planned on helping out each year with maintenance at the site -- mowing, repair, litter patrol, and so on.

Dave Kissel, landscape architect from our Bedford, Indiana office, drew up the plans for the area and he did a fine job. We were sure that local residents and visitors would enjoy the area. We asked readers to help us look after this recreation site and help us take care of it. The Capitol Tree project, after all, was shared by our entire communities and we didn't want anything to happen there -- like vandalism.

But we had already had one minor incident occur. Judy Holdren Beaver had planted a small Norway spruce right beside the stump of the Capitol Tree to honor and remember her grandparents, who had lived there around the turn of the century. Marie Holdren (Judy's mother), of New Matamoras, had been in touch with me about the new tree. They were extremely proud of it and so was I. It was a beautiful young tree and a fitting memorial.

I ended by saying that it was a crying shame that someone had slipped in there after dark one night and dug it up. I told readers that we would replace it and see what happens. I wrote that *"obviously, we can't go in there every week and plant another tree. So, we'll need everyone's assistance in helping us care for the area. Either that, or close down the site and chalk up another victory for the rowdies."*

Your.....Wayne National Forest column that I wrote on May 16, 1988:
Investment in our young people.

That's the type of investment which will surely pay dividends in the future. Our young people, of course, are our future and I'd like to tell you what some folks are doing to ensure that it is a bright one.

We'll go back to the beginning, which again was the Wayne National Forest's Capitol Christmas Tree project. Many worthwhile programs got their start because of the activities surrounding that event. I suspect that for years we will be tracing the beginnings of many additional programs to good will and public support that surrounded the Capitol Tree project.

When the tree was cut last November, among the 700-plus people in attendance were Roy Palmer -- from Hocking Technical College (HTC); Ron Cornell -- The Ohio Forestry Association; and Jack Haessly - Haessly

Hardwood Lumber Co. These three men were very impressed with the entire ceremony and the coordination involved. They were especially impressed with the involvement of the young people who we had helping us out.

Those young people were none other than Calvin Martin's Frontier High School FFA group and Terry Schafer's Forestry Class from the Washington County Career Center. Several other young people, primarily Frontier students, helped out that day, also.

Roy, Jack, and Ron got to thinking that it would be great to take advantage of the Capitol Christmas Tree enthusiasm, do something positive for our youths, and somehow mesh that together with their interest and involvement in forestry and natural resources.

What they came up with was this: Hocking Tech put up $450 and Haessly Hardwood matched that amount. The money is to be used as scholarship funds for students entering Hocking Tech in any of the natural resource fields. The name associated with the awards will be:"Capitol Christmas Tree Scholarships."

Calvin Martin, who has been instrumental in urging his students to enter natural resource work, was able to chip-in $200 from the FFA toward the scholarship fund. The FFA earned that money, and more, from a couple of Wayne National Forest work projects this year.

What came out of this great idea was the awarding of scholarships to three high school seniors, who will be entering Hocking Tech next Fall -- Eric Wagner and Matt Farnsworth of Frontier High, who will be studying Parks and Recreation Management; and Bill Close of the Career Center, who will study Timber Harvesting at HTC.

On May 19 I went to the Capitol Tree site with Roy, Ron, Jack, and Judy Sinnott, who is the Information Director at HTC. There we were joined by Bob Forbes, Frontier High's principal, Calvin, Terry, and the three students, who were each presented with the very first Capitol Christmas Tree scholarships.

The feeling among all those involved is to try to make the scholarship awards an annual event. By so doing it will encourage local kids to further their education -- and further it in the natural resource fields which will be so important to us in this area of the state in future years.

It's another success story spawned by the Capitol Tree ceremony; and everyone who helped us out last fall played a role in making this come about. We thank you, and our young people thank you.

I didn't mention the Capitol Christmas Tree in my weekly column again until October 24, 1988. In that column I announced that Al Wolter had recently retired from the U.S. Forest Service and was taking a new job back in Ohio as Director of Communications with the

Columbus-based Wildlife Legislative Fund of America. Al had worked on the Wayne National Forest in Ironton as the District Ranger in the 1970s. I actually worked for him in the mid-1970s at Ironton as what was then often referred to as a "junior forester."

Most recently Al had served as the Forest Service Deputy Director of the Office of Information in Washington, D.C. You may remember from a prior chapter in this book that he had assisted us with setting up meetings with Forest Service and USDA officials during our trips to D.C. during the Christmas Tree delivery and during the Lighting Ceremony. Al helped us out in any way he could, and he was there when they lit our tree on December 9. He had also set up my meeting with Assistant USDA Secretary and former major league baseball pitcher, "Vinegar Bend" Mizell, which, with me being such a big baseball fan, was one of the highlights of my trip to D.C.

On October 31, 1988 I told readers that the support stand, which had braced the butt of our Capitol Christmas tree during its shipping to Washington, D.C., was being put to good use once again. We had recently loaned it to the Huron-Manistee National Forest in Michigan, so that they could use it to transport the 1988 Capitol Tree to D.C. After using it, they returned the stand to us.

The plan was that in subsequent years we would offer the stand to be used by other National Forests. Then, after each year we would have an engraved plate attached to the stand, indicating which forest and state used it that year. The stand was to become a rotating trophy of sorts.

We planned to have the stand put into some sort of permanent display at the Washington County Career Center, except for a month or two each winter when it was being used. The Welding Class at the Career Center was the group that had actually constructed the heavy-duty, adjustable stand, with materials and design coordinated by Roy Wetz - R.O. Wetz Transportation, Ray Johnson - Apache Tank, and Dave Archer - Pioneer Pipe.

It was another lasting memory of the great time we had with the Wayne National Forest's 1987 Capitol Christmas tree.

On November 28, 1988 I wrote about Christmas trees and which species seemed to be favored by local residents: white pine, Scotch (Scots) pine, Fraser fir, and Norway spruce; and, of course, I mentioned that the previous year's U.S. Capitol Christmas Tree had been a Norway spruce.

I mentioned that several readers had sent me notes about the 1987 event and saying basically that "we should do that again." I told them that, yes, it was a great time, but I wasn't sure I could do it again. I had "aged 10 years" during that process. Of course, with how the selection process for the Capitol Tree goes, I told them that it was doubtful that it would ever come to Ohio again. That would be "great if it did, but don't hold your breath."

Barb Anderson and the folks from the Huron-Manistee National Forest near Cadillac, Michigan had been in frequent contact with me, with questions about their tree and asking advice about certain things. They seemed to be doing a great job up there with the 1988 tree, a balsam fir.

Casimier Wojakowski had also been in touch. He was, once again, directing the cutting operations. He sent along his best to all and said he hoped to visit the Marietta area in 1989 -- this time as a tourist, not as a lumberjack.

The New Matamoras Historical Society was selling 1989 calendars that were very nice, featuring three photos related to the Capitol tree. We had about 15 or 20 of the calendars for sale at our office in Reno for $4.00 per calendar.

Also, it was very interesting to note the nice write-ups about the Capitol Tree event in the Frontier School District's annual report, which was published in November, 1988. In particular, the FFA, the band, and the chorus had all played major roles in the success of the 1987 project.

And one last thing I mentioned to readers was that *"John Carson tells me the Frontier Band Boosters are selling small ornaments, which were cut from the actual Capitol Tree itself. You'll recall the main stem of the tree was brought "home" in January specifically for that purpose. Credit Gil Courtney and Roy Wetz for that maneuver. Better contact the boosters for an ornament. They'll probably go like hot cakes."*

My March 20, 1989 column was a tribute to Barb Hamilton, who had recently passed away. Barb had been a key member of our Capitol Christmas Tree Planning Committee. She helped in so many ways.

When I found out that Barb was a native West Virginian (so was I), we seemed to really hit it off. And then I learned that her late husband was Scotty Hamilton, who had been West Virginia University's first basketball All-American. With me also being a WVU grad and Mountaineer basketball fan, I was keenly interested in that story. I asked her many questions about those days and she never seemed to tire of answering me.

Barb Hamilton was such a nice person and my talks with her remain one of the highlights of my Capitol Christmas Tree experience. That entire March 20, 1989 column is featured in the Exhibits section of this book.

On December 4, 1989 I told readers that the current year's U.S. Capitol Christmas Tree had run into some recent problems. Readers often asked me about things like that and I tried to keep them updated as much as I could.

Following the tree that we provided in 1987, the Huron-Manistee National Forest in Michigan provided the tree for the nation's capitol in 1988. Casimier Wojakowski, the retired lumberjack from the Upper Peninsula of Michigan who traveled to Ohio to direct our cutting operation in 1987, supervised the felling and wrapping of the 1988 tree.

For readers who remembered Casimier and his knowledge, I wrote that *"I'm sure it is no surprise that the Michigan event went off just like ours did -- without a hitch."*

Another link to Ohio was present at that 1988 cutting, too. It was the heavy duty tree stand, which was built by the Washington County Career Center's Welding Class, per specifications of Wojakowski and Roy Wetz of R.O. Wetz Transportation in Marietta. The tree stand was used to support the weight from the trunk of those heavy trees as they were shipped to Washington, D.C.

I also wrote *"that the tree stand is now back in our possession and will soon go back up to the Career Center where it will be displayed. Although it wasn't used for the 1989 tree in Montana, the folks running the 1990 event in Colorado have already contacted me about using the tree stand there."*

By the time I wrote this column, Casimier was already scheduled to go to Colorado to direct the 1990 cutting. The plan for the tree stand was that each year after the cutting and shipping operations, it would be returned to us and eventually to the Career Center for display. A metal label was to be attached each year telling which National Forest used the stand. After a few years of traveling around the country, this stand would be quite a "trophy."

Now, back to the problems in 1989. That year's tree, an Engelmann spruce, came from the Kootenai National Forest in Montana. In an unfortunate turn of events, the tree twisted and fell backwards during the cutting operation. Thank goodness no one was injured, but it scared a lot of people as they hurried for cover. Unfortunately, the top 16 feet of the tree broke off as it hit the ground.

The Montana folks, with thousands of back-up trees to choose from, simply went down the road a ways and cut another tree. We wouldn't have had that luxury with our local Norway spruce. That's one reason we were so extra careful with it. An oak, a maple, or a tulip poplar wouldn't have made a very good back-up Christmas tree, would it?

In retrospect, perhaps the Montana folks could have used Casimier and even our tree stand. Who knows? But his expertise was invaluable to us. And the Colorado folks, after hearing about the Montana debacle, were certainly looking forward to having both Wojakowski and our stand on hand for their 1990 cutting.

That was the last time I wrote about the Capitol Christmas Tree until my **final newspaper column nearly a year later on September 10, 1990.** I wrote that *"as the old saying goes, all good things must end someday."*

I announced that I would soon be leaving my job with the Wayne National Forest and that our family would be moving to Paducah, Kentucky, where I was taking a job as Public Affairs Forester with Westvaco Corporation, a major manufacturer of paper and paper products.

I told readers that *"as for leaving the U.S. Forest Service, that's not an easy decision to make. Working here on the Wayne National Forest has been an exciting and challenging job. The people of southeastern Ohio, especially Washington and Monroe counties, have been great to work with."*

I went on to list several of the highlights of my 10 years working there and, of course, one of those highlights was the cutting of the U.S. Capitol Christmas Tree in 1987. I said *"that event, national in scope, will go down as one of the most remembered events in local history. We were proud to be the guiding force behind that."* That column is featured in its entirety in the Exhibits section of this book.

POSTSCRIPT

In the late summer of 2018, when I read a newspaper article from Salem, Oregon's Capital Press about the current year's Capitol Christmas Tree, it immediately brought back memories of 1987. Yes, there were major differences. Our tree, of course, came from the Wayne National Forest in Ohio; the 2018 tree was coming from the Willamette National Forest in Oregon. Our tree was a Norway spruce; their tree was a noble fir. The Oregon tree would travel about 3,000 miles to reach its final destination – the West Lawn of the U.S. Capitol. Our tree had to travel a little over 300 miles to get there.

But there were many similarities, too. District Ranger Nikki Swenson is credited with persistent lobbying of her superiors to get the tree to come from her area of Sweet Home, Oregon. She knew what the honor would mean to her community. That made me think back to the times I had pestered our Forest Supervisor, Harold Godlevske, about the Marietta Unit providing the Capitol Christmas Tree.

Several times I called Harold or caught him during breaks at various meetings to lobby for the honor. And when he made a visit to our area on a field tour, I ensured that we drove past several candidate trees for him to see. My efforts eventually paid off, as did Swenson's. She noted that she had once cornered Regional Forester Jim Pena in an elevator to plead her case; and another time talked with him in a stairwell.

Only a few people are ever aware of all of the background efforts leading up to the final selection of a Capitol Christmas Tree.

Swenson knew what the honor of providing the Capitol Tree would mean to her community. I had those same thoughts back in the 1980s. Of course, I tied our efforts into the bicentennial celebrations of both the Northwest Ordinance and the founding of the City of Marietta. Swenson tied-in her efforts to the 50th anniversary of the National Trails System Act and the 175th-year commemoration of the Oregon Trail, both notable events. During the first part of its trip east, the Oregon tree will roughly travel the reverse path of the famous Oregon Trail.

Swenson was quoted in September 2018 as saying, *"there are so many small details"* to consider. How well I remember. In addition to the cutting of the main tree, Oregon is sending a number of smaller companion trees designated for various Congressional and government offices in D.C. And local Oregon residents and school children are making several thousand ornaments to accompany those trees to the Capitol. We did the same things and it took the efforts of many local people to make this all happen.

Swenson also noted the time and effort spent on locating a tree, planning its cutting, determining its route to D.C., scheduling events, and finding ways to encourage community involvement – all of which we did in Ohio in 1987.

She told of how the Willamette had narrowed their candidate trees to five before Jim Kaufmann, Director of the Capitol Grounds, had traveled to Oregon several months ahead of the cutting to make the final selection. We had done the same with Paul Pincus, who at the time was the Landscape Architect working in the office of the Architect of the Capitol.

Swenson said they had to consider accessibility to their site by truck and trailer, as well as getting a crane into the area for the felling operation. And she noted that they were trying to keep the location of the final tree a secret for security reasons. Ditto, ditto, ditto – all things that we had to do, also.

Oregon's selected tree for 2018 is the first time a noble fir has ever been chosen as the U.S. Capitol Christmas Tree. Our Ohio Norway spruce was the third time that species had been selected, but that selection from the Wayne remains the only time that a Capitol Tree has come from a Midwestern national forest known primarily for its deciduous or hardwood trees – oaks, maples, yellow poplar, hickories, and so on.

It is true that previous trees had come from states with many hardwood trees – Tennessee, West Virginia, Pennsylvania, and North Carolina for instance – but the national forests in those states also contained a significant number of high elevation conifers, thousands in fact. Realistically, in Ohio, we probably only had 10 or 12 suitable trees on the entire Wayne National Forest from which to choose. I guess in hindsight that we went out on a proverbial limb to lobby so hard for the 1987 tree to come from Ohio. But it all worked out for us, just as it worked out in 2018 for the folks from Sweet Home, Oregon and the Willamette National Forest.

EXHIBITS

Where U.S. Capitol Christmas Trees Have Come From

Year	Species	Ht.	Source of Tree	State
1964	Douglas fir	24 ft.	Buddies Nurseries	PA
1965	Douglas fir	24 ft.	Buddies Nurseries	PA
1966	Douglas fir	24 ft.	Buddies Nurseries	PA
1967	Douglas fir	24 ft.	Buddies Nurseries	PA
1968	White pine	30 ft.	Finksburg	MD
1969	White pine	40 ft.	Westminster	MD
1970	Norway spruce	40 ft.	Monongahela NF	WV
1971	Black spruce	45 ft.	White Mountain NF	NH
1972	Balsam fir	50 ft.	Cherokee NF	TN
1973	White spruce	51 ft.	Allegheny NF	PA
1974	Fraser fir	41 ft.	Pisgah NF	NC
1975	Balsam fir	41 ft.	Ottawa NF	MI
1976	Red spruce	41 ft.	Monongahela NF	WV
1977	White spruce	52 ft.	Nemadji SF	MN
1978	Norway spruce	60 ft.	Savage River SF	MD

1979	White spruce	52 ft.	Nicolet NF	WI
1980	White spruce	48 ft.	Green Mountain NF	VT
1981	White spruce	50 ft.	Hiawatha NF	MI
1982	Balsam fir	50 ft.	Riley Bostwick WMA	VT
1983	White spruce	52 ft.	Chequamegon NF	WI
1984	White spruce	58 ft.	Superior NF	MN
1985	White spruce	56 ft.	Ottawa NF	MI
1986	Shasta red fir	54 ft.	Klamath NF	CA
1987	Norway spruce	60 ft.	Wayne NF	OH
1988	Balsam fir	50 ft.	Manistee NF	MI
1989	Engelmann spruce	60 ft.	Kootenai NF	MT
1990	Engelmann spruce	65 ft.	Routt NF	CO
1991	Blue spruce	60 ft.	Carson NF	NM
1992	White spruce	62 ft.	Chippewa NF	MN
1993	White fir	65 ft.	San Bernardino NF	CA
1994	Balsam fir	58 ft.	Green Mountain NF	VT
1995	Douglas fir	60 ft.	Plumas NF	CA
1996	Engelmann spruce	75 ft.	Manti-LaSal NF	UT
1997	Black Hills spruce	63 ft.	Black Hills NF	SD

1998	Fraser fir	50 ft.	Pisgah NF	NC
1999	White spruce	70 ft.	Nicolet NF	WI
2000	Blue spruce	65 ft.	Pike NF	CO
2001	White spruce	74 ft.	Ottawa NF	MI
2002	Douglas fir	70 ft.	Umpqua NF	OR
2003	Engelmann spruce	65 ft.	Boise NF	ID
2004	Red spruce	70 ft.	George Washington NF	VA
2005	Engelmann spruce	60 ft.	Santa Fe NF	NM
2006	Pacific silver fir	65 ft.	Olympic NF	WA
2007	Balsam fir	55 ft.	Green Mountain NF	VT
2008	Subalpine fir	78 ft.	Bitterroot NF	MT
2009	Blue spruce	85 ft.	Apache-Sitgreaves NF	AZ
2010	Engelmann spruce	67 ft.	Bridger-Teton NF	WY
2011	Sierra white fir	65 ft.	Stanislaus NF	CA
2012	Engelmann spruce	73 ft.	White River NF	CO
2013	Engelmann spruce	88 ft.	Colville NF	WA
2014	White spruce	88 ft.	Chippewa NF	MN
2015	Lutz spruce	74 ft.	Chugach NF	AK
2016	Engelmann spruce	80 ft.	Payette NF	ID

2017   Engelmann spruce 79 ft. Kootenai NF   MT

2018   Noble fir   80 ft.   Willamette NF   OR

NF – National Forest

SF – State Forest

WMA – Wildlife Management Area

Letter to the Forest Supervisor, dated 1/13/84

We would like to make a proposal to the Region that the Wayne National Forest provide the Capitol Christmas Tree in 1987. The Wayne has never furnished the tree, and the exposure and publicity would be excellent for the Forest. Each year there is national, regional, and state media coverage of the cutting ceremonies, which would help raise our identity level considerably.

Such an event also helps to gain local support and make residents proud of "their" National Forest. State and local government officials are usually involved in the ceremonies too, which goes a long way toward their support of National Forest programs.

The Marietta Unit has found a couple of Norway spruce trees that would be suitable for the Capitol Tree. You saw one of them on your trip over there last spring. Norway spruce has been used for the Capitol Tree previously, the most recent time in 1978. Red spruce and white spruce have also been used several times.

The Region's schedule for the Capitol Christmas Tree goes as follows:
1984-Superior NF-75th anniversary of the Forest

1985-Ottawa NF- 50th anniversary of Toumey Nursery

1986-Allegheny NF-Centennial of PA Forestry Assoc.

1987-Chippewa NF-Tentative (no coinciding events)

1988-Huron-Manistee NF-50th anniv. Of Manistee NF

1989-Hector Land Use Area-35th anniversary

1990-None

1991-None

1992-None

1993-Chequamegon NF-60th anniversary

1994-None

1995-Monongahela NF-75th anniversary

The 1987 date would be nice if we could tie it to some event or anniversary. We may have just the thing: 1787 was the year the Northwest Ordinance was passed. Marietta was the first permanent settlement in the Northwest Territories. The Ordinance opened up for settlement what was essentially the "first frontier," north and west of the Ohio River. During the 100 and 150-year celebrations, Marietta had many dignitaries attend, such as U.S. Presidents, Governors, the President of France, Ambassadors, etc. They plan on something similar for the 200-year celebration. Many of the special events will be put on in 1988 because 1788 was when the Marietta settlement began to flourish. But 1787 was the beginning and is historically important.

If we could furnish a tree in December of 1987, it would be a perfect way for the Wayne to assist with the 200-year celebration and lead in to some of Marietta's 1988 events. I'm positive we can get national TV, magazine, radio, and newspaper coverage of the event, which would be a great plus for the Wayne.

I'm sure the Region would be willing to give us the 1987 slot and have the Chippewa take 1990, '91, or '92, whenever they see the possible high-visibility, national tie-ins to 1987 for the Wayne. Marietta has some committees already working to prepare for the 200th anniversary events and we could coordinate nicely with their efforts.

Enclosed are snapshots of two trees on National Forest land – one at Sheets Run and one behind the Brown Building. As you can see, they would make beautiful candidates.

We can submit measurement data quickly and any additional information the Region requires. This is an opportunity that doesn't come along often and we would certainly like to take advantage of it.

Dan Kincaid

for GARY R. COLEMAN
District Ranger

Author's Note: These 'copies of photos' don't show up real well, but it does give you an idea of what we were "pitching" to the Forest Supervisor for his consideration. I have a copy of this actual letter in my files.

**CUTTING CEREMONY PROGRAM
1987 U.S. CAPITOL
BICENTENNIAL CHRISTMAS TREE
WAYNE NATIONAL FOREST
WASHINGTON COUNTY, OHIO
FRIDAY, NOVEMBER 20, 1987**

Welcome –   Sandra Matthews
Washington County Commissioner

Honor Guard –   American Legion Post 378,
New Matamoras

National Anthem - Frontier Marching Band

Pledge of Allegiance - Frontier FFA

Invocation -   Rev. Dwight Umbel
New Matamoras Church of the Nazarene

**Introduction of
Special Guests–**   Dan Kincaid
Supervisory Forester
Marietta Unit, Wayne NF

Remarks -   Frank Voytas, Forest Supervisor,
Wayne & Hoosier NF's

Christmas Music - Frontier Chorus
Frontier Marching Band

Benediction -   Rev. Kurt Landerholm
Newport United Methodist Church

150

Those Introduced at the Cutting Ceremony

(<u>Author's Note</u> – These are in the approximate order that I introduced them on November 20, 1987. This is reconstructed from old tapes, so please forgive any misspellings, incorrect titles, or omissions. But it certainly gives you an indication of those present and the high level of support and interest that our event generated.)

Ron Cornell – Executive Director, Ohio Forestry Association, Columbus

Marge Rinard – Acting Director, Monroe County Park District

Jim Corbett – New Matamoras City Council

Ralph Starkey – Ohio Division of Youth Services, Columbus

Hcbcr Piatt – Washington Township, Monroe County

Wayne Schafer – Former Washington County Commissioner

Sandy Matthews - Washington County Commissioner

Dick Young - Washington County Commissioner

Nancy Hollister – Mayor, City of Marietta

Lillian Knudson – Wife of former Wayne NF, Athens District Ranger, Ray Knudson

Pat Elisar – Wife of former Wayne NF, Athens District Ranger, Al Elisar

Tom Johnson – State Representative, Ohio's 96th District

Al Foulger – Director, U.S. Forest Service Experiment Station, Delaware, OH

Robert Kaden – Marietta Bicentennial Commission

George Joy – Frontier Local School Board

Mrs. Lester Dye – Ludlow Township, Washington County

Kurt Simon – USDA Soil Conservation Service, Washington County

Dave Early – Benton Township, Monroe County

Ed Beaver – Independence Township, Washington County

Charlie Stone – Ohio Division of Wildlife, Washington County Game Protector

Harry Hall – Various civic and taxpayer organizations, Washington County

Buddy McKeefer – New Matamoras City Council

John Maynard – Aide to Senator Metzenbaum

Jack Clift – Southeastern Ohio Oil & Gas Association

Ernie Hulsey – Former Monroe County Commissioner

Rusty Morris – Frontier Local School Board

Robert Hill – Northwest Ordinance Bicentennial Planning Commission and Political Science Professor, Marietta College

John Herlan – Newport Township, Washington County

Roland Schaar – Madison, WI - The 1st District Ranger, Wayne NF, Athens District (1935-1940), who was introduced by current Acting Athens District Ranger, **Jim Apgar**

Jim Miller - Northwest Ordinance Bicentennial Planning Commission

John Miley – State Vocational-Agriculture Supervisor, Columbus

Calvin Martin and all of his Students – Frontier High School FFA

Terry Schafer and all of his Students – Washington County Career Center FFA, including Student FFA President **Brian Brooks**

Lowell King – Vice-President, Frontier Local School Board

Pam Sloan – Publisher, Monroe County Beacon newspaper

Diana McMahon – Correspondent, Parkersburg News (and New Matamoras resident)

Gil Courtney – President, Peoples Savings Bank, New Matamoras

Donna Knowlton – Ohio Lottery Commission

Stuart Parsons – Ohio State University and State FFA

John Schmidt – New Matamoras City Council

Irma Highman – Executive Director, SCS, Monroe County

Don Busch and Carlos Miller – Busch Crane Rental, Vienna, WV

Bob Kimball – Flinn's Septic Service, Williamstown, WV

Pete and Jeff Edgar – Howard Edgar Construction

Casimier Wojakowski – Timber Felling Specialist/Lumberjack, Escanaba, Michigan

Greg Black – Black's Tree Service

Danny Thompson – Carlton Oil Corporation

Louie Haynes – Stowe Equipment and Stihl Chainsaw Representative

Teresa Heilmann and Kathy Chenoweth – Washington County Extension

Roy and Chip Wetz – R.O. Wetz Transportation

Mack and Kenny Haessly – Kenmack Lumber

Dave Decker – Independence Township, Washington County

John Crist – USDA Forest Service, State & Private Forestry, Morgantown, WV

Annetta Richardson – Reporter, Parkersburg News

Sandra Binegar, Carolyn Phipps, Judy Holdren Beaver – Descendants of Joseph and Mary Holdren, the originals settlers of the land where this tree was cut.

Jim Delong – New Matamoras City Council

Ruth and Norman Drissell – Marietta Bicentennial Commission

Dave Barrett – Washington County Joint Vocational School

Thanks to **John Beugel, Matt Farnsworth, Greg Danver, Mike Pethtel, Donnie Allen, Roger**

Weddle, and Gil Courtney for several nights of site security.

John Hoff – Superintendent, Frontier Local School District

Bob Forbes – Principal, Frontier High School

Gale Eddy – President, Little Muskingum Watershed Association and former Chief of the Little Muskingum VFD

Steve McMahon – Chief, Newport VFD

Jim Greenwood – Newport Township, Washington County

Roger Weddle – Assistant Chief, New Matamoras VFD

Pat Hulsey – My friend and former Trustee for Benton Township, Monroe County

Jean Pickering – who painted signs commemorating this event and which will accompany the trees to the U.S. Capitol

Glenn Dierkes – Monroe County Commissioner

Mark Gruetze – Managing Editor, The Marietta Times newspaper

Ohio Forestry Association – Doug Brenneman, Chairman, Board of Trustees (and President of

Brenneman Lumber Company, Mt. Vernon, OH); **Roy Palmer**, First Vice-President (and representing Hocking Technical College, Nelsonville, OH); **Jack Haessly**, Second Vice-President (and President of Haessly Hardwood Lumber Co., Newport, OH); **Darrel Roberts**, Member, OFA Board of Trustees (and with Mead Paper Corp., Chillicothe, OH); and **Garry Marcum**, Member, OFA Board of Trustees (and with Stone Container Corp., Coshocton, OH).

Marjorie Davis – USDA Agricultural Stabilization and Conservation Service

Linda Bailey – Little Muskingum Watershed Association

Foster Reed – Lawrence Township, Washington County

Paul Junk – Washington County Engineer

Frank Beugel – Benton Township, Monroe County

Wilbur Jones – Jackson Township, Monroe County

Jamie Haught – Benton Township, Monroe County

Sharon Sue English – Washington Township, Monroe County

Floyd Early – Grandview Township, Washington County

Doris Amos – Treasurer, New Matamoras City
Council
Gail Depuy – Lawrence Township, Washington
County
Patricia Putnam Godfrey
Hope Barnhouse
Beth Martin
Beulah McFarlane
And last, but certainly not least (I see you hiding back
there), let me recognize my wife, **Vicki Kincaid.** On
the count of three, everybody turn around and look at
her! No, don't do that. Just kidding, dear.
(<u>Author's Note</u>: Again, I apologize for misspellings, incorrect
titles, or other inaccuracies, as well as for those who were
present that day but I missed. I am going from memory and
from transcribing the often difficult to understand audio
from that day. There were other Township Trustees present,
but I was unable to make out names from the audio
recordings. Suffice it to say that every Township in the
eastern half of Washington County, as well as the southern
half of Monroe County, was represented. In any event, this
list gives some indication of the wide variety of "officials"
who came to watch and support the cutting of the U.S.
Capitol Christmas Tree. In retrospect, the level of support
was quite amazing. There are just over 100 names listed
above. That means there were also several hundred others in
attendance that day, including local citizens, news reporters,
and Forest Service employees, as well as Frontier High
School students, band members, and the choir.)

**SEND-OFF CEREMONY PROGRAM
1987 U.S. CAPITOL
BICENTENNIAL CHRISTMAS TREE
HERMANN FINE ARTS CENTER
MARIETTA COLLEGE, MARIETTA, OHIO
SATURDAY, NOVEMBER 21, 1987**

Honor Guard	-	VFW Post 5108
National Anthem	-	Marietta High School Band, Marshall Kimball, Director
Pledge of Allegiance	-	Boy Scout Troop 203 Led by Butch Hawkins
Invocation	-	Rev. Donald Shuler First Baptist Church, Marietta
Welcome	-	Mayor Nancy Hollister
Thanks and Introductions-		Dan Kincaid, Supervisory Forester, Marietta Unit Wayne NF
Remarks -		Frank Voytas, Forest Supervisor, Wayne and Hoosier NFs
Dedication -		Barbara Lovely-Executive Dir., Marietta Bicentennial Comm.

Presentation of Flags to Accompany the Tree:

U.S. Flag: Bernard Cleveland, Jr., VFW Post 5108

State of Ohio Flag: Nancy Hollister

Washington County Flag: Sandra Matthews

Bicentennial Flag: Barbara Lovely

School Awards -   Iwana Simon

Christmas Music -   Marietta High School Band

Benediction -   Tim T. Wallace, Minister Reno Christian Church

(FRONT COVER OF BOTH CEREMONY PROGRAMS- Prepared by Washington County Commissioner, Sandy Matthews)

1987 U.S. Capitol Bicentennial Christmas Tree

In honor of the Bicentennial of the Ordinance of 1787 and the 200th Birthday of Marietta, the first permanent settlement in the Northwest Territory created by the Ordinance, this year's Christmas tree for our nation's Capitol in Washington, D.C. has been selected from a section of Wayne National Forest bordering the Ohio River in Southeastern Ohio.

Foresters estimate the tree was planted in a river bottom around 1900 by a homesteader, in what is now the Frontier Local School District. The tall, stately Norway spruce towers above neighboring hardwood trees in the forest. Now, thanks to the efforts of many hardworking people, one little seedling of nearly a century ago will find a unique place in history.

Individuals, organizations, and businesses too numerous to list have donated money, time, energy and enthusiasm to this Bicentennial Capitol Christmas Tree project. Their efforts are deeply appreciated. Special thanks go to Dan Kincaid, Supervisory Forester at Wayne National Forest's Marietta Unit; Teena Sechler, Public Information Officer, Wayne and Hoosier National Forests, Bedford, Indiana; and Acting District Ranger Jim Apgar, District Ranger Chuck Myers, and Business Management Clerk Connie Morris, all of Wayne National Forest.

Councilwoman was friend of forest, city

It was just about this time two years ago that I first came to know Barb Hamilton.

The Wayne National Forest had just been chosen to furnish the nation's Capitol Christmas tree for 1987 and we formed a steering committee to help guide us through the project. Hamilton's name was one of the first recommended to us, and she was very eager to assist in any way she could.

Along with her friend, Iwana Simon, one of Hamilton's most important contributions to the Capitol Christmas Tree effort was to involve city and county school children in the project.

They contacted principals and teachers and before long it seemed as though everyone was doing something – making ornaments, Christmas cards, exhibits, posters, putting on skits and plays. It was unbelievable. Everything was related to the Capitol tree through the bicentennial theme.

When we delivered the main tree and several smaller ones to Washington, D.C., boxes of homemade ornaments, cards, and posters were presented to Ohio's Congressional delegation; and they were certainly impressed. I remember especially the reactions of Sen. John Glenn and Reps. Clarence Miller, Douglas Applegate, and Michael Dewine.

Hamilton and Simon got contests started among school children and presented awards to the winners during the send-off ceremony at Marietta College.

Hamilton did much more, too. She helped arrange for the Marietta High School band to play during the send-off. She helped make arrangements at the college and with the city. And on two separate Monday mornings she met me bright and early at Peoples Bank on Second and Putnam to help set up window displays about the Wayne National Forest, the Capitol Christmas Tree, and the Marietta Bicentennial.

Hamilton never missed many meetings either and, believe me, there were lots of them. It took the efforts of many people to pull things off and she did more than her share.

Barb was always pleased when I asked her about her husband Scotty's All-American basketball days at West Virginia University. She was quite a sports fan and never seemed to tire of my questions. That made her even more special to me.

All of us here were saddened when we heard of her recent death. We felt we had lost a close friend.

But we also are glad we had the chance to work with such a kind and caring lady. She helped make Marietta, Washington County, and the surrounding area a better place in which to live.

Dan Kincaid is a forester with Wayne National Forest, Box 132, Route 1, Marietta, Ohio 45750 (373-9055). His column now appears on Tuesdays.

(<u>AUTHOR'S NOTE</u> – The following story appeared in the December 1987 issue of Redbook Magazine. It was written by Teena Sechler and appears here with her permission. Teena was the Public Information Officer for the Wayne and Hoosier National Forests and assisted with many aspects of the 1987 Capitol Christmas Tree event.

Legend has it that a "drummer" or traveling salesman gave away spruce seedlings to the wives of many settlers in the Ohio region over the years as a way to get them to look at the wares he was selling. Speculation was that the Norway spruce we cut from Wayne National Forest originated in that manner since the property had been part of a private farm for many years prior to it becoming part of Wayne National Forest.

Teena's piece is a fictional story, so certain aspects do not match with our tree. For example, a post-cutting aging of our spruce tree indicated that it was likely planted sometime just after 1900, not during the Civil War era.

But our tree could still have been a gift from a drummer or salesman even in, say, 1902. Nonetheless, Teena's fictional story was spawned by the legend of those early drummers and her story was very interesting, well received by readers, and an important contribution to our overall Capitol Christmas Tree publicity efforts.   – dbk, 2018)

A DRUMMER'S GIFT

By Teena Sechler

A Christmas Legend – This Christmas, a Norway spruce from a forest in Ohio will stand in front of our nation's Capitol. There is a legend that this tree was planted by a poor farmer's wife more than one hundred years ago. It was given to her by a drummer, a kindly man who rode in a wagon from homestead to homestead, selling pots and pans. Here is the story of that man and that woman and their very special bond.

The woman ran her rough hands over the shiny copper kettle and then put it back reluctantly. She smiled sadly and stepped back from the drummer's wagon. "I'm sorry, but there's nothing I can afford," she told him. "Thank you kindly for stopping." She looked embarrassed and brushed back a stray strand of blond hair. "There's sassafras tea on the stove, if you'd like some before you go."

The drummer tipped his dusty cap and said that would be real fine. She smiled shyly now and hurried off into the house. Two big-eyed children who had been clinging to her skirt stayed behind, staring at him with curiosity.

Visitors were rare in this part of the country. It was too far inland from the busy Ohio River and too far south from the rapidly settling flatlands. These hills attracted the poorer settlers and life here was hard. More and more the drummer was seeing abandoned farmsteads, boarded up, the families having given up and gone looking for better prospects elsewhere.

The woman returned with the tea. She carried it carefully in both hands and when she handed it to him he saw that the cup was porcelain. He looked up at her and she smiled proudly. "Pretty, isn't it?" she said. "It was my mother's."

He looked more closely at her and thought suddenly how like his wife she was. Memories of his bride, who had agreed to come west from Philadelphia, leaving all the fine things she'd grown up with, came back to him. He remembered how excited she had been when they moved onto their homestead and built the log house on the hill. How hard she had worked and how tired she had grown. The tiredness seemed to seep into her soul. There years in a row she had miscarried a baby. The sparkle had faded from her eyes and her step had slowed. Then, the fourth year, the fourth baby had been lost. His beautiful Anna had lain quietly in the dark house while her life drained out of her. He had buried her beside the little spruce in the yard. Then he'd ridden away from the farm and had never gone back.

The blond woman touched his arm. "Is something wrong?" she asked.

He shook his head and wiped roughly at his eyes, embarrassed. "No, Ma'am, this tea is real good, thank you kindly," he said. He gave the cup back to her and quickly climbed up on his wagon seat. "I'll be back through in a few months, if you need anything." He released the brake and shook the reins loose. The old wagon creaked and jostled under him as it swung back out on the main road and moved off to the next homestead.

As his wagon bounced over uneven ruts, the pans, washboards and spoons clanking, he thought again of the woman and of all the women who lived out their hard lives in these hills. And he thought of his Anna, who had known so little joy and had smiled so rarely in those last years.

In his mind he saw her grave beside the Norway spruce. How tall the tree must be now, he thought. Suddenly he sat up straighter, the beginning of an idea forming in his mind. The little spruce had first grown in Anna's parents' yard in Philadelphia. When she had packed to go with him, she had asked to take it along. Her father had carefully dug up the tree and loaded it in the wagon for the trip west. Anna had taken great care in replanting it by their new house and had carried water to it regularly. On warm summer evenings they sat together in the doorway and she often told him how much happiness the little spruce brought her. Watching it grow reminded her of home.

If the tree could bring his Anna joy, couldn't spruce trees bring joy to other women in isolated and far from the homes they'd grown up in? He began to whistle and pushed the dusty felt hat back on his head. "Yes, Anna, I believe they could!" he said aloud, and the mules pulling the wagon pricked up their ears and trotted faster.

It was four months before he pulled up again in front of the blond woman's house. The children ran to meet him and then stood hesitantly by the gate. Their mother, bent over in the garden, straightened and shaded her eyes to see who was there. He thought he saw a smile as she recognized him and raised her hand to wave, then wiped both hands on her apron as she came to greet him. Farther up the hill, he saw a man working an ox, pulling stumps from a field. The man paid no attention to the dust-covered drummer peddling pots and pans.

The woman's face was flushed from the sun and the hem of her skirt was thick with dust. The initial enthusiasm he had seen in her face at the prospect of a visitor soon vanished as she approached the wagon. "It's good of you to stop again," she explained, "but my husband still hasn't got a crop in and we don't have any money yet, so I dare not even look." She twisted her apron nervously. "I can get you water if you're thirsty."

He thought she looked more tired than before. The blond hair beneath the bonnet looked dull and dirty and the faded gingham dress didn't hide the fact that she was much thinner. "Water would be nice. And I brought you a gift," he said sweeping off his hat and bowing with a grin.

"Oh, I can't accept any gift!" she said, her eyes widening in alarm.

"It's okay," he assured her. "Come, see what I've brought," he said, beckoning for her and the children to come around the back of his wagon. He took out a basket and lifted its canvas cover. Inside were several seedling Norway spruces, each bundled in moss. He lifted one out and gave it to the little girl. "It's a spruce tree from the North. If you help your mother plant it and take care of it, it'll grow tall. They're beautiful trees...." His voice faded.

He looked up at the woman. "It was seeing you that gave me the idea," he said. "You reminded me of my wife Anna. She had a spruce such as this and she loved that tree." He shrugged and tucked the canvas back around the remaining trees in the basket and placed them in the wagon. He looked at the ground, at his scuffed, worn boots. "I wanted to bring you, and all the other women like you, joy. That's all. I wanted to make it up to my Anna and bring you joy." He wiped at his eyes with his sleeve. "I best be going. You and your ma take care of that tree," he said to the little girl. He tousled her hair and swung up onto his wagon.

The drummer gave every woman along his route a seedling tree until the basket was empty. Then he went East to restock his supplies and returned with two more baskets of trees. Again, he gave them out to the lonely women in the hills of southeastern Ohio.

The women planted them next to their homes, watered them, and watched them grow. The spruces were a bit of home for many of the women and a reminder of kindness for all of them. They waited for the drummer to come again, to show him how well the trees were being cared for, to thank him.

But the drummer never came. His wagon and his mules were requisitioned by the Union Army to carry supplies to field units in Virginia. There was trouble with the Southern states, talk of war, of secession. A sniper, with an old rifle and ideas of glory, shot and killed the drummer as he crossed a creek bed one morning at dawn.

The drummer's trees grew tall. The blond woman to whom he had given that first tree planted the little spruce by her front gate. She cared for it while her children played in the yard and smiled to herself when she saw how it grew. Her husband was killed in the war the following spring, but she stayed put with the children for awhile, until she married again. Then the house was boarded up and she and the children moved away.

The fields grew over with scrub oak and a storm that winter blew part of the roof off the house. The next winter the walls caved in. Only the tree seemed to thrive, towering higher each year over the house's skeletal remains. Travelers along the old road would often wonder at the unexpected sight of the tall spruce and many stopped to rest in its shade. The tree became a landmark.

During the Depression years, many of the hill farms were lost because people couldn't pay the taxes. The government acquired large plots of land, including the farm where the Norway spruce grew. In the 1950s this area was designated the Wayne National Forest.

In early 1987, a search was made for a Christmas tree to be placed in front of our nation's Capitol. A forester who remembered seeing the majestic Norway spruce suggested it be chosen. After its photograph and dimensions were submitted through the Forest Service, the Capitol architect came and personally approved the tree.

If the drummer could know what became of his gift to the poor farmer's wife, he would be pleased. This Christmas, the great spruce – his tribute to Anna – will shine brightly in front of the United States Capitol in Washington, D.C.

Teena Sechler is a forester at the Wayne-Hoosier National Forest. This is her first published story. While it's widely believed that a drummer distributed Ohio's Norway spruces, the details of this story are Sechler's own speculation. **REDBOOK, December 1987.**

The VHS Tape –
THE CAPITOL CHRISTMAS TREE

<u>AUTHOR'S NOTE</u> – The following script for this video was written by Lynn Kantner, U.S. Forest Service, and the tape was produced by her son, Ray Beach. Portions of the videotaping were done by Lynn's other son, Cullen Beach. Some tape provided by Gil Courtney was also dubbed-in, as well as a few Forest Service photos. I provided the narration for the final product. I was hesitant to narrate Lynn's script because I didn't think I had a good narrator's voice. But they finally convinced me that because I had the most complete knowledge of all the events, the narration would thus sound more authentic. I hope that was the case.

The video contains some excellent visual shots and scenes, many of which do not appear in the various other videotapes that were taken during that time. It is the most complete and comprehensive visual account of the events of November and December 1987. Those who have copies are fortunate indeed. Future historians and reviewers will hopefully be able to refer to this video tape for information about the 1987 U.S. Capitol Christmas Tree.

I will show my narration in italics and quotes, while other information about the tape appears in block-style font. Throughout the narration there are all types of still photos and video footage being shown to depict what the script is saying. I felt like providing this script of the tape would provide readers with yet another relevant item related to the 1987 Capitol Christmas Tree event.

The tape opens with some Forest Service radio chatter from the evening before the Cutting Ceremony regarding the moving in of some of the heavy equipment needed for the following day.

Then it begins with this audio:

"What you're about to see is the story of a tree......"

The title appears:
The U.S. Forest Service Presents a Ray Beach Video - THE CAPITOL CHRISTMAS TREE

These words then appear on the screen:
This is the story of the first Capitol Christmas Tree from Ohio, a Norway spruce from the Wayne National Forest and the people of New Matamoras, Newport, and Marietta.

Throughout this first part of the video there are scenes of it snowing on the day of the cutting, various pre-cut shots of the tree itself, and of people visiting the tree site to take photos on the days preceding the cutting ceremony. Then the script begins (and throughout all the script sections of the tape, there are many excellent shots of various scenes connected with the planning, cutting, send-off, lighting, and other related scenes):

"What you're about to see is the story of a tree. You'll see a lot of people, too. People who helped make this story possible. Behind this story and these people and, of course, behind the tree are many more people, thousands literally, who in some way contributed to the story.

People from Marietta, Newport, and New Matamoras, small towns in southeastern Ohio; and other communities and people living in Washington and Monroe counties; band members from Marietta and Frontier High Schools; Future Farmers of America; Carlton Oil Corporation; Black's Tree Service; Wayne National Forest; Busch Crane Rental; R.O. Wetz Transportation; Kenmack Lumber; Howard Edgar Contractor; Washington County Career Center; the Marietta Bicentennial Commission; and the Capitol Christmas Tree Committee.

There were groups and individuals who donated time, money, work, and even trees. You'll see a lot of these people. But there are many you won't see who worked behind the scenes, so to speak: Like the hundreds of school children from all over Ohio who worked to make the beautiful hand-made ornaments that finally graced 30 Christmas trees throughout our nation's Capitol.

You won't see these people, but they are there just the same – just like the individual lights that blended together to create the aura of the beautiful Christmas tree – a Norway spruce that was a gift to the American people in 1987 from "the heart of it all" in Wayne National Forest.

So, this is the story of that tree, planted at the turn of the century in the yard of a farm house on the banks of the Ohio River, and how in 1987, that tree graced the lawn of our nation's Capitol and will for a long, long time be remembered by a lot of people as the first Capitol Christmas Tree from this state.

The land where the 85-foot tall Norway spruce stood is now part of Wayne National Forest. The tree was planted in a time when the land looked very different. It was planted as a seedling in the yard of a homestead overlooking the Ohio River. A house stood behind the tree once; a road ran past; and children played in the yard. Now, only the foundation stones of the house remain. In earlier times this was a hunting ground for Indians and later was claimed by both the French and the English. Ownership of these lands came to the United States by the Treaty of Paris in 1783 after the Revolutionary War.

Surveying of this vast wilderness began shortly afterward, interrupted frequently by skirmishes with Indians. A new system of rectangular surveys was used, which improved upon former surveying systems, for the first seven ranges. These seven ranges are all in Ohio.

The government put up these lands for sale and in 1787 a group of shareholders called the Ohio Company of Associates bought a large tract beginning just west of the seven ranges. This included the land that would later become the tree site. Actual settlement of the Ohio Company's purchase began in 1788 with the arrival of 48 pioneers at the confluence of the Muskingum and Ohio Rivers, which is now the site of Marietta.

The river bottom hollow where the tree grew is called Sheets Run. It lies at the lower end of the Long Reach of the Ohio River, an unusual straight stretch of the river which was noted by many early travelers. The Sheets Run tract was bought and settled in 1816 by Joseph and Ruth Holdren. The land eventually went to Joseph Irwin Holdren (the *second son of Ruth and Joseph.) He and his wife Mary raised 12 children there. Joseph Irwin Holdren ran a sawmill and farmed 198 acres of land. He also brought in the first oil well in the township. He and Mary later moved away and sold the farm.*

The property was bought and sold several times until the Grimes family sold it to the U.S. government in 1969 to become part of the Wayne National Forest. The house is gone and the heirs of the families who lived there are scattered. Who actually planted the tree is unknown, but it's likely that it was planted by Joseph I. and Mary Holdren some time just after the turn of the century.

My name is Dan Kincaid and I work for the Wayne National Forest in Marietta, Ohio. In 1981 I started a campaign to have Ohio supply the 1987 Capitol Christmas Tree. I thought it would be a special way to commemorate the Bicentennial of the Northwest Territory, of which Ohio was a part and Marietta was the first permanent settlement.

The Capitol Christmas Tree has traditionally been chosen from states like, Michigan, Minnesota, or Vermont, northern states more noted for their forests, particularly of evergreen trees. In fact, for the 24 year period that the national Forest Service has been providing the Capitol Tree, no Ohio tree had ever before been honored.

So, the work began six years before the event of December 9, 1987. That was when the switch was flipped by Speaker of the House of Representatives, Jim Wright, and 4,000 lights illuminated Ohio's gift to the people of our country – the people's tree, the Capitol Christmas Tree.

The tree was given final approval by Paul Pincus, the Landscape Architect for the U.S. Capitol, one year prior to the cutting. A backup tree was also selected, and even a third, just in case something unexpected happened to the main tree. Marilyn Ortt, a local botanist for the State of Ohio, helped find some of the backup trees. Marietta Mayor Nancy Hollister, Barbary Lovely of the Marietta Bicentennial Commission, and Phyllis Richerson of the Marietta Tourist and Convention Bureau helped convince Pincus that we could do everything necessary to ensure a beautiful tree; and the wheels were officially set in motion.

A Capitol Christmas Tree Committee was established to carry out the various tasks and to help raise necessary funds, since the Forest Service budget cannot be used for this sort of activity. The core of the committee included: Barbara Lovely and Phyllis Richerson; Barb Hamilton of the Marietta City Council; Gil Courtney, President of the Peoples Savings Bank in New Matamoras; Sandra Matthews, Washington County Commissioner; Marilyn Ortt; Iwana Simon; Marty Kitchen, City of Marietta Recreation Director; Dave Bergman, Lynn Malowney, Bernice Wilson, and John Piehowicz of the Ohio Department of Natural Resources; and Chuck Myers, Jim Apgar, Teena Sechler, and myself of the U.S. Forest Service."
*(**NOTE**: Some members would come and go over time, and additional members such as Harry Cogswell of Apex Feed and Supply in Marietta; and former Washington County Commissioner Wayne Schafer would take on important roles. Also, local U.S. Forest Service employees John Kerr, Dave Greenwood, Gloria Eighmey, Lynn Kantner, Connie*

On the screen:
Last Meeting Before the Day of Cutting

There is no script reading for this next portion of the
videotape. It is recorded video and audio of a Capitol
Christmas Tree Committee Meeting at the Marietta Unit
Office of Wayne National Forest on November 19, 1987. It
includes:

- Jim Apgar discussing an 18-foot Colorado blue
  spruce that was cut over in the Athens area and was
  destined for the Senate Private Dining Room.
- Marty Kitchen, Barb Hamilton, and Sandy Matthews
  discussing plans for the Send-Off Ceremony on
  November 21.
- Dan Kincaid discussing how many of the Christmas
  cards were still remaining to sell. This was one of our
  primary fundraising activities.
- Sandy Matthews discussing the program handouts
  for the Cutting and Send-Off ceremonies.
- Jim Apgar telling the group that the first District
  Ranger for the Athens Ranger District from 1935-
  1940, Roland Schaar, was coming to both
  ceremonies. He lived in Madison, Wisconsin and was
  in his 80s. He was flying down to attend.
- Lynn Kantner going over the list of dignitaries who
  might be attending the cutting ceremony. We had
  mailed out about 225 invitations.
- Gil Courtney talking about the buses that he had
  lined up to take local residents and the Frontier High

School band to the Lighting Ceremony in Washington, D.C. on December 9.

- Dan Kincaid talking about site security and traffic control on Route 7 during the Cutting Ceremony. We had been in contact with both the Washington County Sheriff and the Ohio Highway Patrol for these matters.

- Barb Hamilton letting us know about the arrangements she had made for punch and cookies and a small reception area inside the Hermann Fine Arts Center at Marietta College following the Send-Off Ceremony.

- Teena Sechler mentioned that she had received a request for another small Christmas tree to bring with us to D.C. (We had originally been told to bring 27, then it was 29, and now 30. Fortunately we anticipated this happening and were planning to bring a few extras anyway. These were the smaller 6-8 foot trees supplied to us by the Ohio Christmas Tree Growers Association.)

Then back to the script:

"I contacted District Rangers and Forest Service employees from other National Forests to find out how they physically accomplished the cutting, wrapping, handling, and hauling of the tree.

A central character whose name kept coming up in the communications was Casimier Wojakowski from Escanaba, Michigan, who was an expert at cutting and felling large trees. He had been involved in the cutting of several past

The next section of the tape has a considerable amount of footage of Dan Kincaid, Lynn Kantner, and Casimier Wojakowski walking around the tree site on the day prior to the cutting. It is very good video and recorded conversations. Casimier wanted to get a good look at the site prior to the actual cutting. He remarked how "clean" this site was compared to many he had dealt with in the past, in terms of brush and other trees that might interfere with cutting the main tree.

He explained his overall plans for the felling operation. I went over all the equipment we had lined up for the next day and he said that was good – a crane, bucket truck, dozer with a winch, heavy duty pickup and winch, and others. I jokingly told him that all we needed now was someone who knew what to do with all that equipment and Casimier got a big laugh out of that.

Then more script:

"Before the actual day of the tree cutting, a lot of things had to be organized and coordinated. 28 additional donated trees accompanied the main Capitol Tree and these came from all over the state of Ohio. They had to be cut, wrapped, and delivered to Marietta, where they were stored until the day when they would make the journey to Washington. Once in Washington these 28 trees would go to the offices of various Ohio Congressmen and several other locations, including the Senate Dining Hall, the Supreme Court, and the U.S. Department of Agriculture lobby.

So, about two weeks before the day of cutting the main tree, small trees of various sizes and varieties started arriving at our office. The Ohio Division of Forestry Nursery is located just across the road from our office and officials there donated a storage building for the trees. The weather was so mild that we might well have lost some of those trees without the cold storage building. It was so warm, in fact, that we had to hose down the trees daily to keep them moist and cool. We even brought in quantities of sphagnum moss to wrap around the trunks. Every day Dave Greenwood, Gloria Eighmey, Bill Engle, Bob Florence, and Art Nicholson from our office went to the nursery, checked the trees and wrappings, hosed them down, and made sure everything was just right."

There was video footage of all of this: Going to the nursery; Dave and Gloria tying on bags of sphagnum moss to tree trunks; Dave using a hose to water down trees; Dave showing Lynn Kantner and Ray Beach the trees – blue spruce, Douglas fir, Fraser fir, Scotch pine, and others; Dave explaining their care and also where some of them were headed to in D.C.

Back to the script, read around some very good video shots:

"We also started round-the-clock surveillance of the Capitol Tree about two weeks before the actual Cutting Ceremony. Looking back, I would say that the location of that tree was the worst kept secret in the history of Washington County. It was pretty hard to keep the actual location of the tree a secret with all of the publicity the tree was getting. It's pretty hard to hide an 85-foot tall Norway spruce tree anyway. They're few and far between in this area.

Southeastern Security and Investigation gave us five donated days of surveillance; Washington County Sheriff Richard Ellis and Lt. Herman and his crew at the Ohio Highway Patrol assisted with extra patrols and monitoring of the area throughout November. Volunteer citizens and our own employees filled in the rest of the time. Jokes about mishaps to the tree helped relieve some of the mounting tension.

Guards reported visitors coming to take pictures, touch the tree, to stand back quietly and watch the sunrise, or just sit and fix the scene in their memories. Thankfully, there wasn't one negative incident of souvenir seekers or vandalism. I think that says something pretty special about our local folks.

We started moving in all the necessary equipment to the site on the day before the scheduled tree cutting ceremony. For so many years since the house and farm buildings had disappeared, the tree stood in relative quiet. Slowly over the years since the last family left the farm house, the area had returned to nature's more humble creatures. Squirrels, rabbits, deer, and field mice filled in where man, wife, children, horses, and farm animals had been. Brush, weeds, and finally trees closed in around the stately spruce and became its silent neighbors. From its vantage point, the tree still watched over the activities of people on the Ohio River and perhaps kept track of industrial progress in a way. Perhaps the tree had become accustomed to the quiet or perhaps it missed the hustle and bustle of human activity.

It's surprising how many of us that day had these feelings. With all of the noise and commotion intruding on the site, I

*Everything was in place by dusk and quiet covered the site
like a blanket. Were we really ready? We all lingered longer
than needed, caught in the emotion of what was going to
happen. It was a magical few moments then, like Christmas
eves remembered as a child. After all, we were caught up in
a ceremony of proportions beyond our control now. So was
the tree.*

*On Friday morning, November 20, 1987 the tree cutting
ceremony, the event we had planned for and anticipated for
over a year, was ready to begin. All of our local employees,
those from Athens, and other officials gathered in the dark
before dawn at the Marietta office. Uniforms were clean and
pressed, boots were shined; everyone knew what their
respective roles would be and they were prepared to carry
out whatever orders came their way. The official time clock
started and cars, trucks, and personnel started rolling. A
special crew remained at the office to handle chores at that
end."*

There was footage of all things mentioned in the above
paragraphs. Then the video began to show footage of the
crowd gathering on-site before the Cutting Ceremony. If you
look closely, I'm sure you will see several people you know.
And yes, Smokey Bear was on hand for the younger kids (of
which there were many; it was evident that parents wanted
their children to experience this historical event.)

*"Over 700 people gathered along the banks of the Ohio
River to watch the ceremony. It was a cold, crisp, clear day,*

typical of mid-November in these parts. The Frontier Local High School chorus and band initiated the proceedings about 9:00 a.m. with festive Christmas music."

All of the following proceedings were captured on this video. Sandy Matthews, Washington County Commissioner and resident of the Frontier Local School District (in which the tree was located), served as program emcee and opened the ceremony. The audio is fairly clear for most of what follows. This is not narrated by me, but captured in real-time audio.

Sandy Matthews – "On behalf of the 1987 Capitol Christmas Tree Committee, I want to welcome you all to this historic occasion. Our committee has been working with anticipation of this day for the past 10 months. We are pleased to have been selected to provide the Capitol Christmas Tree from the Wayne National Forest, Washington County, Ohio in observation of the Bicentennial of the Northwest Territory. This is a once in a lifetime event and we here today will be a part of history. We welcome all of you who have come to help us cut, wrap, and send off this stately Norway spruce – our gift to the nation. At this time with the Honor Guard from the New Matamoras American Legion Post 378 and the Frontier High School Marching Band, we will now have our national anthem." [Music plays]. "At this time the Frontier FFA will lead us in the pledge to the flag."

Next came the invocation and my introduction of numerous guests per the official program, both of which appear in the Exhibits section of this book. There is very good video coverage of these items in the tape.

The video tape then shows the rest of the official program with remarks by Frank Voytas, Jim Apgar, and Roland Schaar; and the Frontier High School choir singing. I then introduced Casimier Wojakowski and all of the equipment operators and helpers for the cutting, wrapping, and loading of the tree.

I concluded by saying, "If we lose this tree today, it's these guys' fault." [Laughter from the crowd.]

I then informed the crowd that the Frontier band would be going to D.C. to play during the official tree lighting ceremony on December 9. "We're all excited for them and we have several bus loads of people lined up to go over there and show Washington, D.C. what Washington County, Ohio is all about." [Cheering from the band.]

Sandy then came forward and recognized the band once again and thanked them for all of their hard work and efforts. Throughout all of this there are nice shots of the crowd, the band, and the equipment standing ready for the cutting to come.

The official first cut was made by Sandra Binegar of Newport and her cousin Judy Beaver of Johnsville, Ohio, both descendants of Joseph Holdren, the original homesteader of the site."

Numerous other ceremonial cuts with an antique crosscut saw followed - by various dignitaries and officials. There is good footage of this. And most of those who participated in the cuts are listed elsewhere in this book. Art Martin of the Wayne National Forest supervised this part by handling the saw between cuts to ensure safety. The saw was on loan from Hocking Technical College in Nelsonville. This final portion of the official ceremony concluded just before 10:00 a.m. and I thanked everyone who had come out that morning. I asked them to move off the site for safety reasons, so that the official cutting of the tree could begin.

"By 10:00 a.m. a 30-foot circle around the tree was cleared and Mr. Wojakowski had workers assembled for the felling. A crane donated by Busch Crane Rental of Vienna, West Virginia was used to secure the spruce."

The video then shows excellent scenes of Casimier Wojakowski instructing the operators for proper location of their equipment and talking with Mack Haessly on the direction of the tree felling operation, the notching of the tree, and the final cut. We had selected Mack, a seasoned and professional chainsaw operator, to make the official cuts with a chainsaw donated for that purpose by Poulan Chainsaws.

A reporter from Channel 5-TV in Cleveland, Ohio literally jumped in before things started - to ask Casimier a few questions; and Ray Beach was able to get good footage of this, including the audio.

Ray then captured excellent footage of the operators moving their equipment into the final positions: the crane operator; Black's Tree service attaching cables and ropes to the tree from their boom bucket; Danny Thompson and the Carlton Oil vehicle and crew; Pete Edgar's dozer; and more. There are scenes of Chip Wetz; Kenny Haessly with his log skidder; as well as Casimier and me talking and jerking one of the guide ropes into place. Throughout all of this phase three Wayne National Forest employees –John Kerr, Art Martin, and Dale Newell - were shown numerous times assisting and directing things as laid out by Mr. Wojakowski. We were just about ready to go.

"As things proceeded, crews working from different vantage points had to be in touch with Mr. Wojakowski discussing just what the next step would be. He decided that the lower branches needed to be removed from the tree, so crews from Black's Tree Service of Marietta cut them away."

Finally, Mack Haessly began his cut with Casimier at his side ensuring that the notch was proper for the required direction of felling. The videotape shows the entire operation all the way until the tree is on the ground. It is extremely interesting watching Casimier direct the various operators on when and how much to move, and how much tension to apply in various directions to gently lay the tree on the ground without damaging it. After the tree was on the ground, measurements were taken to decide where to cut off the bottom 25 feet and to place the brace just above that point to support the tree while the limbs were being wrapped.

"Forest employees and sawyers from Kenmack Lumber Company felled the tree before Noon under the watchful supervision of Mr. Wojakowski. You can't just jump out of the way and yell "timber!" when you're cutting a big 85 foot Norway spruce. So, as the tree was lowered the crane backed up ever so slowly, so that the branches would fold naturally underneath the tree. After months of planning, the

actual cutting went rather fast. It was a moment to be savored, but it was in many ways a great relief.

The rest of the day was spent wrapping the tree and preparing it for its journey to Washington, D.C. Wrapping involves folding the branches upward and tying them in snuggly. That's not easy to do with a tree whose branches have a 35-foot spread at the bottom. We had to pull those branches to within 10 feet, so that they fit on the flatbed trailer for transporting on the highways. You have to do it gradually, too.

Thankfully, Mr. Wojakowski knew exactly what had to be done. He got some employees from Carlton Oil Corporation; FFA students from the Washington County Career Center and Frontier High School; and Jeff Edgar and they did exactly as directed. Wojakowski told me that it normally takes six hours to wrap a tree once it's on the ground and that it had taken as long as two days depending upon the kind of tree , the weather conditions, and the wrapping crew. But out there that day, the work went so well that it took only four hours.

After the wrapping was completed, Danny Thompson from Carlton Oil actually "rode" the tree as it was lifted, right on to the flatbed truck; he made sure that it was lowered just right, on to the cradle. The cradle was specially made per Wojakowski's specifications by the Washington County Career Center's Welding Class. The cradle held the butt of the tree above the flatbed to prevent damage to the branches. That cradle, by the way, went to Michigan for the 1988 Capitol Christmas Tree and from now on will do that job annually for other national trees.

Further damage was also prevented by snuggling the tree in the spruce boughs cut by Black's Tree Service. Without proper wrapping, wind vibrating around the flatbed during transport can "spank" the needles off the tree. There's an awful lot to think about."

There are great scenes and action shots of all of the preceding operations in this video.

Ray then cuts to Jim Apgar and me talking about the sprinkling of snow that had begun to fall and I told him that I had ordered it on a government requisition about 30 days ago. "They required 30 days lead time to make it happen," I told him. "Well, it's been a great day," Jim said. I told him that, yes, it had really worked out nice. And he said, "See you in D.C."

Lynn Kantner seemed to be everywhere taking photos that day. We did a group shot of all the Forest Service employees in front of the tree. And Ray scanned his video camera around to get footage of all the workers and others who were still present.

"You know, it started to snow at the first cut on the tree and the sky really opened up and laid down a heavy blanket when the tree finally came to rest gently on the ground. It was not only beautiful, but also worked to the benefit of the tree because very little dirt or mud got on it. The snow finally stopped just as the tree was loaded and covered with branches from the sister tree.

The sister tree was another Norway spruce which was felled about a quarter of a mile down the road. It was probably planted about the same time as the one we picked as the national tree and could very easily have been a brother. That tree was our back-up and the branches were not only used to protect the main tree in transit, but were used in Washington to fill in the thin places on the main tree.

When the truck pulled out of the site to go to Marietta for the next day's send-off ceremony, the sun returned to close the whole thing with a fitting and spectacular sunset.

The Forest Service people and some of the Christmas Tree Committee had one more meeting at our office on the morning of the Send-Off Ceremony in Marietta. Everyone had already put out a lot of energy, but there was one more thing left to do." [There is a group photo and some video of that meeting included in the tape.]

"On Saturday, November 21 about 500 area residents gathered in front of Marietta College's Hermann Fine Arts Center to send off the Capitol Christmas Tree to Washington. Marietta High School's marching band, "The Wall of Sound," led the crowd in the singing of "O Christmas Tree" and other Christmas carols. Dignitaries spoke and various flags were dedicated and sent along with the tree."

[The tape shows the flags being presented and Casimier Wojakowski being introduced. He made some very complimentary remarks about the area, the Christmas tree committee, and the workers who had helped him cut, wrap, and load the tree the day before. There were lots of video shots of the crowd gathered that day. Many school children came forward, introduced by Iwana Simon, and received awards for their efforts in making ornaments, cards, posters, and putting on skits and plays about the tree. The band sang

The First Noel and Silent Night, and then played Jingle Bells. Tim Wallace, Minister of the Reno Christian Church, gave the Benediction. People mingled and had punch and cookies afterward inside the Hermann Fine Arts Center.]

"The Capitol Tree and 28 smaller trees were stored in two local warehouses until the following weekend when, on trucks donated by R.O. Wetz Transportation and Kenmack Lumber, the journey to Washington, D.C. began."

"We were a small, but impressive caravan as we left Marietta that morning [Sunday, November 29, 1987]. *There was R.O. "Roy" Wetz, Gil Courtney, Bob McElfresh, Kenny and Mack Haessly, Lynn Kantner, and myself in a van and a car loaded up with handmade tree ornaments; and two 18-wheelers sporting big signs announcing to everyone that this was "their" tree on its way to Washington, D.C.*

As we rolled across West Virginia and Maryland with our tree sticking out five to six feet beyond the end of the lead truck, we had a lot of people waving at us and honking their horns. I remember Bob McElfresh saying that many other truckers hailed him on his CB radio that day. After all, his was the only rig hauling the Capitol Christmas Tree and they were wishing him a safe journey; wanting to hear the whole story; singing Christmas carols to the tree; and just generally spreading good will and Christmas spirit along the highway.

Kenny and Mack shared the driving of the second truck, which carried all the rest of the trees destined for the various buildings and offices throughout the Capitol City. The trip took seven hours. We stored the trees in a Rockville, Maryland police yard and spent the evening in a local hotel.

Here we met with Teena Sechler, the Public Information Officer for the Wayne and Hoosier National Forests. All of this had been planned ahead of time, even the next morning when the U.S. Capitol Police met us in Rockville and escorted us right into Washington, D.C. In fact, we drove right on to the Capitol lawn. [Monday, November 30, 1987].

Despite the cold and the early morning hour, a number of spectators were there to greet us, including Congressmen Miller, Applegate, DeWine, and Regula. Paul Pincus was there, of course, to take over because the tree was now his responsibility. Forest Service officials from the Washington Office also came out to greet us.

For the next two days, Lynn, Teena, and I delivered the rest of the trees and the hundreds of beautiful ornaments, hand-made by children from various schools in Ohio. Congressmen had expected the trees, but none of them were quite prepared for the beautiful gifts made by the school children. John Glenn was so touched that he had us wait while he carefully unwrapped each gift. I only wish all of the school kids could have seen their Congressmen's faces when they opened the ornaments.

Well, the culmination of all this was the Tree Lighting Ceremony at 5:00 p.m. on Wednesday, December 9, 1987. Approximately 500 people from Washington County were there with Ohio Governor Celeste and other Ohio dignitaries. In fact, the national anthem was sung by our own Mary Carson from New Matamoras. The Frontier High School band, under the direction of Lynn Johnson, played a medley of Christmas carols. Gil Courtney, President of Peoples Savings Bank in New Matamoras, and Phyllis Richerson, of the Marietta Tourist & Convention Bureau, had arranged for the seven buses needed to take the local people and the band to Washington. Ohio's Congresswoman and several Congressmen spoke to the crowd of 1,000 or more that had gathered to watch the official dedication and lighting of the tree."

The videotape shows much of this, including remarks by the Architect of the Capitol, George White, the Master of Ceremonies and an Ohio native. He introduced Speaker of the House Jim Wright (TX), who gave a short speech and then flipped the switch that lit the lights on the Capitol Christmas Tree at 5:24 p.m.

Marietta Mayor Nancy Hollister and Ohio Governor Richard Celeste then gave remarks, as did Senators Glenn and Metzenbaum. Congresswoman Oakar and Congressmen Regula, Applegate, Eckart, and Miller also made short speeches. Miller noted the 200th anniversary of the Northwest Ordinance (1787), the City of Marietta (1788), the U.S. Constitution (written in 1787, ratified in 1788, and went into effect in 1789). He also noted the on-going nuclear disarmament talks currently being negotiated just down the street by President Ronald Reagan and Soviet leader Mikhail Gorbachev.

Congressman Applegate, whose District the tree came from, gave a shout out in his remarks to "Gil Courtney; Kenny and Mack Haessly, Mary Carson, and Dan Kincaid." And I certainly had not expected that.

The Navy Band played music before and after the ceremony. Afterwards, receptions were hosted by Senator Glenn,

Governor Celeste/Mayor Hollister, and Marietta College Director of Alumni Affairs, George Merkel.

The narration concludes with:
"So that's the story about a tree, an "immigrant" tree from Norway that made it all the way to Washington, D.C to become the People's Christmas Tree in 1987. It seems fitting to me that the tree represented the early immigrants who settled the Northwest Territory and who started this whole thing; and how the descendants of those people worked together to make this event one which will long be remembered in the history of Washington County and the Wayne National Forest."

The credits roll at the end of the tape and include:

Narrated by - Dan Kincaid

Written by - Lynn Kantner

Video by - Cullen Beach

Additional footage by - Gil Courtney

Photos by - Wayne National Forest

Video made possible by - Wayne National Forest

Capitol Christmas Tree Committee

Marietta Bicentennial Commission

Directed by - Ray Beach

(Various other credits are listed for those who helped Ray with the editing, sound, dubbing, etc.)

Dedicated to the Memory of -

<u>Barb Hamilton</u> (Capitol Christmas Tree Committee Member) who had passed away before final production of this video

And

<u>Jud Matheny</u> (father of Lynn Kantner and grandfather of Ray and Cullen Beach) who had also passed away

Date of the video completion - 1989, by Ray Beach

From Ohio Woodlands Magazine:

OHIO TRUCKERS VOLUNTEER TO HAUL CAPITOL CHRISTMAS TREE TO NATION'S CAPITOL

by Dan Kincaid, Forester, Marietta, and Member of OFA Board of Trustees, and Teena Sechler, Public Information Officer, Supervisor's Office, Wayne National Forest

Ohio is known for many things: baseball, automakers, cornfields, railroads, a great river, and the buckeye. But rarely when one thinks of Ohio do 65-foot evergreen trees come to mind. Yet this Christmas, the tree for the nation's Capitol in Washington, D.C. came from southeastern Ohio's Wayne National Forest.

Two Ohio companies, R.O. Wetz Transportation of Marietta, and Kenmack Lumber of Newport, located in Washington County, helped to make this possible. Embodying the spirit of patriotism and pride in their community, these two companies offered their trucks, drivers, fuel, and time to assist in giving this very special gift to the people of America.

"It's been about the most special project we've ever been involved with," said R.O. Wetz. "We've really enjoyed working with the communities and the Wayne National Forest."

Neither company has made a business of transporting large trees, so the challenges associated with wrapping, loading, and hauling the trees were unique, but one that both companies accepted with enthusiasm. Wetz shrugged off skepticism, saying from the beginning, "We can do it—if you put enough heads together, you can always find an answer."

To help with the cutting and wrapping of the tree, the Forest Service brought in a volunteer from Escanaba, Michigan. The tree, with a 35-foot branch spread, had to be bound tightly to fit on an 8-foot truck bed without damaging its branches.

The two trucks hauled 30 trees. Wetz' truck hauled the main tree and "filler branches," stripped from a tree of the same size to be used to repair any defects in the tree so it will be perfectly symmetrical. A trailer was donated by Ravens Metal Products, Inc. of Parkersburg to haul the long tree. The truck from Kenmack Lumber hauled five large trees, 18-24-feet tall; 18 8-foot trees for members .of the Ohio Congressional staff; and six trees for the U.S. Department of Agriculture. Mack Haessly commented, "It's been a real pleasure taking this tree to D.C., an experience that we were real proud to be part of; we were just happy to help out."

The 1987 Capitol Tree came from the Marietta area of the Wayne National Forest to help draw national attention to the state during the bicentennial celebration of the signing of the Northwest Ordinance. Cutting the tree at Christmas also kicked off the 200th anniversary of the founding of the city of Marietta, which was the first settlement in the new territory.

The tree which the Forest Service had selected for the Capitol is not a tree native to Ohio, but the story of how it may have come to be is very American. Its history is unique and fits in so well with the idea of an expanding frontier and entrepreneurship at its best that it seemed especially fitting that this tree would have the honor of going to the United States Capitol.

The tall, stately Norway spruce that stood on the Capitol lawn in Washington, D.C. once towered above the neighboring hardwood trees on an old house site in the Forest. The tree is believed to have been planted about 1900. The Norway spruce is rarely found that far south, yet many house sites dating to the mid to late 1800's in that part of southeast Ohio had Norway spruces in their yards.

In the past, Capitol Christmas trees have come from most of the New England and Lake States. The amount of coordination and work involved in getting a Christmas tree to the Capitol is extensive. The Forest Service, working with the Ohio Department of Natural Resources, organized a committee of local community leaders to work on various parts of the project.

No government funds could be used on the project. The committee was responsible for generating all the necessary funds for financing the Capitol Tree effort. Transportation was by far the biggest expense in the project, so the generosity of the two trucking companies was a significant load off the committee, which would otherwise have had to raise the money.

The Wayne National Forest's 1987 U.S. Capitol Christmas Tree would never have gotten on the ground and to Washington, D.C. without the donations and volunteer efforts of the following:

R.O. Wetz Transportation, Marietta;

Kenmack Lumber, Inc., Newport;

Black's Tree Service, Marietta;

Busch's Crane Rentals, Vienna, WV;

Carlton Oil Corp., Newport;

Howard Edgar Contracting, Newport;

Ravens Trailers, Parkersburg, WV;

Frontier High School, Future Farmers of America, New Matamoras;

Washington County Career Center, Forestry and Welding classes.

Also, special thanks to the ODNR, Division of Forestry, for assistance on many aspects of the project.

The Capitol Christmas Tree program began in 1965. The idea was initiated by John McCormack, at that time Speaker of the House. That first year, a live Douglas fir was selected and actually planted on the Capitol grounds, with the intent of maintaining a living symbol of Christmas. It was to have been re-used annually but, as is often the case in transplanting large trees, it died three years later.

The Forest Service took over responsibility for the Capitol Christmas Tree in 1969. The tree generally comes from the East to minimize transportation costs. A different National Forest is selected each year, with Forests scheduled several years ahead.

In addition to the main tree, several other trees from Ohio were needed to be used in various government offices in Washington, D.C. Trees have been supplied for the Botanical Garden, the Supreme Court, the U.S. Department of Agriculture building, and the Senate and House Dining Rooms, among others. These trees were provided by a variety of private sources in southeastern Ohio.

When the trees were delivered in Washington, D.C., the trucks were met by a delegation of Congressmen and photographers. After the trees were unloaded, the truckers were given a tour of the Capitol by Representative Douglas Applegate. Haessly said, "The chance to see the Capitol and eat in the House Private Dining Room as a guest of Congressman Applegate is something we will always remember!"

From Ohio, The Heart of It All, it was best wishes to the nation.

Right, Mack Haessly of Kenmack Lumber Co.

All wrapped up, ready to go.

L to R: OFA members at the Cutting Ceremony – Roy Palmer, Gary Marcum, Dan Kincaid, Ron Cornell, and Jack Haessly

(<u>AUTHOR'S NOTE</u> – Teena Sechler and I co-wrote the preceding article, as well as supplying the three photos. The story appeared in the Winter 1988 edition of Ohio Woodlands, which I believe came out in January 1988. This quarterly publication of the Ohio Forestry Association went to all OFA members, as well as a copy being sent to every high school library in Ohio. The front cover of that magazine was a full page color photo of the tree standing in the woods, shortly before it was cut in November of 1987. It's a little difficult to see because the tree is featured in the main frame of the photo, but Lynn Kantner of our local Wayne National Forest office is sitting on a tree stump in the lower left, pointing up toward the tree. I took this photo and supplied a copy to OFA. (See Photo chapter of this book for the cover photo.)

I was also honored to have been asked to write another article in that issue of Ohio Woodlands. It was a **Member Profile** of Norm Haessly, the father of Jack Haessly, who was involved in several facets of the Capitol Christmas Tree project. Norm was in his 70s by this time and had been involved in the hardwood lumber business since the early 1930s. By 1954 Jack had entered the family business with his dad. They established Haessly Hardwood Lumber Company near Marietta in the early 1960s and it became one of the most outstanding companies of its kind in the United States. Jack continues to run the company today, along with his two sons. The company also includes a sister company on the same site, Inland Wood Products, which produces wooden pallets. But it all began with Norm, a pioneer and major force in Ohio's hardwood lumber industry. I was fortunate to have known Norm and I'm proud to call Jack a close friend.

VARIOUS OTHER ARTICLES

My weekly newspaper columns obviously offered the most complete and accurate written accounts of activities related to the 1987 U.S. Capitol Christmas Tree project. I wanted to give credit to the many volunteers who assisted in various efforts, so my columns are the only place that many of those thank you's appeared. Also, my timelines are accurate, as is the background information leading up to the 1987 event. This book, **A Gift to the Nation**, includes my weekly columns in the Exhibit section.

However, there was quite a bit of additional related coverage; mostly news coverage, but some feature articles and other types of information, too. We made copies of those other articles that we were aware of, plus many people sent us clippings from newspapers and magazines in their areas.

Lois Severin, of our Wayne National Forest office in Reno (Marietta Unit), collected and copied these additional articles. She presented a set of those to me as one of my "going-away" gifts when I left Ohio for a job in Kentucky in September of 1990. It is with a huge thanks to Lois, who has since passed away, that I am able to list these for the historical record.

Although I don't have the time nor space to reprint all of these related articles in their entireties, on the following pages I have listed the copies that I do have; and it reflects the widespread popularity of and public interest in the event. I have listed the author, the publication, the date if available, and a few notes about each article.

As with a lot of news coverage, there are some errors in the various reports, but, in general, they are mostly correct. Just a quick "for instance" is that one of the articles referred several times to the truck/trailer driven by "Kenmark" Lumber, rather than the correct Kenmack Lumber. There are other errors in some of the coverage, but that's the nature of news reporting, especially when reporters are extremely busy, facing time constraints, deadlines, and so on.

Here is that additional coverage that I have copies of:

- Donn Appleman, Editor of the Ohio Christmas Tree Association Newsletter, wrote a July 1987 story on the front page of that publication giving the background of the upcoming event, what all had gone into it to that point, and what would be happening later in the fall. He said that the Forest Service had asked his organization to provide 31 smaller trees, 8 to 12 feet tall, for various Congressional offices and other facilities in D.C. He asked that any members willing to donate a tree for that purpose to contact him. Donn also ran a photo, which I sent him, of the Capitol Christmas Tree as it stood in the Wayne NF.
- On 9/9/87 the Marietta Times ran a photo of one of the clear, crystal apothecary jars made by Fenton Glass to commemorate the Capitol Christmas Tree, along with a story announcing where a set of three different sized jars could be purchased and the prices. This was one of our local fundraising projects. The story noted that the first sets of the jars were going to be purchased by Marietta Mayor Nancy Hollister and Washington County Commissioners Dick Young, Sandy Matthews, and Glen Miller. The jars featured

an etching of a large Christmas tree in front of the
U.S. Capitol with the logo "1987 Capitol Christmas
Tree – Wayne National Forest."

- On 9/10/87 the Marietta A.M. newspaper also ran
  some information about the availability of the jars
  with a photo of me flanked by Glen Miller and Nancy
  Hollister, who purchased the first sets of jars.

- On 10/1/87 Barbara Lovely, Executive Director of the
  Marietta Bicentennial Commission, mentioned in her
  "Start of it All" column in the Marietta Times about
  the cutting and send-off ceremonies coming up in
  late November for the Capitol Christmas Tree. She
  mentioned the commemorative Christmas cards and
  glass canister sets being sold as souvenirs, as part of
  the fund raising efforts for the project. She also told
  of the U.S. Capitol Landscape Architect, Paul Pincus,
  coming to the area several months previous to give
  the final approval for the tree which we had chosen to
  be the Capitol Tree.

- On 10/3/87 a note in the Marietta Times said that the
  "Washington County Commissioners probably have
  throbbing hands today" from signing about 140
  special invitations for both the Capitol Christmas
  Tree Cutting Ceremony on November 20 and the
  Send-Off Ceremony on November 21. Also signing
  the invitations were: Marietta Mayor Nancy
  Hollister; Frontier Local School Superintendent John
  Hoff; and Terry Hoffman, Acting Wayne National
  Forest Supervisor.

- Teena Sechler, Public Information Officer for the
  Wayne and Hoosier National Forests, wrote an article
  for the October 1987 edition of the Wa-Hoo Lookout,

which was an internal Forest Service newsletter. She provided the background of the 1987 tree, how it came to be selected from the Wayne National Forest, the history of the U.S. Capitol Christmas Tree program, and explained the legend of how Norway spruce trees came to be planted on homesteads throughout the Ohio country. Teena thanked all of those assisting with the project and concluded her article by saying, "Many of us have wondered during the past year if we could really pull this off, but we're now confident it's going to happen and will likely be one of the best things the Wayne has ever done for their public image in Ohio."

That October 1987 issue of the newsletter also announced the retirement of Forest Supervisor Harold Godlevske. When I first began my efforts in 1981 to get the 1987 Capitol Christmas Tree to come from the Marietta, Ohio area, the only Forest Service person who didn't think I was crazy was Harold (and possibly Athens District Ranger Bob Joens). Of course, the closer we got to the actual cutting, send-off, and lighting ceremonies, the more that everyone jumped on board. Harold initially networked on his end, I networked on my end and, with tenacity over a period of a few years, we finally received the necessary approval from our superiors in Milwaukee, WI and Washington, D.C. to provide the tree. Of course, it still needed final on-the-ground approval from the Capitol's Landscape Architect, and we got that in 1986. This is all explained in earlier chapters of this book. I was sad to see Harold leave before we finally got the tree cut and shipped to D.C., but I want everyone to know that without his initial support the whole event would never have gotten off the ground.

- On 10/21/87 Barb Hamilton and Iwana Simon, who were both on our Capitol Christmas Tree Planning Committee, announced in the Marietta Times that they were seeking elementary and junior high school projects for the Capitol Tree contest.
- Barbara Lovely mentioned in her "Start of it All" column in the Marietta Times on 10/29/87 the dates and times for the Capitol Tree ceremonies and the availability of the souvenir cards and glass canisters.
- On 10/30/87 the Martins Ferry (OH) Times Leader announced that the Capitol Tree Christmas cards and the sets of three commemorative apothecary jars (16, 32, and 48 ounces in size respectively) were being sold at the Monroe County Park District Office in Woodsfield.
- The Ohio Magazine's November 1987 issue featured a couple of paragraphs in its calendar section listing information and the dates for the upcoming Cutting and Send-Off Ceremonies for the U.S. Capitol Christmas Tree.
- The November 1987 Newsletter of the Northwest Ordinance and U.S. Constitution Bicentennial featured a column about the tree, giving some of the background and listing upcoming dates for the cutting, send-off, and lighting ceremonies.
- In the 11/3/87 edition of the Martins Ferry (OH) Times Leader, Bob Hecker interviewed me for a story about the Capitol Christmas Tree; and about the Wayne National Forest's history, scattered land ownership pattern, and land acquisition plans for the

future. I told him that the Capitol Tree project was "a once-in-a-lifetime event. It'll be the first time the Capitol Christmas tree has ever been chosen from the Wayne," I told Hecker, "and I feel safe in saying it'll be the last."

- On 11/7/87 Jess Mancini of the Marietta A.M. newspaper wrote an article about the upcoming Capitol Christmas Tree activities. He quoted me, Marietta Mayor Nancy Hollister, and Phyllis Richerson of the Marietta Tourist & Convention Bureau. Mayor Hollister said, "This is an opportunity for Washington County and the community that's never going to happen again."

- On 11/8/87 the Cincinnati (OH) Enquirer ran a story by Irene Wright about the tree, along with a photo of it standing in the Wayne National Forest prior to the cutting. There was an accompanying graphic map showing the location of Washington County in relation to Hamilton County in the state of Ohio; as well as a more detailed map showing the location of Marietta and surrounding communities. In the story Wright quoted Paul Pincus, myself, and Bob Forbes, Principal of Frontier High School. I was quoted as saying, "I feel like it's probably the biggest event for the Wayne National Forest in its nearly 50-year history." My friend Don Girton, who had served as Forest Supervisor for the Wayne and Hoosier National Forests in the 1970s, had sent me a copy of the story. Don had retired from the Forest Service a couple of years previous as the Director of the Office of Information in D.C. He now operated a Christmas tree farm in the Cincinnati area and saw the story in the Cincinnati Enquirer. Don's tree farm was actually on the Kentucky side of the Ohio River, near Cincinnati, in Cold Spring, KY.

\- On 11/10/87 the Marietta Times ran a story outlining all of the dates and times for activities over the next month related to the Capitol Christmas Tree. A photo we supplied them of the tree standing in the forest also ran on this date.

\- Roger Kalter also ran a story in the Marietta Times on 11/10/87. He interviewed me extensively and I must have had too much coffee that morning. I told him that some "may snicker, but this tree (will be) standing in front of the United States Capitol. Dignitaries from around the world will see it. U.S. citizens will see it. This is not some Mickey Mouse place out in the hills; this is the U.S. Capitol," I said. I also told him that the eyes of the nation would be focused on southeastern Ohio. "This shows, as a community, we can be involved in something significant that has positive effects. I also told Roger that, "this appears to be the biggest thing ever to happen in Wayne National Forest and certainly in the Marietta Unit." Kalter mentioned some of the Wayne National Forest history and some of the events leading up to and scheduled to occur around the Capitol Christmas Tree. Before all of the caffeine began wearing off, I said to Roger, "This is undoubtedly a once-in-a-lifetime happening for our area. If the U.S. Capitol Tree ever comes from southeastern Ohio again, it will sure surprise me. And if it by chance does, then I'm sure we'll all be six feet underground by then." I don't know why I was so wound up during that interview. Roger and I were friends and he was a great guy, so it couldn't have been anything that he said. I guess it was just my passion for the whole project that was showing up – and also the coffee and caffeine!

- The Parkersburg (WV) Sentinel reporter Jo Horvath wrote a story in the 11/10/87 edition of the newspaper about the Little Hocking Elementary School's fifth grade classes planting a three-foot tall Norway spruce to commemorate the cutting of the main Capitol Tree from the Wayne National Forest. Teachers Libby Arnold and Kathy Hamrick coordinated the activity which also included a poetry contest and a poster contest. According to Horvath's article, Missy Ward won the poetry contest and Laura Bickle won the poster contest. "Since we are taking a 65-foot Norway spruce out of the county, we thought we'd put a three-foot one back," said Hamrick. The Little Hocking school's activities were just one example of the many school activities taking place around Washington County in honor of the Capitol Christmas Tree.
- In the Marietta Times on 11/12/87 Barbara Lovely, Executive Director of the Marietta Bicentennial Commission, wrote a "Start of it All" column with a thorough background of how the tree was selected to come from our area, the probable history of its planting origin, and notes on what would be happening in the next few weeks.
- Teena Sechler of our Supervisor Office in Bedford, IN sent out a news release on 11/13/87 providing a history of the land where the Capitol Christmas Tree

was located. It was based on research done by
Elizabeth Cottle of Marietta who had compiled it as a
Volunteer for the Forest Service. Several reporters
referenced this news release in future articles. The
research reaffirmed that the likely planters of the
Norway spruce were Joseph I. Holdren or his wife
Mary around 1900 or shortly thereafter. The property
had been in the Holdren family since about 1816. It
later changed hands a couple of times before the
Grimes family sold it to become part of the Wayne
National Forest.

- Roger Kalter's article in the Marietta Times on
11/17/87 told about the cutting of a Norway spruce
from the yard of Diane and Luke Arnold of the Oak
Grove section of Marietta. It said that the tree was
scheduled to be put up in the USDA patio in D.C. Pete
Suerken of the Ohio Division of Forestry and Marilyn
Ortt of the Marietta Tree Commission coordinated
locating the tree, which was cut down by John Kerr of
our local Wayne National Forest office. Luke Arnold
said the tree was getting too big for his lawn and this
would save him the trouble of having it cut and
hauled off. The 24-foot tree had originally been
planted by Arnold's parents, who lived in Vincent,
and was transplanted to the Oak Grove location in
1974. Diane Arnold said that Luke's parents, who had
come in to town for the cutting, "were pretty excited."
Oak Grove Elementary students gathered and sang
"Oh, Christmas Tree," shared Christmas stories, and
read poems. Later that day a 12-foot Colorado blue
spruce was scheduled to be cut from the yard of Jess
Latimer in Marietta. (I believe this tree went to the

USDA Office in D.C.) Kalter's story also related how a tree was cut the day before from the Harold Jeffers farm near Chesterhill in Morgan County. It was scheduled to go in the Supreme Court building. That was a larger tree and was somewhat "difficult to handle without damaging it," I told Kalter. "We used a log loader to help us." I also told Kalter that the previous Friday 21 smaller trees had arrived from the Ohio Christmas Tree Growers Association. All of these companion trees to the main Capitol Tree were stored at the Ohio Division of Forestry Nursery in Reno prior to shipping them to various Congressional offices in D.C.

- An 11/17/87 article in the Athens Messenger told of cutting an 18-foot blue spruce from the Mabel Howell Tree Farm that was headed to the Senate Private Dining Room. Acting Athens District Ranger Jim Apgar of the Wayne National Forest coordinated the ceremony, which was attended by about 60 people. A photo of Howell and Apgar during the ceremony was featured, along with a photo of Art Martin, Forestry Technician at Wayne National Forest, actually cutting down the tree.

- On 11/18/87 the Marietta Times ran a photo showing Dave Greenwood of our Wayne NF office helping to load the Jess Latimer tree in Marietta onto Dave Padgitt's truck for transport to Reno. Padgitt was with the Ohio Division of Forestry fire control office in Barlow. This tree was scheduled to be put up in the lobby of the USDA office in D.C.

- Richard Ellers, staff writer for the Cleveland (OH) Plain Dealer, wrote a pre-cutting story on 11/18/87 about the tree and listed upcoming dates. He interviewed me, Marietta Mayor Nancy Hollister, and captured a few quotes from Marietta Tourist & Convention Bureau Director Phyllis Richerson. Ellers referred to the tree as "hidden at the end of a country lane just off Ohio Rt. 7" and as "the 'Cinderella' of Ohio's Wayne National Forest." He also wrote that, "From the obscurity of a former farmstead in Washington County, the tall, graceful spruce has been selected to reign this holiday season as the official Christmas tree of the U.S. Capitol in Washington, D.C."

-   On 11/18/87 Patrick Jackson of the Zanesville (OH) Times Recorder wrote about a small Douglas-fir Christmas tree that was being cut from the Larry Sarabaugh farm near Adamsville. This tree, along with 20-some others coordinated by the Ohio Christmas Tree Growers Association, was going to be sent to D.C. and placed in one of the offices of the Ohio Congressional delegation.

-   The Marietta Times, 11/19/87, announced that a tree planting to commemorate the Capitol Christmas Tree would be held on the afternoon following the Cutting Ceremony at the Marietta Bicentennial Grove. The grove was located on the ceremonial mound at Camp Tupper on the Fourth Street side.

-   The Marietta Times also ran a story on 11/19/87 announcing times for the following day's Cutting Ceremony. They noted that "crews armed with booms, winches, saws, and other heavy equipment will gather Friday to cut the tree that soon will grace the Capitol Building in Washington, D.C." The Times also noted that students from Fairview Elementary School in Marietta traveled to the site to view the tree on the day before it was cut.

- On 11/19/87, Marietta Times Managing Editor, Mark Gruetze, and his Editorial Board, ran an opinion piece saying that the selection of the tree from our area was another reason for residents to feel good about where they live. They noted the tie-in to the history of the Northwest Ordinance and listed a timeline for the cutting, send-off, and lighting ceremonies. They said that when Speaker of the House, Jim Wright, "turns on the lights of the decorated tree" on December 9, "Washington County can share the joy of a gift to the entire nation." The Board wrote that we can whisper to ourselves, "Hey, that's from us."

- A note in the Marietta Times on 11/19/87 read that the Frontier Board of Education had formally approved sending band director Lynne Johnson and the marching band to Washington, D.C., where it would play during the tree lighting ceremony on December 9.

- On 11/20/87 the Spirit of Democracy newspaper in Woodsfield ran a lengthy story detailing the selection of the Capitol Christmas tree, its history, and a lead-in to the cutting, which would occur later that day. Two photos accompanied the story: 1) an unidentified person standing in the woods, looking up at the tree a few weeks before it was cut; 2) a photo of Nina and Norman Johnson walking with their dog on their farm along the Jericho Low Gap Road in Monroe County. The Johnson's furnished two Christmas trees to be sent to D.C. along with about 28 others from around eastern Ohio. One of their trees was slated for the office of Congressman Applegate.

- On 11/20/87 the Marietta Times quoted Washington County Sheriff, Richard D, Ellis, as saying that this was the first time in his 23 years as sheriff that he had guarded a Christmas tree. "But, then again, it's the first time we've had a tree going to the U.S. Capitol," he noted. Ellis and his deputies, along with Forest Service personnel, citizens, the Ohio Highway Patrol, and a security firm had been "guarding" the tree for several days prior to the cutting. "I'll be glad when it is cut," Ellis said. "I was getting a little paranoid about a (possible) newspaper headline reading 'Sheriff Lets Vandals Destroy U.S. Capitol Tree'."
- The 11/20/87 edition of the Parkersburg (WV) Sentinel ran an article giving a brief summary of the Cutting and Send-Off ceremonies.
- The Marietta A.M. ran a story on 11/20/87 announcing the time schedule for the Cutting Ceremony and the Send-Off Ceremony. It also mentioned that a tree from the Harold Jeffers Tree Farm in Morgan County would go to the Supreme Court; a tree for the Senate would come from the Norman Johnson farm in Monroe County; Mabel Howell's Tree Farm near Athens would provide a tree for the Senate Private Dining Room; Leo Bro from Ironton would provide a 24-foot Norway spruce for the U.S. Botanical Gardens; another 24-foot tree would come from Marietta for the USDA Patio; and that various other trees from around Ohio would be

sent to D.C. to adorn other USDA locations, the U.S.
Forest Service office, and offices of the Ohio
Congressional delegation. These trees were all sent to
us at our Reno (Marietta) Office and we stored them
across the road in an Ohio Division of Forestry
Nursery warehouse until they were shipped on a
Kenmack Lumber tractor trailer to D.C. for delivery.

-   Tom Hrach wrote a story on 11/20/87 in the Marietta
    Times summarizing the tree cutting and quoting
    Casimier Wojakowski and Judy Beaver. He
    mentioned Jim Miller, who noted the tie-in to the
    Bicentennial of the Northwest Ordinance. Miller was
    Executive Director of the State Commission on the
    ordinance and the bicentennial. I had talked to Miller
    a couple of times over the previous months and he
    was really appreciative of our efforts to publicize the
    tree in relation to the bicentennial of the Northwest
    Ordinance. Hrach's story was accompanied by a
    photo of Frontier High School band member Pauly
    Harris playing her trombone for the National Anthem
    during the Cutting Ceremony.

-   Annetta Richardson of the Marietta A.M. newspaper
    wrote a long story on 11/21/87 detailing the cutting of
    the tree the day before. County Commissioner Sandra
    Matthews told her that "this is a once-in-a-lifetime
    happening. (It's) our gift to the nation." Casimier
    Wojakowski told Richardson that "this tree is as good
    as any I've sent (to D.C.)" After getting the tree on the
    ground, I told Richardson that "in many ways it was a
    real relief." As it began to snow, I also told her that "I
    had put in a government requisition for snow. Can
    you think of a better send-off?" The 72-year old

Wojakowski said that there was more media coverage for this cutting than any of the many Christmas tree cuttings he had ever been involved with. I concluded by telling Richardson, "When I got the idea and started the whole ball rolling (in 1981), I never thought it would be such a big thing. (But) it's been very special. We have every reason to feel proud." A photo of Casimier and me tightening one of the guide ropes attached to the tree accompanied the story. Another photo showed Wojakowski directing Mack Haessly on which of the lower limbs to remove from the tree after it was felled and where to make the final cut removing part of the butt of the tree. And a final photo showed students from Washington County Career Center helping wrap branches on the tree.

- Another side story by Richardson in the 11/21/87 Marietta A.M. talked about the "legends" surrounding the tree, such as who planted it and when. I was quoted as saying, "There's a lot of fact and fiction to the legend surrounding the Capitol tree's origin. It's the topic of great conversation in Washington County. We haven't counted the rings officially yet, but it's fun to speculate about what could have been." Richardson talked with Sandra Binegar and Judy Beaver, both descendants of the Holdren family, the likely planters of the tree. A photo of the two ladies making the first ceremonial cut of the tree was featured. Beaver had "mixed emotions about cutting down the tree. It's a great honor, but it was part of our family. I guess if it had to be cut from somewhere, then I'm happy it was here." In another newspaper story Binegar was more philosophical about the tree, saying that she was proud of it being cut and that if it had been left in the woods it would have eventually just fallen down and rotted. Both ladies said they wished that their fathers had been alive to see the tree cut. Richardson mentioned Teena Sechler's story "A Drummer's Gift" in Redbook magazine which related a possible origin of the tree. I concluded by saying that, "This is a real special event for all of us. I've taken a lot of pride in the project and I hope it leaves a lot of good memories and good feelings for the local community for many years to come. Whatever the history (of the tree's origin), I think Ohioans can be proud of this tree – their gift to the nation."

- Michael Lafferty, reporter for the Columbus (OH) Dispatch, wrote a story on 11/21/87 about the Cutting Ceremony. He interviewed Judy Holdren Beaver, who told of the history of the tree and the property it was cut from. She said, "It's a wonderful honor for the tree to come from Washington County." And she also said that "it feels like a little bit of our family went with the tree." Dispatch photographer, Jeff Hinckley, included a photo of the tree lying on the ground after it was cut. He took the photo from above, out of a bucket truck.

- On 11/21/87 Irene Wright, along with staffer Charlie Fry, wrote another article for the Cincinnati Enquirer. It was accompanied by two photos: one of Casimier Wojakowski directing the cutting of the tree and one of our crew loading the wrapped tree on to the Wetz Transportation trailer on November 20. The article quoted Lois Severin of our Wayne NF office, who said "the cutting went fine, and the tree came down about noon"; John Hoff, Frontier Local School District Superintendent ("I believe this topped any previous event in this area," he said.); and Thelma Holdren and her son Don, who told of the tree being planted on the original Holdren homestead prior to the land becoming part of Wayne National Forest.

- On 11/21/87, the Pleasants County Leader, just across the Ohio River in St. Marys, WV, ran a short note about the Cutting Ceremony that had taken place the previous day; also accompanying the note was a full length photo of the tree prior to cutting with the New Matamoras American Legion Post 378 in the photo.

- Richard Ellers, staff writer for the Cleveland (OH) Plain Dealer, wrote a story for their 11/21/87 edition about the Cutting Ceremony. A photo showed Casimier Wojakowski in action as the tree was cut and lowered. Ellers quoted Wojakowski, me, Sandra Binegar, Nancy Hollister, and Frontier High School band member, Sarah Carson, who said, "Are we ever excited about the trip (to D.C)!" She said that Massillon (OH) was the farthest the band had previously traveled and that some of the band members had never been out of state except to West Virginia.

- Above the banner on the 11/21/87 front page of the Marietta Times was a graphic with the caption "Capitol Tree Cut at Frontier." Inside was a story about the cutting of the tree along with a photo of the ceremonial "first cut" by Judy Beaver and Sandra Binegar – with a crosscut saw. The ladies were both

descendants of the Holdren family, which planted the
Norway spruce in the early 1900s. Other related
photos in that issue were: 1) Students from Frontier
High School's Vo-Ag program helping tie-down the
branches of the tree, readying it for transport; 2) A
photo of the crane and bucket truck getting ready to
attach cables and ropes to the tree prior to final
cutting; 3) A photo of Mack Haessly making the final
cut at the butt of the tree before it was gently lowered
to the ground by the crane. Haessly used a saw
furnished by the Poulan Chainsaw Company, which
had traditionally furnished a saw for that purpose for
the previous several years; 4) A photo of me and
Casimier Wojakowski adjusting a rope prior to gently
lowering the tree to the ground.

- A sidebar story, titled "Bits and Pieces from a Day of
Chopping and Sawing" appeared in the 11/21/87
issue of the Marietta Times with short topics: 1)
Several people examined the stump after cutting to
help estimate the tree's age. Phil Perry, forester from
Wayne National Forest's Athens office, counted the
rings and determined the tree was about 75 years old.
He also noted that the rings showed an apparent
injury of some sort about 31 years previous; 2) I was
quoted as saying that the tree's location had been
"one of the worst kept secrets in Washington County"
and that several thousand people probably knew
which tree was set for the cutting; 3) But we had
stationed volunteers on-site for 10 nights prior to the
cutting to provide security. Local law enforcement
agencies and a local security company also provided
security. We didn't want anything to happen to that

tree! We didn't have many back-ups if something
happened to it; 4) Marilyn Ortt had worked one night
shift rotation to keep an eye on the tree – under
starry skies and a 55 degree temperature. She said,
"The night I spent under the tree branches was one of
the best nights I've ever had camping;" 5) For
Frontier High School teacher Calvin Martin and his
Vo-Ag students the tree cutting was more than just a
ceremony. It was also a day spent working to wrap
the tree and to be used as an educational
opportunity; 6) Bob Forbes, Frontier High School
principal, wasn't sure at first if there would be
enough room at the site for all of his students who
wanted to attend. Of course, some of his students
were there working, participating in the ceremony,
including the band and choir. But finally, less than a
half hour before the cutting ceremony was to begin,
he announced that any student who wanted to attend
could do so. Buses were provided to take them there.

- On 11/21/87 Tom Hrach wrote a story in the Marietta
Times about Casimier Wojakowski, who said, "This is
the furthest I've ever gone (to cut a tree). But I think
it's really worth it." I had contacted Wojakowski in
July and told Hrach, "He has done this kind of thing
for 29 years in several different states. There just
aren't many people with his job description."
Casimier told Hrach our tree was just average, but
once they got it set up and decorated in D.C., that it
would look fine. He said that he thought the best
looking large Christmas trees came from Wisconsin,
Michigan, and possibly Vermont. Wojakowski had
previously directed the cutting of the 1981 Capitol

Christmas Tree from the Hiawatha National Forest in
Michigan; the 1983 tree from the Chequamegon
National Forest in Wisconsin; and the 1985 tree from
the Ottawa National Forest in Michigan. He had also
handled five tree cuttings headed to state capitols in
Wisconsin and Michigan, as well as numerous large
trees cut and shipped to various businesses and other
locations in the Chicago area. Hrach also included in
his story a timeline for the tree from November 21
through December 9 (the Lighting Ceremony.)

- An 11/22/87 photo in the Marietta A.M. showed
Marilyn Ortt shoveling dirt during a tree planting at
Camp Tupper in Marietta to commemorate the
cutting of the Capitol Tree. The caption noted that
about 12 people attended the brief occasion. Standing
in the background I can make out Frank Voytas,
Roland Schaar, Jim Apgar, and Dave Greenwood –
all of the Forest Service. Greenwood coordinated
digging the white pine tree from Wayne National
Forest land to present to the Marietta Tree
Commission for the ceremony.

- On 11/23/87 Robin Broughton wrote a story for the
Marietta Times about the Send-Off Ceremony. She
quoted Barbara Lovely as saying, "This tree carries
the wishes of Wayne National Forest, Ohio,
Washington County, and Marietta, but it also carries
the wishes of each of us as individuals participating at
this unique moment in history." Broughton quoted
Marietta Mayor Nancy Hollister, "This majestic
queen is our special gift to the nation. It comes from
us representing the historical significance of
southeastern Ohio." A photo also ran showing

Marietta High School band members Tonya Bargerhoff and Mary Augenstein leading the crowd in a rendition of "O, Christmas Tree" at the ceremony. Singing in the background were Barbara Lovely, Don Shuler, and Nancy Hollister.

- The 11/23/87 Marietta A.M. also ran a photo of Bargerhoff and Augenstein singing at the Send-Off Ceremony at Marietta College, as well as another photo of part of the crowd at the ceremony with the tree in the background loaded on the R.O. Wetz Transportation trailer.
- On 11/23/87 Mrs. Franklin Holdren of New Matamoras wrote a letter to the editor of the Marietta Times explaining the history of the Holdren family and their settling of the property where the Capitol Christmas Tree was cut. The tree had likely been planted by the Joseph Holdren family around the turn of the century
- Marilyn Ortt's Tree Commission column ran in the Marietta Times on 11/24/87. She mentioned that the Wayne National Forest donated a white pine tree for the city's Bicentennial Grove in honor of the Capitol Christmas Tree. Dave Greenwood and Gloria Eighmey of our office carefully dug the tree from National Forest land, potted it, and Dave presented it to the city and Mayor Hollister. Ortt mentioned Forest Service personnel who were present during the planting included Frank Voytas, Terry Hoffman, Jim Apgar, Roland Schaar (ret.), and Teena Sechler.
- On 11/26/87 the Parkersburg (WV) News noted that the Capitol Christmas Tree would arrive in D.C. on 11/30/87.

- On 11/26/87 staff writer Bob Hecker of the Martins Ferry (OH) Times Leader wrote an article about the Capitol Christmas Tree, focusing on the historical aspect of the property where it grew. He interviewed cousins Mary Mahnken and Sandra Binegar, both descendants of the Holdren family, which likely planted the tree soon after the year 1900.
- On 11/26/87 the Monroe County Beacon in Woodsfield ran four photos of the Cutting Ceremony: 1) showing the extent of the crowd on the site that morning, noting that TV stations from as far away as Youngstown, OH and Pittsburgh, PA were present; 2) a photo of Woodsfield resident Donna Knowlton and New Matamoras' Gil Courtney making a ceremonial cut on the tree with a crosscut saw; 3) a full length shot of the tree standing prior to its being cut; 4) a photo of me making introductions during the ceremony.
- On 11/28/87 Scott Solomon wrote in the Marietta Times about North Hills Elementary School in Marietta and teacher Barb Case using discarded slate shingles from her house to decorate as part of the contest among schools for the U.S. Capitol Christmas Tree celebration. Teena Sechler of the Forest Service and local residents Iwana Simon and Barb Hamilton took the lead in coordinating this contest. Awards were given out the day of the Send-Off Ceremony to various school children throughout Washington County. Sechler suggested that some of the slate decorations be sent to Congressional offices along with the trees being donated by the Ohio Christmas Tree Growers Association. A photo of Case and her

class ran with the story. The students were shown
with their decorated slates, all of which were titled
"The Giving Tree."

- Staff reporter for the Marietta Times, Roger Kalter,
wrote a story on 11/28/87 about the companion trees
being shipped to D.C. on the Kenmack Lumber truck
and trailer. The 30 or so smaller trees had been
stored in a cool warehouse at the Ohio Division of
Forestry (ODOF) Nursery in Reno. I was quoted in
the article, as was Marilyn Ortt of the Marietta Tree
Commission, who was also a member of our Capitol
Christmas Tree Planning Committee. Ortt was
helping load the smaller trees, which were slated to
go to Congressional offices and other D.C. buildings.
She was being assisted by Tony Lauer, Roger Taylor,
and Mack Haessly, Jr. of Kenmack Lumber. Earlier
that day Dave Greenwood, Gloria Eighmey, Bob
Florence, Art Nicholson, and Bill Engle from Wayne
National Forest were also on hand. John Eaton of the
ODOF assisted by allowing use of their forklift to load
a couple of the larger trees. Ortt said she was being
"particular about the loading" of the trees to ensure
safe transport to their destination. An accompanying
photo showed Haessly Jr. using the forklift to load
one of the larger trees.
- A short note in the 11/28/87 edition of the Marietta
Times mentioned that a tree was recently planted in
the city's Bicentennial Grove commemorating the
Capitol Christmas Tree.
- On 11/30/87 the Marietta Times ran a story about
delivering the Capitol Tree to D.C. Two photos were
featured: one of Bob McElfresh of R.O. Wetz

Transportation pulling out of Marietta on November 29 as the truck driver for the main tree; and the other of Wayne National Forest's Dave Greenwood loading the tree that was cut from Jess Latimer's yard in Marietta and which was slated to go to the lobby of the U.S. Department of Agriculture building in D.C. That tree and several others were hauled by Kenmack Lumber on a separate truck and trailer. McElfresh and I were quoted in the article. Bob mentioned the CB chatter on his radio as we made the seven hour trip from Marietta to Rockville, MD the first day. One trucker asked McElfresh if he could have the tree and Bob responded, "The only way you could get this baby through your house is to cut a hole in the roof."

- On 12/1/87 the Associated Press wire service ran a clip about delivering the tree to D.C. It featured quotes from Bob McElfresh and me and was carried by a number of media outlets, including the Steubenville (OH) Herald Star and the Logan (OH) Daily News.

- On 12/2/87 The Escanaba (MI) Daily Press ran a front page photo showing Casimier Wojakowski directing the cutting of our Capitol Christmas Tree along with a comprehensive article about his life and career. Inside there were two more photos – one of Casimier tugging on the guide rope on November 20 and another of Casimier at his garage in Michigan showing a collection of large ropes that he used for his various tree felling operations. The article referred to Casimier as "the nation's axe-man" and to the various state and national trees that he had handled over the years as the "jolly green giants."

- On 12/7/87 the Marietta Times ran a photo showing workers at the U.S. Capitol decorating the tree. The caption also noted that about 15 seats remained available on the fifth New Matamoras bus and to contact Gil Courtney if you wanted one of those seats to attend the Lighting Ceremony.
- On 12/8/87 The Athens Messenger ran a photo of Mabel Howell with the 5th grade class of Morrison Elementary. She was donating a blue spruce to the school to commemorate the Capitol Christmas Tree in honor of the students visiting her Tree Farm on November 17 to witness the cutting of an 18-foot blue spruce by Wayne National Forest personnel that would go to the Senate Private Dining Room.
- Sean Flynn wrote a nice article in the Marietta Times on 12/8/87 about the Frontier High School band and its preparation for the trip to D.C., where they would be playing at the Lighting Ceremony. Gil Courtney, Nancy Hollister, and band members were quoted.
- The Marietta Times on 12/8/87 ran a short story, along with the itineraries for the five buses from New Matamoras and the two buses from Marietta that were taking local people to the lighting ceremony in D.C. The story quoted Phyllis Richerson, Executive Director of the Marietta Tourist and Convention Bureau, as being amazed in the interest for this bus tour, which now had 75 people signed up to go. "I thought we'd be lucky to get 35 to sign up," said Richerson. "I never dreamed there would be this much interest." She went on to mention that there was a real good mixture of people going on the trip – grandparents, tourists, grandchildren, and others.

One of the tourists was Robert Amos, from New South Wales, Australia, who was in Marietta visiting friends. Amos said that he was going to try and get as close to the tree as possible during the lighting ceremony so that his sister back in Australia could see him on TV.

- A short note in the Marietta Times' In the Valley section on 12/8/87 noted that New Matamoras resident Mary Carson would be singing The Star Spangled Banner during the Lighting Ceremony.
- On 12/9/87 the Marietta A.M. newspaper ran a photo of Congressmen Clarence Miller and Doug Applegate standing in front of the truck that delivered the tree to the west lawn of the U.S. Capitol on November 30.
- On 12/9/87 the Marietta Times ran a story stating that Gil Courtney and John Carson were already working with the Capitol officials to bring the trunk of the tree back "home" at the end of its duties in D.C. Their idea was to saw up the trunk and make souvenirs and keepsakes from the tree. Courtney was President of Peoples Savings Bank in New Matamoras and an official with the Matamoras Area Business and Civic Organization, as well as a key member of our Capitol Christmas Tree Planning Committee. Carson's wife, Mary, sang the national anthem at the Tree Lighting Ceremony in D.C. The Carson's were also from New Matamoras.
- On 12/9/87 staff writer Jess Mancini wrote an article in the Parkersburg News that described the Lighting Ceremony that would take place later that day. He quoted Phyllis Richerson, Gil Courtney, and Nancy Hollister.

- On 12/9/87 I ran a short note in the Marietta Times' In the Valley section letting local residents know that we only had a very few commemorative jars and Christmas cards left to sell; and that we were completely sold out of the ornaments.
- On 12/9/87 the Athens Messenger newspaper ran a very nice article about New Matamoras resident Mary Carson, who would be singing the national anthem at the Lighting Ceremony. Carson had sung at various school, church, and other events since she was young, but was quoted as saying, "I never dreamed I would sing at the Capitol of the United States." (Carson's daughter Sarah was a member of the Frontier High School band, which also played during the ceremony.)
- On 12/9/87 the Marietta Times ran an editorial highlighting that night's tree lighting ceremony and praising the community support and volunteerism that had surrounded this tree event.
- On 12/9/87 Gil Courtney handed out a list of people riding on the five buses from Frontier School District, along with a proposed itinerary for the day. The buses were to leave no later than 5:20 a.m., stop to eat in Lavale, MD, and arrive in Washington. D.C. around 12:45 p.m. Around 1:30 p.m. the buses would leave for a driving tour around the D.C. area with stops scheduled for the Lincoln Memorial, Vietnam Monument, and Arlington Cemetery. They planned to pass other sites such as the Library of Congress, the U.S. Mint, the Jefferson Monument, the Kennedy Center, and the White House before arriving back at the Capitol for the 5:00 p.m. Lighting Ceremony.

After attending a reception for all Ohioans, hosted by Governor Celeste and Mayor Hollister in the Dirksen Building, the buses would leave around 7:00 p.m. to head back home.

- The front page of the Marietta Times on 12/10/87 featured a full photo of the lit Capitol Christmas Tree with the U.S. Capitol in the background. Three separate stories filed by reporter Sean Flynn also appeared in this issue.

- In one story Flynn wrote about the previous day's lighting ceremony. He quoted Frontier High School Vo-Ag teacher Calvin Martin as saying that the entire event had been a good educational lesson for his students. Martin also told of Frontier students helping with the cutting and the wrapping of the tree on November 30, as well as helping set up the bleachers and other preparations the day before the Cutting Ceremony. The story also told of Gil Courtney, along with assistance from Frances Cochran, Joanne West, and Valerie McPeek, putting together a program handout and schedule for everyone on the five Frontier-area buses who attended the Lighting Ceremony. On the back of the program was a list of everyone who made the trip. Two photos accompanied this article: one of Mary Carson singing the Star Spangled Banner during the Lighting Ceremony and one that showed Mayor Hollister, Senator Glenn, Governor Celeste, and Senator Metzenbaum sitting at the ceremony.

- A second Flynn story on 12/10/87 detailed the lighting ceremony itself. He quoted from Mayor Hollister's short speech. "We send you our magnificent queen of the forest. Quite simply, Merry Christmas from the Wayne National Forest, the Great State of Ohio, New Matamoras, Newport, and Marietta - Ohio's first bicentennial city." Flynn also quoted me following the lighting of the tree. "I feel great. I'm telling you, it's like a burden lifted right off of my shoulders. This was a real job there for awhile!" Considering everything that could have gone wrong over the previous couple of years, but didn't, you can understand how I felt. I knew that if anything had gone wrong during the process, it was going to zero right back on me. That's why I felt relieved when it was over. But I concluded my discussion with Flynn by saying, "I'll tell you one thing: This is something a lot of the county people will remember all their lives. It really will be."

- Flynn's third story in the 12/10/87 issue of the Marietta Times told of the tears in the eyes of Frontier High School band director, Lynne Johnson, after her band had performed an excellent and flawless collection of Christmas songs at the Lighting Ceremony. She recalled that three years earlier, Frontier didn't even have a band and that until the Cutting Ceremony along the banks of the Ohio River on November 20, the band had never performed outside of a football stadium. "I don't think they (the band) really realized what it was until they got here and saw the tree, looked at the Capitol, and saw all of the people. But they did an excellent job," Johnson reflected with pride. Band member Shannon McKnight said, "After this, more people are going to want to be in the band 'cause we made it to

Washington – something they said Frontier would never do."

Gale Matthews, whose granddaughter Missy played trumpet in the band said, "It's a big day. We've come to hear her at football games, but never anything like this. But you know how grandparents are." Nine members of the Matthews clan, including Washington County Commissioner Sandy Matthews (Missy's mother) rode the buses to the ceremony.

Bus driver Francis Butcher said, "Most people could have just watched it on TV, but this really shows people's enthusiasm."

And Gil Courtney, who had organized the five-bus caravan called it "Americanism at the grassroots." He had hoped to fill three buses for the trip, but ended up needing five. Watching the band perform, Courtney said, "This is a real, real treat. Those kids, they were scared, you know, like any kids would be. But they just did a super, super job. They weren't holding anything back." A photo accompanying the article showed band members performing in front of the Capitol. Included in the photo were: Debbie Thompson, Brad Ritchie, Teresa Hurst, and Brenda Himmesger.

- On 12/10/87 the St. Marys (WV) Oracle ran an item about the Capitol Tree and announced that I would be speaking on the subject at the Pleasants County Historical Society on 12/16/87. The article said that many descendants of the Holdren family, who planted the tree around 1900, lived "on both sides of the Ohio River in this area."

- Also, in the 12/10/87 edition of the St, Marys Oracle, Betty Smith, in her <u>Taking Notes</u> column, announced my upcoming presentation to the Historical Society, and mentioned the Capitol Tree Lighting Ceremony in D.C. in relation to the Reagan-Gorbachev summit.
- Barbara Lovely's 12/10/87 "Start of it All" column in the Marietta Times noted the community pride in the tree and its tie-in to the bicentennial celebration. Lovely was Executive Director of the Marietta Bicentennial Commission.
- On 12/10/87 the Parkersburg (WV) News wrote of the previous day's lighting ceremony with quotes from House Speaker Jim Wright of Texas, who flipped the switch to light the tree; Ohio Senators Howard Metzenbaum and John Glenn; Marietta Mayor Nancy Hollister; and Ohio Governor Richard Celeste.
- USA Today's "Quote of the Day" on 12/10/87 was by House Speaker Jim Wright from Texas, who had lit the Capitol Tree the day before. Wright said that the tree was "Bigger, I dare say, than one of its kind that might have been brought from Texas."
- On 12/11/87 the Zanesville, OH newspaper ran a photo of Congressman Clarence Miller giving remarks during the Lighting Ceremony, with the lit tree in the background.
- The 12/12/87 edition of the Marietta Times featured two items of interest. One told of the Frontier High School Future Farmers of America chapter presenting honorary FFA jackets to Congressmen Applegate and Miller. The other was a humorous thing that happened when seven local officials visited

the White House the day after the lighting ceremony in D.C. Those officials included Marietta Mayor Nancy Hollister, former Mayor George Cranston, Washington County Commissioners Glen Miller and Dick Young, and others. Only one of the officials set off the metal detector when they arrived, the group's lone Democrat, Dick Young. That led Young's friend, Miller, to joke that "it must have been a Democrat detector."

- On 12/15/87 the Marietta Times ran a note telling about the Washington County Career Center making the support bracket for the tree's base.
- On 12/16/87 Diana McMahan, Correspondent for the Parkersburg (WV) News, wrote a very detailed story about the bus trip from New Matamoras to D.C. McMahan, a New Matamoras resident, made the trip along with her 5th grade son.
- On 12/16/87 the Marietta Times ran a note reminding people to watch Ed Johnson's upcoming Agricountry segment on WBNS-TV Channel 10 featuring the Cutting Ceremony.
- Barbara Lovely's excellent 12/17/87 column, "Start of it All," in the Marietta Times, told of the Lighting Ceremony and what the tree had meant to both local people and the nation.
- On 12/17/87 Norma Jean Antill wrote a column in the Monroe County Beacon giving an excellent account of the bus trip to D.C. for the Lighting Ceremony. She mentioned numerous places that the group visited during the day prior to the lighting. She also listed those passengers who rode on bus number four during the trip. The top of her column featured

the front of the commemorative Christmas card that
was designed for the 1987 Capitol Christmas Tree
event.

- We received many thank you notes from various
elected officials and other dignitaries after the
Lighting Ceremony. One of the most heartfelt was a
personal letter I received from Congressman Louis
Stokes of the Cleveland area, dated 12/18/87, who
thanked us for our efforts on behalf of all Ohioans.
He also thanked us for visiting his office and
delivering a small tree and ornaments to him on
December 1.
- The cover of the Congressional Quarterly, dated
12/19/87, featured a photo of the Capitol Christmas
Tree lit up with the U.S. Capitol in the background.
- On 12/21/87 Transport Topics, the national
newspaper of the trucking industry, featured a front
page photo of the tree being unloaded at the U.S.
Capitol. The caption stated that the tree from Wayne
National Forest and 22 other smaller trees from
southeastern Ohio were hauled to D.C. by R.O. Wetz
Transportation Co. and Kenmack Lumber. Inside the
newspaper was a short story about the project.
- In its In The Valley section on December 21, 1987, the
Marietta Times ran a note that souvenir Capitol
Christmas Tree shirts were available for purchase
from Creighton Sports Center in New Matamoras.
- Both Congressman Clarence Miller and Capitol
Landscape Architect Paul Pincus sent me a copy of
the 12/21/87 Washington Post article by staff writer
Michael Kernan that featured a photo of the lit tree in
front of the Capitol, praising it as the most beautiful

of the many Christmas trees adorning Washington, D.C. that season. Kernan wrote that the White House Tree (or the National Tree, as it is referred to) "is disappointing this year. It simply isn't in the same league with the Capitol Tree." High praise, indeed, for our Norway spruce tree from Ohio.

- Casimier Wojakowski sent me a copy of an article that appeared in his hometown newspaper, The Escanaba (MI) Daily Press, on 12/23/87 about the Capitol Christmas Tree.
- On 12/23/87 the Marietta Times noted that souvenir Capitol Christmas Tree shirts were being sold by Creighton Sports Center in New Matamoras. One style had a picture of the lighted tree on the front with a sentence that read, "I was there when they lit the tree. Dec. 9, 1987 at 5:24 p.m." Another style had a picture of the tree standing in the forest before it was cut and it read "Capitol Christmas Tree 1987."
- Judy Holdren Beaver wrote a letter to the editor of the Marietta Times on 12/23/87 telling everyone how much she had enjoyed the whole event and thanking several of us for our efforts in making it happen.
- The Marietta Times featured another full front-page photo on 12/24/87 of the Capitol Christmas Tree, shining brightly with the Washington Monument illuminated in the background.
- On 12/24/87 the notes from the Chief of the Forest Service's Staff Meeting noted that Washington, DC's – TV Channel 9 interviewed several residents, visitors, and children who proclaimed the 1987 U.S. Capitol Christmas Tree from the Wayne National

Forest in Ohio to be "the most spectacular in the city."

- A Letter to the Editor in the Washington Post, 12/26/87, extolled the beauty of the Capitol Christmas Tree.
- The Bellaire (OH) Times Leader ran a short article on 12/28/87 about the Capitol Tree at the Lighting Ceremony, as well as a photo of Governor Celeste giving remarks at the ceremony.
- On 12/28/87 an editorial ran in the Marietta Times listing the Top Ten local things to remember from 1987. One of those things, of course, was the Capitol Christmas Tree event.
- On 12/30/87 staff writer Tom Hrach of the Marietta Times, wrote about Mayor Nancy Hollister preparing to begin her second term on January 1, 1988. She was quoted as saying, "We've really benefitted from the good publicity from the Capitol Christmas Tree." She credited the cutting of the tree for bringing national attention to Washington County and Marietta, as well as helping celebrate the bicentennial of the Northwest Territory.
- On 12/30/87 the Marietta Times ran a short note telling readers how to purchase a two-hour tape from Dean Beaver of Newport. The tape included the cutting, send-off, and lighting ceremonies for the Capitol Christmas Tree.
- The front page of the Marietta Times on 12/31/87 showed a graphic of the 19 primary stories that had occurred locally over the previous 12 months. One of those listed was the November 20 cutting of the

Capitol Christmas Tree. Reporter Sean Flynn wrote
an accompanying article about all of the events.
- On 1/1/88 in its "Year in Review" story the Marietta
Times ran a photo of Casimier Wojakowski directing
the felling of the Capitol Christmas Tree just as it was
being gently lowered to the ground.
- Annetta Richardson, Staff Writer for the Parkersburg
(WV) News, wrote a nice comprehensive article on
1/4/88 about the Capitol Christmas Tree.
- A short note appeared in the Marietta Times' In The
Valley section on 1/4/88 stating that because of the
popularity of this year's Capitol Tree, officials were
going to leave it standing for several extra days.
- I received a nice note from Casimier Wojakowski on
1/5/88. He had received the clippings I had mailed to
him, as well as some sent to him by Judy Beaver and
Roy Wetz. He had watched the Lighting Ceremony on
CNN and told me that he was "very honored that you
trusted me to harvest your tree."
- A Letter to the Editor of the Monroe County Beacon,
by Hannah Holdren Holland, on 1/7/88, detailed
some of the history of the site where the tree was cut,
as well as some details of the event itself.
- Barbara Lovely's 1/7/88 column, "Start of it All," in
the Marietta Times mentioned the Capitol Tree as
part of the local bicentennial celebrations. Barbara,
who served on our Capitol Christmas Tree Planning
Committee, was Executive Director of the Marietta
Bicentennial Commission.
- Short articles ran in the Marietta Times on 1/14/88
and 1/16/88 (with photo), as well as the Parkersburg
News on 1/9/88 – No authors listed - About the butt

sections of the tree being brought back to be made
into keepsakes. Another similar article by Sean
Flynn, Staff Writer, appeared in the Marietta Times
on 1/7/88.
- Thelma Holdren wrote a letter-to-the-editor of the
Marietta Times on 2/2/88 thanking everyone for
their efforts on the Capitol Tree project. She said the
event "will be remembered and talked about with
pride for many, many years to come." She was a
descendant of the Holdren's who likely planted the
tree near Sheets' Run soon after 1900.
- Received a nice note from Barbara Lovely on 2/10/88
thanking us for our Capitol Christmas Tree project
and tying it in to the Bicentennial celebrations.
- Diana McMahan wrote a story for the Parkersburg
News on 11/20/88 about the 1989 calendars on sale
from the Matamoras Area Historical Society. Each
month featured a different historical photo from the
New Matamoras area. The front cover of the calendar
featured a photo of the 1987 Capitol Christmas Tree
in front of the U.S, Capitol. (U.S. Representative
Douglas Applegate also planned to use the same
photo for his annual calendar to be sent to
constituents.) The back cover of the Matamoras
calendar featured a photo of Mary Carson singing the
National Anthem at the Lighting Ceremony in D.C.
and a photograph of the Holdren family homestead
sometime in the early 1900s. The photo shows some
Holdren family members, their home, and in the
background a small spruce tree which grew to
become the U.S. Capitol Tree in 1987. The photo was
supplied to the Parkersburg News and the Historical

Society courtesy of Sandra Holdren Binegar, a descendant of the original Holdren's.

- On 11/21/88 Roger Kalter wrote a story in the Marietta Times about me giving advice to Barb Anderson, who was coordinating the 1988 Capitol Christmas Tree effort for the Huron-Manistee National Forest in Michigan. Their tree was a 50-foot tall balsam fir. Anderson also ordered glass ornaments from the same company, Casto Glass, which we used to make our ornaments the previous year. The Huron-Manistee NF was using the event to help celebrate the 50th anniversary of their forest. Anderson noted that their event "has meant nothing but good publicity for the forest" and that they would have several local people traveling to D.C. for the Lighting Ceremony on 12/14/88. The biggest recommendation I made to Anderson was to use Casimier Wojakowski to direct their tree cutting and she did just that. Casimier and his wife were hoping to join the bus trip to D.C. for the 1988 Lighting Ceremony. He told Kalter that he wouldn't forget the Ohio tree. "Marietta went all out," he said. "They had as much publicity as all of the other trees (that I have been involved with) combined. I thought efforts (in Ohio) were remarkable."
- A photo in the 12/3/88 Marietta Times showed Bill Johnson, Forestry Technician from the Huron-Manistee National Forest, helping guard the Capitol Tree as it stopped at the Michigan State Capitol in Lansing. In the photo it showed their tree's butt being supported by the metal brace built by our Washington County Career Center the year before.

- A 12/6/88 photo in the Marietta Times showed the
  Michigan tree being erected with a crane on the west
  lawn of the U.S. Capitol grounds. The caption also
  referenced our 1987 Ohio tree.
- Someone in West Virginia sent me a photo from the
  12/22/88 Pocahontas County (WV) Times of a 24-
  foot tall red spruce tree from the Monongahela
  National Forest that would be cut and sent to the
  USDA office in D.C. It was cut from the grounds of
  the Greenbrier Ranger District Office in Bartow, WV,
  where I had worked in 1974 and 1975. Former
  District Ranger Roger Bucklew and Forestry
  Technician Harold Lambert had planted it on site in
  1973, the year before I arrived there for my first job
  with the U.S. Forest Service. Bartow, WV is also the
  community where my mother, Braunda Matheny
  Kincaid, had grown up.
- Dave Sereno's 9/30/89 story in the Marietta Times
  told of the 50th anniversary of R.O. Wetz
  Transportation. Owner Roy Wetz noted that one of
  his company's highlights over the years was hauling
  the Capitol Christmas Tree to Washington, D.C. in
  1987. After it was cut from Wayne National Forest,
  they had stored the tree for several days in one of
  their local warehouses prior to the final haul to D.C.
  "We actually babysat that thing for two weeks
  keeping it watered so it wouldn't be destroyed," Wetz
  recalled.
- A similar article about Wetz was written for the
  Parkersburg News on 10/1/89. Roy's son, Tag, noted
  that one of the company's 'red letter' days was

"hauling the (Capitol) Christmas Tree from the Wayne National Forest in 1987."

- A story in the 12/11/90 Paducah (KY) Sun told of that year's Capitol Christmas Tree, an Engelmann spruce, coming from the Routt National Forest near Walden, CO to help celebrate the 100th anniversary of the town. The story was accompanied by a photo of 75-year old Casimier Wojakowski, who traveled from his home in Bark River, MI to supervise the cutting.
- Casimier also sent me a newspaper clipping from his local Escanaba (MI) Daily Press several days later that told of this story, too, along with a photo of him in action that had appeared in the Rocky Mountain News. He had put these items in a Christmas card that the Routt National Forest had designed to commemorate the cutting. Casimier wrote that he and his wife Mildred had traveled to D.C. to watch their first Capitol Christmas Tree lighting ceremony........ "after all these years!"
- Casimicr and I continued to stay in touch. He sent me a clipping from the 12/5/91 Escanaba (MI) Daily Press with a photo showing a 47-foot balsam fir that he helped cut from the Brule River State Forest near Superior, WI. That tree was destined to be set up in the rotunda of the State Capitol in Madison, WI. A head and shoulder photo of Wojakowski also appeared in the article.
- My last correspondence with Casimier Wojakowski was in the summer of 1992 when he was preparing to assist the Chippewa National Forest in Minnesota with cutting their U.S. Capitol Christmas Tree, a 62-foot tall white spruce. This would be the seventh one

that he had supervised cutting. (Back in the early 1980s the Chippewa NF had originally been on the master list to supply the 1987 tree; but they had graciously let the Wayne NF have that year instead, so that we could use it to help celebrate the bicentennials of the Northwest Ordinance and the City of Marietta.)

Reading through this list all these years later, it still amazes me about the tremendous amount of positive publicity this 1987 Capitol Christmas Tree generated for the Wayne National Forest, Washington County, Marietta, Frontier Local School District, New Matamoras, Newport, and many local individuals, companies, and various organizations. The whole event showed the full potential of what our area could accomplish. All of the logistics and coordination were quite amazing. Looking back, I'm not sure how we did it all! I guess we were younger then.

MY WEEKLY NEWSPAPER COLUMNS

The following weekly newspaper columns or segments of columns that I wrote between 1979 and 1990 discussed various aspects of the U.S. Capitol Christmas Tree program. The first column listed below was written while I worked at the Chattahoochee National Forest in Georgia; the rest of the columns were written when I worked for the Wayne National Forest in Ohio. There are a total of 39 columns listed, the majority of them written in 1987, the year the Wayne National Forest furnished the Capitol Christmas Tree, and early 1988. For columns that only had a portion devoted to the Capitol Tree topic, I have put the applicable portions in bold, so that readers can find the pertinent sections easier.

The dates listed at the beginning of each column were the dates when I wrote them, which was, in general, anywhere from three days to a week prior to when they appeared in print. My column appeared each week in two newspapers in Georgia and three in Ohio (and from time to time in two additional Ohio newspapers). Of course, all of the newspapers had different deadline dates for when they needed my articles; different days of the week when they appeared in print; and various other circumstances that changed things from time to time. This got to be a little confusing for me, especially when I was trying to keep my columns timely. So, some of the dates on my columns below may not match up exactly with when things were occurring. But rest assured that there is accuracy in the details of what I was writing.

All of these columns, and others, can be read in full in previous editions of my books:

Your.....Wayne National Forest, Volume I (covering
the years 1981 and 1982);
Your.....Wayne National Forest, Volume II (covering
the years 1983 – 1986);
Your.....Wayne National Forest, Volume III (covering
the years 1987 – 1990).

The 1979 column listed below is included in my book:
Your.....Chattahoochee National Forest (covering the
period between December 1978 – June 1980).

These books are all available on Amazon and can also be
ordered through Barnes & Noble and Books-A-Million
stores.

Since the idea of the Wayne NF supplying the Capitol
Christmas Tree originated with me, since I served as the
local on-the-ground Forest Service coordinator, and since I
had the platform of writing a weekly column for several
southeastern Ohio newspapers, I'm certain that the total
content of these writings represents the most complete
accounting of what happened: How the idea originated; how
it came to be approved; key players and who all was involved
at various times between 1981 and 1987; the related
activities, including the Cutting Ceremony, Send-Off
Ceremony, and the Lighting Ceremony in D.C.; volunteer
and fundraising efforts; cooperating agencies, organizations,
individuals, and companies; community involvement; and,
of course, the many aspects of public relations that occurred.

That is why I have largely based this book on the chronology
of those weekly columns. That is not to say that everything
involved with the event was covered in my columns. So, I
have talked with numerous people who were involved;

reviewed video tapes and photos; and read as many newspaper, newsletter, and magazine accounts as I could find, so as to make this book as complete as possible.

Despite this, I may have left something out; remembered it differently than others; or got dates or names wrong. If this has happened, I apologize. There was no intent on my part. The primary purpose of this book is to record for history's sake the entirety of a very significant event for the Wayne National Forest, Washington County, New Matamoras, Newport, Marietta, and Frontier Local School District. And I believe I have done that.

I'm not getting any younger, and many folks involved with the 1987 event have now passed on. That is why I felt like now was the time to gather as much information as possible and put it into this book.

Thank you to all readers for allowing me this opportunity. I felt privileged to have coordinated the 1987 Capitol Christmas Tree event. But it certainly couldn't have happened without the involvement of, quite literally, a few hundred people. And I, once again, take this moment to thank everyone who was involved for their assistance in helping make the 1987 event truly historic. Now, for the newspaper columns, 1979-1990.

December 20, 1979 –
I've had some people ask about the Christmas tree that is put up every December at our nation's Capitol in Washington, D.C. Where does the tree come from? What kinds of trees are used? When did the program begin? How does the U.S. Forest Service help select the tree?

The Capitol Christmas Tree program began in 1965 with the big push coming from the Speaker of the House at that time, John McCormack. That year, a live Douglas fir tree was selected and actually planted on the Capitol grounds. The thinking was to maintain a living symbol of the Christmas spirit and to re-use the tree in ceremonies each year. Unfortunately, after the 1968 season the tree died.

In 1969 the Forest Service became the agency responsible for the Capitol Christmas Tree program. That year three different trees were pieced together to make the one large tree. The results were not satisfactory. The tree was very difficult to put together and it didn't look that good either.

In 1970 the procedure for selecting the tree was again changed and this procedure has remained in effect since that time. Basically, here's the process:

1) The tree is selected from forests east of the Mississippi River. This involves Regions 8 and 9 of the U.S. Forest Service. The reason for this is that it would be very difficult to transport a large tree from the western United States all the way to the Capitol.
2) Foresters working at the field level are asked to nominate potential trees, based upon size, form, shape, and ease of removing it from the woods.
3) The Architect from the U.S. Capitol, in conjunction with Forest Service officials, makes a final selection and performs an on-the-ground inspection of the tree.
4) The tree is carefully cut, removed from the woods, and transported in one piece to Washington, D.C.

Some local communities have even held going-away ceremonies for "their" tree and the townspeople then accompanied it by caravan to the Capitol.

In 1970 the first tree was selected from the Monongahela National Forest in West Virginia; in 1971 it came from the Cherokee National Forest in Tennessee; and in 1972 it came from the White Mountain National Forest in New Hampshire. I wasn't able to find what species of trees were used during those years. Two trees, 1977 and 1978, were cut from state forests, but coordination was led by the USDA Forest Service.

From 1973 – 1979 the tree species and their sources were:

1973 – White spruce - (Pennsylvania)

Allegheny National Forest

1974 – Fraser fir - Carolina)

Pisgah National Forest (North

1975 – Balsam fir - (Michigan)

Ottawa National Forest

1976 – Red spruce - (West Virginia)

Monongahela National Forest

1977 – White spruce - (Minnesota)

Nemadji State Forest

1978 – Norway spruce - (Maryland)

Savage River State Forest

1979 – White spruce - (Wisconsin)

Nicolet National Forest

This year's tree was 47 years old and 52 feet tall. The tree was lighted about two weeks before Christmas during a ceremony with several dignitaries attending and the Marine Corps Band playing Christmas music. The tree is usually taken down on January 2.

The U.S. Forest Service is very proud to help coordinate the Capitol Christmas Tree program. Perhaps someday the Chattahoochee National Forest will furnish our nation's Christmas tree.

December 14, 1981 -
I've had some people ask about the Christmas tree that is put up every December at our nation's Capitol in Washington, D.C. Where does the tree come from? What kinds of trees are used? When did the program begin? How does the U.S. Forest Service help select the tree?

The Capitol Christmas Tree program began in 1965, with the big push coming from Speaker of the House at that time, John McCormack. That year a live Douglas fir tree was selected and actually planted on the Capitol grounds. The thinking was to maintain a living symbol of the Christmas spirit and to re-use the tree in ceremonies each year. Unfortunately, after the 1968 season the tree died.

In 1969 the Forest Service became the agency responsible for the Capitol Christmas Tree program. That year 3 different trees were pieced together to make the one large tree. The results were not satisfactory. The tree was very difficult to put together and it didn't look that good either.

In 1970 the procedure for selecting the tree was again changed, and this procedure has remained in effect since that time. Basically, here's the process:

1) The tree is selected from forests east of the Mississippi River. (This involves Regions 8 and 9 of the U.S. Forest Service). The reason for this is that it would be very difficult to transport a large tree from the Western United States all the way to the Capitol.
2) Foresters working at the field level are asked to nominate potential trees, based on form, size, shape, and ease of removing it from the woods;
3) The Architect from the U.S. Capitol, in conjunction with Forest Service officials, makes a final selection and on-the-ground inspection of the tree;
4) The tree is carefully cut, removed from the woods, and transported in one piece to Washington, D.C.

Some local communities have even held going-away ceremonies for "their" tree and the townspeople then accompanied it by car caravan to the Capitol.

In 1970 the first tree was selected from the Monongahela National Forest in West Virginia; in 1971 it came from the Cherokee National Forest in Tennessee; and in 1972 it came from the White Mountain National Forest in New Hampshire. (I wasn't able to find what species of trees were used during those years). Two trees, 1977 and 1978, were cut from state forests, but coordination was led by the USDA Forest Service.

From 1973-80 the trees and their sources were:

1973	White spruce Pennsylvania	Allegheny NF
1974	Fraser fir North Carolina	Pisgah NF
1975	Balsam fir Michigan	Ottawa NF
1976	Red spruce West Virginia	Monongahela NF
1977	White spruce Minnesota	Nemadji State Forest
1978	Norway spruce Maryland	Savage River SF
1979	White spruce Wisconsin	Nicolet NF
1980	White spruce	Green Mountain NF Vermont

1981's tree is 65 years old and 52 feet tall. The white spruce, from Michigan's Hiawatha National Forest, will be lighted about 2 weeks before Christmas during a ceremony with several dignitaries attending and the Marine Corps band playing Christmas music. The tree is usually taken down on January 2.

The U.S. Forest Service is very proud to help coordinate the Capitol Christmas Tree program. Perhaps someday the Wayne National Forest will furnish our Nation's Christmas tree.

December 13, 1982 –
Again this year, the Nation has a Christmas tree at the
Capitol that was cut from one of our National Forests. This
year's tree, a 35-year old, 50-foot balsam fir, came from the
Green Mountain National Forest in Vermont, near the small
town of Rochester. And who should be present at the cutting
ceremony but our own Geologist, Lynn Kantner.

Lynn periodically provides geologic advice and expertise to
National Forests in Vermont, New Hampshire, Missouri,
Illinois, and Indiana, in addition to her work for the Wayne
National Forest. She was able to watch the cutting ceremony,
along with the other Green Mountain National Forest
personnel. These ceremonies are quite impressive -- and well
they should be, providing the Capitol with its traditional tree.

The Governor of Vermont helped cut the tree; and there were
short messages by Vermont's Fish and Game Commissioner,
as well as the Green Mountain Forest Supervisor. The entire
town of Rochester turned out for the send-off ceremony, and
local citizens, schools, and organizations provided hundreds
of hand-made decorations to go with the tree. Wouldn't it be
nice if the Wayne National Forest could one day provide the
Capitol Christmas tree?

The Forest Service is the agency responsible for coordinating
the Christmas Tree Program. The tree is selected, several
years in advance, by Forest Service officials and the Capitol
Architect from Washington. The tree is selected from forests
east of the Mississippi River, mainly because transporting
one from the western U.S. would be very difficult. About 3
weeks before Christmas, the tree is carefully cut, removed
from the woods, and transported in one piece to

Washington, D.C. The labor, equipment, and transportation are donated by various groups and individuals.

Speaker of the House, Tip O'Neill, and his grandchildren will conduct this year's special lighting ceremony on December 15. There will be nearly 10,000 lights and ornaments on this year's tree.

Over the last 10 years, the following trees have served as our Capitol Christmas Tree:

1973 - White spruce -   Allegheny National Forest - Pennsylvania

1974 – Fraser fir -   Pisgah National Forest - North Carolina

1975 - Balsam fir -   Ottawa National Forest - Michigan

1976 - Red spruce -   Monongahela National Forest - West Virginia

1977 - White spruce -   Nemadji State Forest - Minnesota

1978 - Norway spruce -   Savage River State Forest - Maryland

1979 - White spruce -   Nicolet National Forest - Wisconsin

1980 - White spruce -   Green Mountain National Forest - Vermont

1981 - White spruce -   Hiawatha National Forest -
                             Michigan

1982 - Balsam fir -   Green Mountain National
                             Forest - Vermont

(**Author's Note** - *In later years I learned that the 1982 tree
actually came from the Riley Bostwick Wildlife
Management Area in Vermont. Even though the USDA
Forest Service was the federal agency coordinating the
cutting of this tree, the area was managed by the Vermont
Department of Fish and Wildlife. Prior to being managed
by the state of Vermont, the property had been owned and
managed by Mr. Bostwick for about 40 years. He had
carefully and professionally managed his property and it
was even included in the American Tree Farm system.)*

December 19, 1983

<u>Outdoor News from Near and Far</u>

*The Capitol Christmas Tree was again selected from one of
our eastern National Forests -- the Chequamegon National
Forest in northern Wisconsin. This was the 20th consecutive
year that a tree has been displayed on the West Front Lawn
of the Capitol. This year's tree, a 52-foot tall white spruce,
was grown on the site of a former CCC (Civilian Conservation
Corps) camp. One reason this particular tree was selected
was to help both the Chequamegon and the CCC celebrate
their 50th anniversaries. The tree arrived in Washington,
D.C. on December 5 and lighting ceremonies were held on
December 14.

There are some possible candidates for a Capitol Christmas
Tree on the Wayne National Forest, too. Maybe within the
next few years Ohio can furnish a tree and go down in history

with other states as a contributor to this annual program. I'm
working on some ideas to make that happen. Wish me luck.

(**Author's Note** – *The two paragraphs above were just
part of my 12/19/83 column. For the previous two years I
had been working behind the scenes to get internal Forest
Service support for the Wayne National Forest to supply the
Capitol Christmas Tree. By late 1983, things had begun to
look good for making that happen. So, I then felt confident
enough to let the reading public know, via my newspaper
column, that something was in the works. You can see from
reading the column below, which was written one year
later, why I was working to make 1987 the year for the
Wayne NF to provide the tree.*)

December 10, 1984

I'm sure most of you saw the newspaper articles last week
about the nation's Capitol Christmas Tree program. As the
article said, the Wayne National Forest has been selected to
provide the Capitol Christmas Tree in 1987. I've been dying
to let everyone know, but I was told to wait for the "official"
news release to come out. For now, all we can say is that we
will furnish the tree. There will likely be no more specifics
announced for a couple of years.

You see, I pushed hard for us to supply the tree and for the
1987 date because it will tie in to the 200th anniversary of
the signing of the Northwest Ordinance. That date will also
serve as a lead-in to Marietta's 1988 bicentennial
celebration, which from early indications will be a year full of
festivities, celebrations, and other activities. The Christmas
tree will be cut in late November or early December of 1987,
transported to Washington, D.C., erected, lights installed

about two weeks before Christmas, and left standing on into January of 1988. So you see, the entire process will be quite a kick-off to Marietta's 1988 festivities.

First, I had to convince Forest Supervisor, Harold Godlevske, that we could find a suitable tree on the Marietta Unit of the Wayne National Forest. I bugged him about this for a couple of years, but to his credit he never got irritated at me and he bought into the idea because of the tie-in to the bicentennial celebrations.

Then, Harold had to convince the Regional Office in Milwaukee that we could do this. Obviously, southeastern Ohio isn't known for having large conifers that would be suitable to stand in front of the nation's capitol. Most of the previous trees have come from the upper Lake States, New England, or the higher elevation Appalachian Mountains. And they weren't oaks, maples, ash, or elms. Also, 1987 was already slated to have a tree come from the Chippewa National Forest in Minnesota.

I won't bore you with a lot of the background (maybe someday I can), but Harold was able to convince the Chippewa to give its 1987 slot to the Wayne (again, mainly because of the bicentennial tie-ins.)

The only other thing I'll mention right now is that some of our Forest Service personnel don't see why the tree can't come from the Ironton or Athens units. They just don't quite get it that the tree <u>has</u> to come from the Marietta Unit because this is where the story of the Northwest Territory, the Northwest Ordinance, and basically the state of Ohio began – in Marietta in 1787 and 1788. Anyway, I'll stand firm on that point and work hard to make sure that the 1987

Capitol Christmas Tree comes from the Marietta Unit of the Wayne National Forest.

For those of you who aren't history buffs, the Northwest Ordinance opened up for settlement all the lands north and west of the Ohio River that now comprise Ohio, Indiana, Michigan, Illinois, Wisconsin, and part of Minnesota. It was an act of immense historic significance in the development of the United States. And, of course, Marietta was the first permanent settlement established in the Northwest Territory under the terms of the 1787 Ordinance. The first settlers left New England in December of 1787 and arrived at what is now Marietta in April of 1788.

We know that by furnishing the 1987 Capitol Christmas Tree, the Wayne National Forest can contribute to the overall efforts of the bicentennial celebration.

Past Capitol Christmas trees have come from Pennsylvania, North Carolina, Michigan, West Virginia, Minnesota, Maryland, Wisconsin, and Vermont. This year's tree, which will be lit at the nation's Capitol on December 12, came from Minnesota. The 1985 tree will come from Michigan and the 1986 tree from Pennsylvania.

The U.S. Forest Service has been the agency responsible for supplying the tree over the years, but the final selection is always made by the Capitol's landscape architect. He ensures that each tree has the proper dimensions, shape, and so on. We will have a number of trees available for him to look at and give final approval for – in a couple of years.

When 1982's tree was cut in Vermont, the entire town of Rochester turned out for a send-off ceremony. Local schools, organizations, and citizens provided hundreds of handmade decorations to be sent along with the tree. One year a town even followed in caravan to Washington, D.C. and helped light the tree. There are endless possibilities of things that could be done. National news coverage is always a part of the ceremony, too.

So, keep your fingers crossed that everything continues to go well and that three years from now, the Capitol Christmas tree will be cut from the Marietta Unit of the Wayne National Forest.

December 16, 1985
Christmas-time kind of sneaks up on you, doesn't it? It seems like one day you're hunting, or raking leaves, and then all of a sudden, it's here. It must have something to do with the days getting shorter. I don't know. It's like that here at work, too. We always plan on having certain jobs completed by January 1st each year. You have to plan ahead because the New Year seems to get here in a hurry.

One Forest Service job that we never let sneak up on us, though, is that of furnishing the nation's Capitol Christmas Tree. Preliminary planning for locating, cutting, transporting, erecting, and lighting that tree takes place weeks, months, and in some cases years ahead of time.

I mention this because, if things go well, the Marietta Unit of the Wayne National Forest will furnish the tree in 1987. The tree would be cut in late November or early December of 1987, erected in Washington several days later, and remain standing on into the New Year of 1988.

This national event will tie-in nicely with the 200th anniversary of the signing of the Northwest Ordinance in 1787 and be a perfect lead-in to Marietta's 200th anniversary celebration as the first permanent town in the Northwest Territory settled under the terms of the Ordinance. That event had enormous historical importance and the 200-year celebrations will no doubt attract quite a lot of national media attention.

Not only Marietta, but the entire Wayne National Forest, surrounding towns, and the whole state of Ohio will be able to participate in and be proud of this event. This will be the first time that Ohio has ever furnished the nation's Capitol Christmas Tree.

There are a few hurdles to clear first, though. One of the most important is approval and selection of a tree by the Capitol Architect. This probably won't occur until the Spring of '87. So, lest I sound too enthusiastic, let there be caution until that time. Prior to then, however, there will still have to be a certain amount of planning and coordination take place; so you can bet the enthusiasm, mine in particular, will continue to mount.

This year's tree, the 22nd one, came from the Kenton Ranger District, Ottawa National Forest, in Michigan's Upper Peninsula. It was a 54-foot white spruce, cut on November 22, and it was lit in a Washington, D.C. ceremony on December 11. Michigan Senator Don Riegle, a former Civilian Conservation Corps employee who helped plant many trees in that area, was one of those participating in the cutting ceremony. (The possibilities are almost endless here in Ohio about how and who might cut our tree).

Pennsylvania will furnish the tree in 1986 and then it becomes the Buckeye State's turn in '87. I can hardly wait. One thing I can promise you. We'll be prepared; we won't let it sneak up on us. Merry Christmas to all of you.

November 10, 1986

By now I'm sure most of you have heard that the Wayne National Forest will furnish the nation's Capitol Christmas Tree in 1987. It's quite an honor for the Wayne, for the local area, and for the entire state of Ohio. It's the first time a tree has been selected from the Buckeye State.

Most trees in the 24-year history of the program have come from states which have a large number of evergreen species to choose from. Ohio is, of course, a state with a relatively small amount of forest land to begin with, and most of that contains hardwood or deciduous trees. So, we are extremely proud and somewhat lucky to be able to supply the '87 tree, which, by the way, will be a Norway Spruce.

Some people seem to be confusing the Capitol tree with the White House tree. The Capitol tree goes up on the Capitol lawn, is generally lit by the Speaker of the House or some other prominent politician following a ceremony, and is widely referred to as the "people's tree." That's one reason different states are given the honor of supplying the tree as often as possible.

The Capitol tree normally receives more publicity than the White House tree and is lit a week or so earlier. It's not uncommon to receive a great deal of national media attention -- TV, newspaper, and radio.

We're just beginning to explore the many possibilities for local and statewide publicity and the many ways in which we hope to involve groups, organizations, other government agencies, businesses, and interested individuals. Most help will be sought on a volunteer basis, as has been the tradition for the past 24 years.

Nothing is final, but we're looking at such activities as a cutting ceremony; a caravan around Ohio possibly climaxing with a send off ceremony from Columbus; local artists providing a sketch for the official Christmas cards which will commemorate the event; local firms to help cut, lower, wrap, and ship the tree; school groups and organizations to prepare posters, ornaments, and cards to accompany the tree to Washington, D.C.; magazine articles; and groups to furnish and sponsor the approximately 20 additional, smaller trees which must be sent to D.C. also. The smaller trees, ranging in height from eight to about 30 feet, go in such places as the Capitol rotunda, the Supreme Court, and the Department of Agriculture.

And, of course, one of our primary intentions all along has been to help publicize and celebrate the bicentennials of both the Northwest Ordinance and the settling of Marietta. Since the tree will be cut and erected in late 1987, and remain standing into the new year of 1988, it will serve both purposes nicely.

We hope to involve the Ohio Division of Forestry, the city of Marietta, the Bicentennial Commission, Washington County schools, the Marietta Tourist and Convention Bureau, the Ohio Division of Wildlife, Washington County Commissioners, and on and on. But making lists is sometimes difficult because you invariably leave someone off. The bottom line is this -- any group in Ohio that wants to help us will be given the opportunity to do so.

It's been a long and rocky four-year road just to get final approval to furnish the '87 tree. Someday I will share with you the actual way this all came about – it was basically two of us who made it happen. The doubters have fallen by the wayside. The major player, without whose active support this would never have happened, was Forest Supervisor Harold Godlevske. Again, some day I will share the background details. Now is not the time.

Other key individuals have been: District Ranger Chuck Myers; former District Rangers Bob Joens and Gary Coleman; other Forest Service employees Teena Sechler, Dave Kissell, Art Martin, Dave Greenwood, John Kerr, and Gloria Eighmey; Ohio Department of Natural Resources botanist Marilyn Ortt; Marietta Mayor Nancy Hollister; Bicentennial Commission President Barbara Lovely; and Tourist and Convention Bureau Director Phyllis Richerson.

Now the work begins!!

January 12, 1987
As is usually the case, the New Year will bring plenty of activity for all of us on the Wayne National Forest. Let's take a quick look at some of the projects with which we'll be involved.
*First and foremost will be completion of the Land Management Plan, which will provide direction on what we'll be doing for the next 10 years. Copies of the draft plan have been available for several weeks now and anyone wishing to send in their comments must do so by January 22, 1987. Once comments are received, they will be analyzed and any

necessary changes will be made to the plan. The finalized Land Management Plan should be available to the public sometime this Summer. At that time we'll inform everyone that the final plan has been completed.

*We plan on constructing another segment of the North Country Trail (NCT) this summer, perhaps another 4-5 miles. Eventually we anticipate a 30-40 mile chunk of this trail going through the Marietta Unit and a significant portion also going through the Athens Unit where it will overlap the Buckeye Trail. The NCT will one day extend from North Dakota all the way to New York state where it will hook up with the Appalachian Trail.

*There will be approximately 3.4 million board feet of timber sold this year between the Athens and Marietta Units. In addition to selling timber, we will be accomplishing several acres of tree planting and timber stand improvement projects such as thinning, pruning, and overstory removal.

*Several wildlife projects will be undertaken including waterhole development, maintaining and/or establishing openings, surveys of old orchards, wild turkey projects, waterfowl habitat plans, and also projects to benefit non-game animals and birds.

*Reconstruction will occur on several miles of roads within the Forest, including Bean Ridge and Felter Road on the Marietta Unit. These old township roads will be upgraded using Forest Service funds, under the terms of cooperative agreements with the counties and townships. Also, our engineers are trying to allow for as many parking areas and pull-offs as possible along the new roads.

*As usual there will be a ton of miscellaneous other projects including abandoned mine reclamation, landscape management, a study of possible natural/scenic areas, archaeological surveys, fire fighting, and so on. We do a little bit of everything and, while it makes for a complex job, it sure does keep things interesting.

***And last, but not least, let's mention the Capitol Christmas Tree once again. The Wayne National Forest, and Ohio, will provide this tree for the Capitol lawn in Washington, D.C. for the first time ever. It will be quite an honor and will take lots of time to coordinate throughout the year. There are literally hundreds of items of publicity and arrangements that have to be made. You'll read more about this as the time approaches.**

There you have it -- an overview of what 1987 holds. If you have any questions or comments, please call or stop by one of our offices. We'd be pleased to talk with you.

April 6, 1987
***In addition to the Wayne National Forest furnishing the Capitol Christmas Tree for 1987, southeastern Ohio will also provide the following trees:**
*** a 24-foot tree for the U.S. Botanical Gardens**

*** a 24-foot tree for the Supreme Court**

*** an 18-foot tree for the U.S. Department of Agriculture patio**

*** an 18-foot tree for the Senate Private Dining Room**

*** a 12-foot tree for the House Public Dining Room**

*** a 12-foot tree for the Senate Public Dining Room**

Early plans are for the trees to come from a state forest, the City of Marietta, an Ohio tree farm, the City of Athens, the City of Ironton, and one other source. A few smaller 8-foot trees have to be sent to Washington, D.C., also. These will be provided by the Ohio Christmas Tree Growers Association.

Members of the Marietta Tree Commission have begun their search for a presentable 18-foot tree from within the city limits. It should be a well-formed, symmetrical tree -- a Norway spruce, if at all possible. If anyone knows of such a tree, or would be interested in donating a tree for this purpose, please contact a member of the city tree commission.

*It's well-known that only a small percentage of this country's population is involved in full-time farming and that these farmers are providing food for the rest of us (and for much of the world, for that matter). But what I didn't realize was that there were so many part-time gardeners who are growing at least a portion of their home food supply, mostly vegetables. The National Gardening Association reports that well over half of all American households produced some of their own food in 1986. This year they are predicting that 50 million people will have a garden, which will make this the number one "national pastime" for the second year in a row. And the food raised is a significant part of many family food supplies.

*It was interesting to note in a recent newsletter that the U.S. Forest Service: provides over 40 percent of all recreation on federal lands; manages over 40 percent of the nation's total inventory of sawtimber; provides over one-third of the lands in the National Wilderness System; provides habitat for nearly 60 percent of the animal species and over 50 percent of the fresh water fish in the United States; manages watersheds, mostly in the West, which provide over half of the nation's total water supply; provides permits for about 14,000 ranchers and farmers, again mostly in the West, for grazing operations; and removes over $1 billion worth of minerals each year.

Quite interesting statistics which point out the many varied activities with which the Forest Service gets involved.

September 14, 1987

Time sure marches on! The date for cutting the Capitol Christmas Tree is just around the corner. It's November 20, to be exact.

We've been busily preparing for all that's involved with this once-in-a-lifetime event and I'd like to mention a few things to bring you up to date. You'll be reading more and more about the Capitol Tree in coming months, so if I fail to mention someone this time, never fear, I'll catch you next time around.

*It seems like only yesterday, but in fact it was way back in 1981 or 1982 when we first decided to go after the 1987 tree. We felt the 200th anniversary of the Northwest Ordinance was significant enough to convince the people in Washington, D.C. that Washington County, Ohio should supply the tree that year. It took 2 or 3 years of calls, letters, etc., with a big push by Forest Supervisor Harold Godlevske, but eventually everyone agreed.

*A Capitol Christmas Tree from Ohio. Now that's a first! Most trees in the past 20 or so years have come from places like Michigan, Wisconsin, Vermont, and Minnesota -- where the National Forests have literally millions of trees from which to choose. In fact, the 1987 tree was originally slated to come from the Chippewa National Forest in Minnesota.

*We weren't home free until Paul Pincus, landscape architect for the Capitol, gave us final approval for our tree in an on-site visit in the Fall of 1986. We received a big boost during Pincus' visit when he heard presentations of support from Marietta Mayor Nancy Hollister, Tourist and Convention Bureau Director Phyllis Richerson, and Bicentennial Executive Director Barbara Lovely, all three of whom continue to work closely with us.

*We received immediate support from the Washington County Commissioners, who saw the value of this project. Sandy Matthews has been involved from the beginning and is helping plan for the November 20 Cutting Ceremony and the November 21 Send-Off Ceremony. Glenn Miller purchased one of the first sets of souvenir jars (along with the Mayor, and Calvin Mendenhall), which will commemorate this event.

*Each year this project is accomplished with as much volunteer effort as possible, so the cost to the government can be minimized. This year is no exception, as time, equipment, and money are being donated. Our Planning Committee includes not only Forest Service employees and representatives of the Ohio Department of Natural Resources, but individuals like Gil Courtney of New Matamoras; Marilyn Ortt, Barb Hamilton, Marty Kitchen, and Iwana Simon from Marietta; Harry Cogswell of Apex Feed and Supply and Wayne Schafer, former County Commissioner. Many area service clubs are also participating.

*Supplies and equipment are coming from R.O. Wetz Transportation – Marietta; Kenmack Lumber – Newport; Busch Construction - Vienna, WV; Black's Tree Service - Marietta; B.F. Goodrich - Oak Grove; and Apex Feed - Marietta.

*We're getting help from Frontier High School, Marietta College, and Marietta High School. Elizabeth Cottle is doing some research work for us. Fenton Glass is making the commemorative jars, River Press the Christmas cards, and Casto Glass Company the souvenir ornaments. Six smaller trees from southeastern Ohio are being sent, along with the main tree, to various Washington, D.C. locations.

*The souvenir jars are going like hot cakes. Better buy a set before they're all gone. We have a few at our offices in Athens (592-6644) and Reno (373-9055) and the Marietta Tourist and Convention Bureau on 3rd Street has 3 sets left, I believe. Cost is $20 a set -- three jars per set and they can also be purchased individually.

*I know I've missed someone or some group. I do apologize, but I promise to go into more detail as we lead up to the November 20 cutting date.

September 21, 1987
*Good news for boaters and fishermen who use our Leith Run Boat Ramp for access to the Willow Island pool of the Ohio River. We recently completed a dredging project which

removed the stumps and silt buildup at the mouth of the creek, where it empties into the main river. It should now be a snap getting from the ramp to the Ohio's main channel without having to worry about hitting a stump or raking bottom or dragging your propeller through the mud.

During extreme low water conditions there may still be a few shallow places up near the boat ramp. But they aren't anywhere near as severe as what we had out by the main river. We hope that within the next few years we can get a small dredging outfit to do minor work closer to the ramp.

We have additional plans for Leith Run, too. We plan to build and install a boarding dock for boaters -- adjacent to the ramp. Within the next five or so years we also have plans to add about 8 to 10 campsites to the area. And perhaps another picnic shelter for group cookouts. These items are dependent upon us getting the dollars, of course, so we'll just have to keep our fingers crossed.

But for now, anyway, the major dredging in finished. We were afraid initially that we couldn't get money until next year, but things fell quickly into place thanks due in large part to the Corps of Engineers -- Huntington District and Dave Kissell, Landscape Architect from our Forest Service Supervisor's Office.

We hope everyone enjoys the better boating facilities.

***I always try to keep my promises. Last week I said I'd probably leave some people off the list of those who have helped out so far with the Capitol Tree project. And sure enough, I did.**

This entire project is supposed to function through contributions and donations, so it'll take cooperation and help from many folks. Missing from last week's list were the following, who have made cash donations: Paul Warren and the folks at Warren Drilling; Sam Cook at Broughton Foods; the Marietta Kiwanis Club; Tony Popp and Marietta Savings; and Jim Meagle and the crew at Dime Bank. We certainly appreciate the help. It will all go toward making the 1987 Capitol Christmas Tree project one which we'll all be proud of.

We also want to thank Mr. and Mrs. Jess Latimer of Marietta and Mr. and Mrs. Luke Arnold of Oak Grove. They are furnishing smaller trees which will go to the U.S. House of Representatives and the U.S. Department of Agriculture Patio, respectively.

And Frontier High School, which will be helping in many ways. Bob Forbes and his people have been extremely helpful and we'll provide a detailed account on all of Frontier's efforts at a future date.

I hope you can all get involved in some way to help make this project one which will be remembered in our area for a long time to come.

*More locations at which to buy the Christmas Tree jars --Sugden's Book Store, Harpers Landing, Wallahalla Gallery, and Huck's Farm Market, all in Marietta; and Hole in the Wall Gift Shop operated by the Mendenhall's on County Road 9 (Eightmile Road) east of Marietta; also, the Marietta Tourist &

**Convention Bureau office, and Wayne National
Forest offices in Reno and Athens.**

October 12, 1987

We now have available the Christmas cards which have been
printed to commemorate the 1987 U.S. Capitol Christmas tree.
In case you've been in Borneo or somewhere for the past
several months and haven't heard, the Wayne National
Forest is providing this year's tree for the nation's capitol.
Specifically, the tree is coming from Washington County,
Frontier Local School District.

The Wayne was chosen to supply this year's tree through a
long approval process and Washington County, being Ohio's
first county, was the logical choice of locations. Also, there was
a natural tie-in to the 200th anniversary celebrations of both
the Northwest Ordinance and the City of Marietta.

The calendar is moving rapidly and before you know it,
November 20 in fact, the tree will be cut and there will be a
formal send-off ceremony the following day in Marietta.
You'll be hearing and reading more about the activities
scheduled for those two days.

Back to the cards. River Press printed about 5,000 Christmas
cards for us. We are required to send 1,000 to Washington,
D.C. for their use. Then, 1,000 each are being sent to Forest
Service offices in Athens, Ironton, and Bedford, Indiana, for
them to sell. That leaves us with 1,000 here at the Marietta
office (actually only about 800 since some have already been
sold).

You'll definitely want to buy some cards, either to send out
for Christmas or just to save as souvenirs. They come

wrapped 10 to a package and they sell for only $3.00 per package. At that price I don't expect the cards to last very long, so if you want some, just come to one of our offices--Marietta, Athens, or Ironton.

The front of the card features the U.S. Capitol with the tree standing in front. In the lower middle portion of the card is an outline of a Christmas tree bulb with a scene depicting how the tree might have looked as it stood in the front yard of a pioneer home over 100 years ago.

To the right is the Ohio River with a sternwheeler heading downstream. It's a very nice design, which was provided by Lynn Murel of our Athens office and a friend of hers, Tim McKenzie. The front cover says "Wayne National Forest, Capitol Christmas Tree-1987."

The inside of the card provides room for you to write a holiday message on the left side and on the right side is the following greeting, which was written by Teena Sechler of our Supervisor's Office:

"In honor of the bicentennial of the Northwest Ordinance
the people of Ohio present to the nation---
a Norway Spruce from the Wayne National Forest.

The tree's history is tied to the story of a young salesman who gave out seedling spruce trees as he traveled through Ohio.

It was planted in the river country on a farm near Marietta, the first settlement in the Northwest Territory.

The 1987 Capitol tree is a special legacy
of the pioneers who settled this country 200 years ago."

From Ohio,
the heart of it all,
with best wishes to the nation…
HAPPY HOLIDAYS.

*On another note, the souvenir jars we've been selling are going very fast. We have less than 100 sets left, so if you've been putting off getting a set, you'd better hurry. Cost is $20 per set of three, or $7.50-small, $8.00- medium, and $8.50- large. We have them at all three Wayne National Forest offices and at several stores and shops in the three towns. Be sure to mark November 21 on your calendar for the big ceremony and send-off for the Christmas tree. It will be held at the parking lot of the Hermann Fine Arts building at Marietta College at 2:00p.m. There will be several dignitaries, speakers, bands, and so forth present. Let's all join in making this an event that will long be remembered in our area.

October 20, 1987
The list of people and companies that are donating time, money, equipment, or supplies for the Capitol Christmas Tree project continues to grow. It's becoming a real community effort to get the main tree and several smaller trees to Washington, D.C.

We'll be having a Cutting Ceremony on Friday, November 20 and a Send-off Ceremony on Saturday, November 21. The first will be held in the Wayne National Forest at the tree site. The second will be held in the parking lot of the Hermann Fine Arts Center at Marietta College. The public is welcome to attend either, or both, of these ceremonies.

We certainly do encourage you to attend because this is undoubtedly a once-in-a-lifetime happening for our area. If the U.S. Capitol Tree ever comes from southeastern Ohio again, it will sure surprise me. And if it, by chance, does, then I'm sure we'll all be six feet underground by then.

As we get closer to the November 20-21 dates, you can read more of the specifics, times, etc. in this column and in other newspaper, radio, and TV announcements. If all else fails, give us a call at 373-9055 for more details.

Back to the donations and volunteers. In addition to others mentioned previously, we have:

Carlton Oil Corporation, Newport -- Donating manpower and use of a truck with a heavy duty winch.

Newport Lumber Company -- Donating plywood for making four signs which will accompany the trees to D.C. and for another sign to be used locally, which will be painted by Frontier High School.

Blauvelt Sign Company, Marietta -- Paint for the signs.

Jean Pickering Sign Painter, Lowell -- Jean will be doing the actual painting and lettering of the four signs.

Gil Courtney of the Peoples Savings Bank, New Matamoras and the Matamoras Area Business and Civic Organization -- Gil has already donated considerable time and effort in helping plan for our festivities. He has helped make arrangements to have equipment furnished for our use and he is coordinating the job, with MABCO of New Matamoras, of supplying a smaller tree to be sent to Washington. This smaller tree will go in the Senate Public Dining Room during the Christmas season.

Frontier High School -- We've had tremendous cooperation
and assistance from John Hoff - District Superintendent,
Bob Forbes - Principal, and Calvin Martin - Instructor. The
main tree is coming from Frontier District and, as such,
these people want to make the event one that will be long-
remembered in their area. Calvin's FFA group will be helping
with several items leading up to and during the cutting
ceremony. Frontier High School will be heavily involved in
the Nov. 20 activities, including such things as the band,
choir, transportation, parking, handing out programs and so
forth.

Washington County Career Center -- Dave Barrett, Dave
Rose, and Terry Schafer have offered any assistance they
have available to us. In particular the forestry class and the
welding class will be helping on a number of items. There's
much more. Stay tuned for further updates. So long for now.

October 26, 1987
*We've just recently completed a nice little recreation site on
State Route 26 just a few miles north of Marietta. It offers
parking, picnic spots, two camp sites, a toilet, and easy
access to the Little Muskingum River. Now, if we can just get
the "yay-hoos" to leave it alone so that people can enjoy it.

That's right. We've barely got the area constructed and we're
beginning to have vandalism. We'll be doing regular patrols
of the area, in conjunction with a couple of other law
enforcement agencies, in hopes of putting a stop to this. Just
last weekend the County Sheriff's Department apprehended
two juveniles who were doing their thing to the building.

For the life of me I can't understand the mentality of the
people who destroy things like this. I don't know if they think

they're being tough guys or what. Anyway, we'll be taking a hard stance on anyone caught vandalizing our areas.

If anyone spots anything unusual or sees anyone damaging things in one of our recreation sites, please get a description, vehicle license number, and any other information you can. Call the sheriff. Call us. Don't let one percent of the people ruin things for the other 99 percent. If we all chip in together, we can stop this stuff.

***The Capitol Christmas Tree project continues to roll along. We've received cash donations from the Marietta Rotary Club and the Citizens Bank of Beverly. These will go a long way toward helping cover expenses for this once-in-a-lifetime event.**

McDonald's on Pike Street and Newport IGA will be furnishing food for the workers who will be cutting down the tree on November 20.

Pete Suerken, John Eaton, and Dave Schatz -- all with the Ohio Division of Forestry -- will be assisting us with gathering and storing the approximately 20 additional trees which go to Washington, D.C. along with the main tree. These smaller trees go to Congressmen's offices, the Senate, House, Supreme Court, Department of Agriculture, and a few other places.

Without the help of these and other volunteers, we'd have a difficult time completing the Christmas tree project. Thanks much.

*By the time you read this, we should have on hand another supply of Christmas cards. We sold the first batch within just a few days -- over 4,000 cards. We weren't going to fool with any reprinting, but so many of you wanted cards that we're having 3,000 more printed at River Press.

This will probably be the last bunch available, so better get some soon. Call us at 373-9055 before coming to the office in Reno, so you can make sure we still have them. Thanks for your support on this community project. These cards should serve as souvenirs and keepsakes for years to come.

November 2, 1987

*Area support for the Capitol Christmas Tree project is very high and continuing to grow. Stowe's Truck and Equipment Company has volunteered time and equipment for the project. Likewise for Jim Mitchell at American Petroel, Incorporated. We really couldn't pull off this project without the donations and volunteers.

*Our primary fundraiser has been selling commemorative jars and Christmas cards. Both promise to be collector's items. We've sold all of our jar sets at this office, but we're calling back the ones which have been scattered at our Forest Service offices in other towns, so we can meet the demand locally.

If you don't hurry, you may be left out in the cold. Some jars are still available at Huck's Farm Market, Apex Feed and Supply, Birdwatcher's Digest, Harper's Landing, and the Marietta Tourist and Convention Bureau. Also, Marty

Kitchen at the Marietta Recreation Department has a few sets left.

In New Matamoras you can either get, or place an order for, jars at the Par-Mar #4 Station. Same goes for Oopsa Daisy Florist in Newport. In Monroe County see Marge Rinard in the Park District office in the Courthouse at Woodsfield.

By the time you read this we may be out of cards. All I can say is give us a call to find out (373-9055). I suppose if the demand is great enough we could order some more from the printer, but I'm not sure if we have time for that.

Some cards may be available, also, at Sugden's, the Tourist & Convention Bureau, from Marty Kitchen, Oopsa Daisy, Par-Mar, and Marge Rinard. If one place is out, call the others, or check with us.

*The 72 ornaments should arrive any day now. They're flat, crystal disks with the "1987 Capitol Christmas Tree" logo on them. We have about 30 of these promised already, so I doubt they'll last very long. Call if you're interested. Cost will be about $5.00 each, I believe.

*Several elected officials, organization presidents, chairmen, superintendents, principals, and so forth received written invitations to the Tree Cutting Ceremony on November 20 and the Send-Off Ceremony on November 21. If you didn't get one, please don't be offended because everyone in the general public is invited to both ceremonies. It seems like when you send out mass mailings or put together lists, you always forget someone or something. But believe me, it's not intentional.

*Next week I'll fill you in with the particulars about the 11/20/87 ceremony at 9:00 a.m. and the 11/21/87 ceremony at 2:00 p.m. So long till then.

November 9, 1987
Well, it's almost here. The Big Day! By the time you read this, we'll only be a few days from the Cutting Ceremony for the nation's Capitol Christmas Tree. That will be held on Friday, November 20, 1987 at 9:00 a.m. near Frontier High School.

Then there's the big Send-Off Ceremony the following day on Saturday, November 21, 1987 at 2:00 p.m. in the parking lot of the Hermann Fine Arts Building at Marietta College.

Now, before I go further let me remind you that everyone and anyone is invited to both ceremonies. These events will be long-remembered in the history of our area and you'll certainly want to be there if at all possible. We sent out some personal invitations to community leaders, elected officials, agency heads, organization presidents, superintendents, commissioners, trustees, and so on, but this was just a matter of courtesy. If you didn't receive one (and we undoubtedly missed someone by mistake), please don't be offended. <u>EVERYONE</u> is invited!!

If you do want to attend the Cutting Ceremony on 11/20/87, here's how to get there: Go to Frontier High School between 8:00 a.m. and 8:30 a.m. and park in the lot on the east side of the school beside their maintenance garage. As you face the high school with State Route 7 to your back, the lot is on the left. There will be shuttle buses which will take you to the actual tree site in the woods. Please arrive at Frontier early, so we can get everyone to the tree by 9:00 a.m. Frontier High School is located right on State Route 7, about 20 miles northeast of Marietta. Following the ceremony the buses will take you back to the high school. Don't linger or you'll have a long walk back.

The ceremonies both days will include welcomes, short speeches by dignitaries, singing, band music, and other related goings-on. It could be chilly or rainy or even snowing those days, so the actual programs will be short. Hopefully, each one will last only about one-half hour.

Two things I don't want you to be disappointed about. First, the tree itself will not be cut down during the ceremony, although there will be some small cuts made by certain dignitaries using a cross-cut saw. For safety reasons everyone must be off the site by 10:00 a.m., when the actual felling operation will begin. The reason? We'll be using a crane, a truck and trailer, a skidder, a pick-up with a winch, and a tree-service bucket, among other things. The site will become a small construction-type area, under the direction of Mr. Casimier Wojakowski from Escanaba, Michigan, and for safety reasons you won't be allowed too close while the tree is coming down.

Second, if things go well on Friday, then on 11/21 the tree will be wrapped and loaded, and laying on a flatbed trailer at the send-off ceremony in Marietta. It will not be set upright, and you won't be able to touch it.

When this Capitol Tree project first began in our minds about 5 years ago, we weren't sure it would ever actually happen. Then in 1986 when we finally became certain it would happen, it seemed as though 11/20/87 would never get here. Well, folks, like a big snowball gathering steam and size as it rolls to the bottom of the hill, the time is now here -

with all the momentum a truly historic event always brings. Many of you have helped make it possible. Please come join us on either day to become part of this truly historic event.

*Many related columns will follow in weeks to come -- thank-you's, a description of the lighting ceremony in Washington, D.C. on 12/9/87, and a final perspective on the whole event. Stay tuned for those.

Immediate thanks now go to the Frontier Lions Club, Central Trust Company, and the Matamoras Area Business and Civic Organization for cash donations; Dave Padgitt of the Ohio Division of Forestry for use of equipment; People's Banking and Trust in Marietta for use of their display window; all Washington County schools for their involvement in class projects related to the Capitol Tree; and Elainea Delatore, Tonya Ice and Brenda Bowersock, students at Frontier High School, for their volunteer help. And I can't forget all the teachers at Frontier, especially Calvin Martin and Randi Buckton, as well as Barbara Benson at Newport Elementary School. Sorry if I've missed someone; I'll catch you in a future column.

A short P.S. – We're getting calls from TV, radio, and newspapers from all over Ohio -- Cincinnati, Akron, Cleveland, Columbus, P.M. Magazine -- you name it. Once again, our area is doing something special that all Ohioans want to know about. See you Friday and Saturday.

November 16, 1987
(<u>NOTE</u>: In order to keep things consistent at the newspaper office, these columns were <u>dated</u> on the Monday before the events occurred, even though the cutting actually occurred four days after the date listed on this column.)

*Whew! The big day has finally come and gone. The nation's Capitol Christmas Tree is safely on the ground -- wrapped and loaded and just about ready for its trip to Washington, D.C. That's right. We've had it stored in a local warehouse for the past few days while we finished gathering the other 25-odd size smaller trees that go to various offices and buildings in the District of Columbia.

The big tree is loaded on the back of an R.O. Wetz Transportation tractor trailer, with plenty of spare branches packed alongside, while all the other trees are loaded onto a trailer being hauled by Kenmack Lumber, Incorporated. These two companies have done a great job helping us get everything ready for the trip to D.C. We certainly couldn't have pulled off this project without their help.

Another thing we couldn't have pulled off without a lot of help was the cutting, wrapping, and loading of the 24-, 18-, and 12-foot trees from our local area, which will end up in the Supreme Court, U.S. Department of Agriculture patio, and a USDA main office.

Here's where the ODNR-Division of Forestry (ODOF) came to our rescue. Pete Suerken, local service forester, orchestrated all the work for those three trees -- how to get them on the ground, when to cut them, and how to get them wrapped for temporary storage.

The ODOF fellows brought over a log loader from Hocking State Forest and, I'll tell you, without that piece of equipment and the two operators -- Rich Jones and Nolan Danner -- we'd have been in big trouble. Then there was Dave Padgitt, from ODOF's Fire Control Office in Barlow. He had his long, tilt-bed truck with him and we used his winch to help load and unload the two larger trees. Floyd Stine from Suerken's crew helped wrap the trees, along with Forest Service employees Dave Greenwood, Gloria Eighmey, John Kerr and Bill Engle.

It was a real team effort and we couldn't have accomplished it without everyone's help.

*Others who have donated time, money, or equipment: Haessly Hardwood Lumber Company -- materials for signs painted by Frontier High School; Gil Courtney -- use of a camper for several days preceding the cutting ceremony (parked on-site for security personnel); Harry Cogswell, Apex Feed -- rope used to tie the main tree; Matamoras Area Business and Civic Organization for three Christmas trees, two of which they got from the Mr. and Mrs. Norman Johnson farm in Monroe County; Marge Rinard of the Monroe County Park District in Woodsfield, who helped with publicity and fundraising sales of jars, cards, and ornaments; Dave Archer with Pioneer Pipe and Ray Johnson of Apache Tank -- furnished time and materials for constructing a brace to help support the tree on the back of the trailer during its trip to D.C.; the Washington County Career Center welding class put the finishing touches on the brace; Howard Edgar Contractor, Incorporated -- dozer work on the tree site; Mike Pethtel, Eric Wagner, Cindi Hier, Elainea Delatore and other Frontier High School students -- painting of two beautiful signs for the events; Dave Kantner, John Beugel, Mike Pethtel, Marilyn Ortt, Gil Courtney, Greg Danver, Matt Farnsworth, Donnie Allen, Rick Taylor, John Kerr, Dave Greenwood, Lynn Kantner, Bill Engle, Art Nicholson, Gloria Eighmey, Anne Davey, and Regina Martin -- overnight security work. It took a lot of people to pull this off. Most have been mentioned previously.

Thanks to each and every one of you from your..... Wayne National Forest.

*I'd also like to give special thanks to the secretary at our Marietta Office – Connie Morris. She was involved in almost all facets of this event. She served on the planning committee; coordinated ordering and selling of the ornaments, cards, and commemorative jars; helped with logistics for both the cutting event and the send-off ceremony; served as our official record keeper for all things connected to this event; answered tons of questions on the phone and with walk-in visitors; and typed all of my newspaper columns, which I scratched out, sometimes I'm sure, in almost unintelligible scribbles. And her able assistant, Lois Severin, who worked closely with Connie, helping out with whatever came up. Both of these ladies staffed our on-site information table at the cutting ceremony, along with Lynn Kantner. A big thank you to all of them!

November 23, 1987
WASHINGTON, D.C. -- Well, yesterday we unloaded Washington County and Wayne National Forest's gift to the nation -- the U.S. Capitol Christmas tree. As the morning began we were met by a police escort in Rockville, Maryland and taken directly to the U.S. Capitol. There we were greeted by Paul Pincus, Capitol Landscape Architect, whose crew helped us unload the main tree, spare branches, 18 trees for congressmen, and 11 other trees destined for offices around D.C. Within a couple of hours it was all over.

What made it really nice was the number of spectators, Forest Service officials, Congressmen, and their aides, who came to meet us. There was plenty of media attention, too.

Those of us who were there had a great time, meeting and talking with everyone. And the pictures! All I can say is that there were plenty of pictures taken: with Congressmen Applegate and Miller who represent our Districts back home; and Congressmen Ralph Regula and Michael Dewine, also from Ohio; and various Forest Service and Capitol officials.

Roy Wetz and Robert McElfresh were with us from R.O. Wetz Transportation, which of course, hauled the main tree, the 55-foot Norway spruce; Mack and Ken Haessly were there from Kenmack Lumber, Inc. -- they hauled the 29 smaller trees; Gil Courtney from People's Savings Bank in New Matamoras accompanied us; as did Randy Carletti of East-West Trailer Company and Dave Edwards - Ravens Trailer; Teena Sechler, our Forest Service Public Information Officer from Bedford, Indiana was with us, coordinating the publicity and arrangements; along with Lynn Kantner of our Marietta Office who helped with many things, including keeping Bob McElfresh alert on the long drive across West Virginia and Maryland.

We've had a great time so far, trying to lay the groundwork for the December 9 Lighting Ceremony on the Capitol Lawn. Thanks to everyone back home who has made this event possible so far. We'll be home soon, but many of us will return on the 9th -- along with six busloads of Washington Countians. And one thing for sure; after that date, it'll be a long time before they ever forget southeastern Ohio or Washington County.

*Notes from here and there:

Casimier Wojakowski, the man who came from Michigan to help us cut our tree, said this crew was the best he's ever worked with; and he's done this several times before for various states and National Forests. He also told me it was the quickest he's ever cut, wrapped, and loaded a big tree. It took only four hours, whereas it usually takes six to eight. He directed things, but as he told me afterwards, "a band leader is only as good as his band." Again, a tribute to the equipment operators and helpers -- Black's Tree Service, Busch Crane Rental, R.O. Wetz Transportation, Kenmack Lumber Inc., Carlton Oil Corp., Howard Edgar Contractor, Frontier High School FFA, and Washington County Career Center.

I apologize to anyone I may have overlooked during either the Cutting Ceremony or the Send-Off. There were just so many folks who helped out that it was a chore to keep it all straight. Also, sorry if I was short or abrupt with anyone -- as my wife said later, "I acted like I was in a tizzy." There was just so much happening that I was on system overload for a couple of days. But now it's better. I'm back to my same old jovial self.

How about a hand for that Carlton Oil crew led by Danny Thompson? They, along with Jeff Edgar, jumped right in and had that tree tied up in no time flat. The Carlton crew included Roger Strickler, Jack Strickler, Danny Thompson, Jr., Harold Edgar, and Frank Edgar.

Want one of those Capitol Tree T-shirts or sweatshirts? They're done very nicely and will be excellent keepsakes. Contact Bill Creighton at Creighton Sports Center in New Matamoras. He can have them done to say New Matamoras,

Bicentennial of the Northwest Ordinance, Wayne National Forest, or whatever you want.

-- It was great to have Sandra Binegar, Carolyn Phipps, and Judy Beaver, all descendants of the Holdren's -- on hand for the festivities. The Holdren's owned the property where the Capitol Christmas Tree was cut.......before it became part of Wayne National Forest. It made a good tie-in with the historical aspect of the whole Capitol Christmas Tree event.

November 30, 1987
*By the time you read this, the U.S. Capitol Christmas Tree and the 29 smaller trees will all be decorated and standing in their respective locations in Washington, D.C. In fact, the big tree itself will be officially lit in a 5:00 p.m. ceremony, December 9 on the Capitol lawn.

Several dignitaries will be there, including most of the Ohio Congressional delegation. Marietta Mayor Nancy Hollister is slated to give remarks concerning the bicentennial of the Northwest Ordinance; the Frontier High School band will be playing a couple of songs; and Mary Carson, of New Matamoras, will be singing the Star Spangled Banner. Earlier that day Calvin Martin and his Frontier Future Farmers of America Chapter will be presenting U.S. Representative Douglas Applegate with a jacket, making him an honorary chapter member.

Capitol Landscape Architect Paul Pincus, who coordinates the annual Capitol Christmas tree event, remarked that he had never seen such widespread local interest in the festivities. I took that as a huge compliment directed toward all of Washington County and surrounding areas, too.

*A big thank you to Southeastern Security and Investigations, who gave us five donated days of surveillance at the tree site on Sheets Run prior to the cutting. This was a tremendous help to us, trying to make sure nothing bad happened to the tree prior to November 20. Also, the same thanks goes out to Washington County Sheriff Dick Ellis, as well as Lt. Herman and his crew at the Ohio Highway Patrol. Both agencies assisted with extra patrols and monitoring of the area in November.

Loading the 29 smaller trees on November 27 was a big job. We put them on a Kenmack Lumber truck and spent most of the day doing it. John Eaton, manager of the ODNR - Division of Forestry State Nursery in Reno, had let us store the trees in one of his warehouses for several days. We also used John's forklift to help load the two 24-foot and two 18-foot trees. Without that forklift I think we'd still be over there trying to load those four trees.

We had a good crew there that day as Bob Florence and Marilyn Ortt helped the Kenmack crew -- Mack Haessly, Jr., Roger Taylor, and Tony Lauer.

*Special thanks to the Frontier High School band and the Marietta Senior High School band, who played during the Cutting Ceremony and the Send-Off Ceremony, respectively. Lynne Johnson and Marshall Kimball, band directors, do a wonderful job with these kids. Also the Frontier High School Chorus, directed by Bill Bigger -great singing at the Cutting Ceremony!

American Legion Post 378 of New Matamoras and VFW Post 5108 of Marietta were honor guards at the ceremonies, while

Frontier FFA and Marietta Boy Scout Troop 203 led by
Butch Hawkins led the pledges of allegiance.

Local ministers handling the invocations and benedictions
were Dwight Umbel -Church of the Nazarene, New
Matamoras; Kurt Landerholm -- Newport United Methodist
Church; Don Shuler -- First Baptist Church, Marietta; and
Tim Wallace -- Reno Christian Church.

*Robert McElfresh drove the R.O. Wetz Transportation truck
to D.C. on November 30, while Mack and Kenny Haessly
handled the Kenmack rig. Gil Courtney and Roy Wetz
followed in separate vehicles. We stayed overnight in
Rockville, Maryland, where the local police department
watched the trees, while we all got a good night's rest.

*For those of you who might have missed it, Teena Sechler's
story "A Drummer's Gift," appeared in the December issue of
Redbook magazine. It's a very good story, describing how the
early "drummers" traveled throughout southeastern Ohio
selling wares to the frontier housewives, and how they gave
seedling spruce trees to them. Teena is Public Information
Officer for the Wayne and Hoosier National Forests.

December 7, 1987
We're winding down now from all the Capitol Christmas
Tree hoopla. For a few years it seemed like it would never get
here, then it happened, and now it's nearly over. It's a good
thing, too, because I don't know if I could have held up much
longer. If I was prone to ulcers, I'd have had about 10 by
now. It's been a lot of fun though, especially in retrospect.

I still have a couple of more columns left in my pen yet, so
you'll likely be reading more about the 1987 Capitol Tree.

Heck, it remains standing into January, 1988, so there's still plenty of time left to talk about it.

Let's tidy up some of my miscellaneous notes, quotes, thank you's, and 'atta boys and next time around you'll hear about the D.C. trip, the lighting ceremony, the bus ride over, and so on.

*Big, big, special thanks to the Capitol Christmas Tree Committee -- a group of folks who helped us plan things and make the whole operation go: Jim Apgar, Gil Courtney, Barb Hamilton, Harry Cogswell, Barbara Lovely, Sandy Matthews, Marty Kitchen, Marilyn Ortt, Phyllis Richerson, Iwana Simon, Wayne Schafer, Connie Morris, and Teena Sechler. Also, in the beginning we had Chuck Myers and four people from the Ohio Department of Natural Resources -- Dave Bergman, Lynn Malowney, John Piehowicz, and Bernice Wilson. Without the efforts of all these folks, and the many hours of time they spent on the project, we couldn't have pulled it off.

*Casimier Wojakowski, who traveled all the way from Escanaba, Michigan to help us cut the tree, said there was more media coverage at our cutting ceremony than all the others he has participated in combined. That covers several states and 20-some years of experience.

I figure he's right, too. We had TV and newspaper coverage from Marietta, Parkersburg, Columbus, Cleveland, Akron, Cincinnati, Dayton, Wheeling, Pittsburgh, Huntington, Charleston, Clarksburg, and several others. Cable News Network also gave us good coverage on the national level for the D.C. ceremonies.

Wojakowski also told me that he was very impressed with the obvious community support and pride in the entire project. As an outsider he recognized that right away. That's certainly a tribute to Washington County and surrounding areas.

*Further thanks for donations toward the project: Swan Lumber Do-It-Center, Marietta -- lumber; Flinn's Septic Service, Williamstown -- porta-toilets; food and lodging for Mr. Wojakowski -- Knight's Inn, Bonanza, Rax, Burger King, First Settlement, Broughton's, Domino's Pizza, Bob Evans Restaurant, and Hardees (all coordinated by the Marietta Tourist and Convention Bureau); fuel for the R.O. Wetz Transportation and Kenmack Lumber trucks from Bill Hollister at Par Mar Oil and Chuck Pannier at Englefield (Duke Oil Co.); and the following Washington County financial institutions which helped cover meal and lodging costs for the truckers who took the trees to Washington -- Bartlett Farmers Bank, Peoples Savings Bank of New Matamoras, Lower Salem Commercial Bank, Waterford Commercial & Savings Bank, and Peoples Banking & Trust Company of Marietta.

*Don't forget to watch "Agricountry" with Ed Johnson on Channel 10-TV, Columbus at 7:30 a.m. on December 19. That's the Christmas show which will feature a several minute segment on our Capitol Tree cutting. Ed and his crew were down here on November 20 for quite awhile to film and interview people. Check your local listings to make sure of the time, but 12/19/87 is the right date. The exact time does vary in some towns, however, but it is always early on Saturday morning.

December 15, 1987

*What a great time we all had in Washington, D.C. on December 9 as we watched the lighting ceremony for the Capitol Christmas Tree. It was truly an experience that all 400 or so of us will never forget.

There was a mixture of emotions, too -- some of us were relieved that it was over; others were sad to see it end; some were in awe of the tremendously beautiful setting and the ceremony; and everyone was proud, extremely proud, that the Wayne National Forest and Washington County were able to participate in such an event.

We're sure that for many, many years to come, when the Christmas season approaches and we read about Capitol Christmas trees, that local people will fondly recall the time when "their" tree was sent to Washington, D.C.

*Earlier in the day on December 9 the Frontier High School Future Farmers of America participated in two exciting ceremonies. They made U.S. Representatives Doug Applegate and Clarence Miller honorary Frontier Chapter members and presented each congressman with an FFA jacket.

The students, under the direction of advisor Calvin Martin, had prepared a formal ceremony complete with remarks and participation by seven FFA members. They did a fine job and each congressman seemed very pleased with the honor. The students were Matt Farnsworth, Greg Danver, Mike Pethtel, Shorty Martin, John Buegel, Mike Berentz, and Bruce Becker.

Superintendent John Hoff and Principal Bob Forbes accompanied the FFA group, as did Fred Yonda who took videos of the ceremonies. I tagged along to get some black and white photos for the group to use in future newsletters, etc.

*The tree lighting ceremony itself was very nice with Speaker of the House Jim Wright of Texas doing the honors. Mary Carson of New Matamoras gave a great rendition of the Star Spangled Banner and Marietta Mayor Nancy Hollister made remarks summarizing the historical significance of our area and how proud we were to give the tree as a gift to the nation.

The Frontier High School band played a couple of numbers and, I'm telling you what, they did a wonderful job. Spurred on by a few hundred friends, relatives, and onlookers they seemed really pumped up for their performance. And it showed by the great job they did. Band Director Lynne Johnson and all the students worked very hard on this one.

Governor Celeste gave some timely remarks, as did Senators Glenn, Metzenbaum, and Representatives Applegate, Miller, Regula, and Oakar, among others. Celeste and Hollister co-hosted a reception for everyone following the ceremony.

Other Forest Service personnel in attendance were Chief - Dale Robertson, Associate Chief - George Leonard, Regional Forester - Butch Marita, Forest Supervisor - Frank Voytas, Deputy Supervisor - Terry Hoffman, Public Information Officer - Teena Sechler, and Acting District Ranger - Jim Apgar.

*Senator Glenn invited several Forest Service people to his office for eggnog and cookies. That was quite a treat being able to talk with him in a less formal setting. He and his wife are very friendly, down-to-earth people. I guess that's not too surprising since they hail from a small Ohio town – New Concord - just up the road from Marietta.

Senator Glenn and I talked about New Concord's other famous son, current Ohio State basketball star, Jay Burson. My wife - Vicki, son - Brent, and daughter - Shannon were there, too, enjoying the conversation. Believe me, we took plenty of photos. Unfortunately, our oldest son Jeff was unable to be there because he was away at college, studying for semester exams.

Vicki and Senator Glenn had a long chat about his boyhood friends in New Concord, the Cooper family, one of whom was the father of Marietta physician, Dr. Warren Cooper. Vicki is a registered nurse for Drs. Cooper and White at Marietta Ob-Gyn Associates.

*Special thanks to Gil Courtney - President of People's Savings Bank in New Matamoras - for organizing the five busloads of people from Frontier District who attended the ceremony. And, to Phyllis Richerson - Director of the Marietta Tourist and Convention Bureau - and Larry and Janet Steinel of Uniglobe for putting together the two busloads of people from Marietta.

George Merkel, Director of Alumni Affairs at Marietta College, put on a very nice reception at the Master Hosts Inn in D.C. following the ceremony, too. He had quite a set-up with cookies, sandwiches, and all the fixin's. It was enjoyable talking with George and his wife, Joan, about Marietta College and everything else as the evening progressed.

There were too many people present to recognize everyone, but it was great to have all three Washington County Commissioners there -- Sandy Matthews, Glenn Miller, and Dick Young. We certainly appreciate their support and involvement in these activities.

December 21, 1987
*I've been asked if there were any "special" little things which happened during the Capitol Christmas tree hoopla which I'll never forget. Sure there were - many of them.

Standing above all else has to be the many friendships we made and the great cooperative efforts of hundreds of local people who made the entire operation such a huge success. I'll certainly never forget that.

Neither will I forget the many cards, calls, and thank you's we've received. We really feel honored to have been part of an event which focused such a large amount of positive publicity on our area. And you know what? We had fun doing it! Thanks to all of you.

Some of the other things which stand out:

*Spending 15 minutes in the office of Assistant Secretary of Agriculture, Wilmer Mizell. We didn't talk agriculture or forestry, either. We talked baseball. Some of you may remember him as "Vinegar Bend" Mizell, who pitched for the Cardinals and Pirates in the late 1950's and early '60's. He autographed a 1957 Topps baseball card for me and apologized for the grief he caused me in 1960 when his

Pirates beat my beloved New York Yankees in the World Series. Somehow, Mazeroski's fluke home run in Game 7 seems easier to take now.

*That meeting was set up by Al Wolter, Assistant Director of the U.S. Forest Service Office of Information (OI). I've known Al for many years. In fact, I worked for him when he was the District Ranger at Ironton on the Wayne NF back in the 1970s. He was very proud that the Wayne furnished the 1987 Capitol Christmas Tree. By the way, Al worked for Don Girton, the Director of OI, until Don retired a couple of years ago. Don was Forest Supervisor of the Wayne and Hoosier National Forests in the 1970s. Small world!

*I'll never forget running all those red lights on the morning of November 30, either, as we received our police escort, taking the tree from Rockville, Maryland to the U.S. Capitol. It was great! All those lights and we didn't even have to stop. If only I could do that when I'm in Columbus.

*And R.O. Wetz' fender bender. Pardon me, Roy, for mentioning it, but heck, it wasn't your fault anyway. DC drivers during the morning rush can be real maniacs and this guy was no exception. He tried to squeeze his size 4 car into a size 3 space and it just wouldn't fit. The big, burly dude appeared ready for an argument with Roy, but when Mack Haessly, Bob McElfresh, Gil Courtney, Kenny Haessly, and I joined Roy, the fellow mysteriously calmed down.

*Linda Roderick and Phil Straw of Congressman Miller's office, Jim Hart of Congressman Applegate's office, and Martha DiSario of Senator Glenn's office were all extra nice to us -- being rookies in D.C. as we were. Thanks go out to all of them!

*It was a real pleasure to meet and talk with the Chief and Associate Chief of the Forest Service -- Dale Robertson and George Leonard -- and also the Secretary of Agriculture, Richard Lyng, and his Deputy, Peter Myers.

*Lynn Kantner of our office was a big help taking the trees to D.C. She rode part of the way in the big truck with Bob McElfresh and she spent a lot of time on the CB radio. Her "handle" was Snowflake. Bob's was Snowball. Lynn and Bob helped us keep our sanity during the 3-hour, 38-mile long traffic jam between Cumberland and Hancock, Maryland. What an experience that was!

*R.O. Wetz said he wasn't sure whether that was Gil Courtney with us or not. He couldn't get a good look at him because he always had either a video camera or a CB mike in front of his face. What a crew! Seriously, though, we had a great time and Gil got a lot of good video footage. We even ate a couple of coconut pies. Right, Gil?

*North Hills School in Marietta recently planted a Norway spruce to commemorate the Capitol Tree and the bicentennial of the Northwest Ordinance. Each Christmas, many folks will remember the tree, when it was planted, and why. What a great project for grade school kids to be involved with.

December 28, 1987

*The final Wayne Land Management Plan will be out in a few days, capping several years of effort between the public and the Forest Service. The Wayne Plan will guide us in our management activities for the next 10 years, so it is a monumentally important document.

We'll be doing some things differently in the future and some things like we always have. It's all in the plan, and one of the primary aspects of the new plan is that it's all there for the public to see -- and to be involved in. We encourage you to join with us in implementing the plan and in helping us monitor its progress -- sort of keeping tabs on how things are working out.

We believe that fostering a good working partnership with the public is one of the ways we can make the Wayne the best National Forest in the country.

Many of you have requested the planning documents or the summary, and you should receive those shortly. For others, you may review the plan at the public libraries in Woodsfield, Athens, Gallipolis, Jackson, Nelsonville, Logan, New Lexington, New Matamoras, or Marietta and at the Marietta College, Ohio University, or Hocking Technical College libraries. We will also have review copies at our offices in Reno and Athens. If you're interested in the Wayne National Forest, please take the time to look over the plan.

***I received copies from several people of a recent Washington Post article which gave detailed descriptions of many of the Christmas trees in and around the Washington, D.C. area.**

The author's conclusion was that the U.S. Capitol tree, furnished by Wayne National Forest, was by far the prettiest one. He felt that the White House tree was not "in the same league" with the Capitol

tree and he went on to call our Norway spruce "spectacular." But we knew that already, didn't we? One more thing to remind us that we were involved in a truly special event this past Christmas season.

*Paul Pincus, the Landscape Architect for the U.S. Capitol, who coordinates the Christmas tree festivities in D.C., also dropped me a note about the Washington Post article. He has been involved in the Capitol Tree program since it began 24 years ago, and he said this is the first time the Washington Post had ever bothered to do an article about it. Another first for our Washington County tree.

*We've received personal thank you's for the Christmas tree effort from Senator Glenn and Representatives Applegate, Miller, and Stokes, among others. We got the feeling that the entire Ohio Congressional delegation was extremely proud of the fact that the Buckeye State furnished this year's tree.

*We received one last order of about 100 Christmas Tree ornaments a few days ago. There were just too many people who were disappointed that they didn't get one. So, Casto Glass whipped us out one more batch. They're first-come, first-serve and will no doubt go fast. No orders or reservations please. Call to see if we have any left and then pick them up at our Reno office.

Once again, thank all of you for your interest in and support of the 1987 Capitol Christmas Tree project.

January 4, 1988

*We've finally completed the purchase of the nearly 3,500 acre Blaney properties, which we've been working on for several years. It was unique to acquire that many acres from one seller in Monroe and Washington counties. There is also a small property in the extreme southeastern corner of Noble County included in the purchase. This is within our National Forest proclamation boundary and it is the first land we've ever owned in Noble County.

We're glad to have this complex transaction finalized and we look forward to buying several more smaller properties during the coming year.

We've also recently completed the acquisition of 2,523 acres of land from Peabody Coal Company in Athens County. The nice thing about this property is that it is all in one consolidated chunk. The area is located in York and Dover Townships and has not been strip mined in the past -- only underground mining.

The adding of these 6,000 acres to the Wayne National Forest represents one of our major accomplishments for 1987.

***In addition to the widely-publicized Washington Post newspaper article about our Capitol Christmas Tree, Channel 9-TV in D.C. carried an evening news feature story on December 23. They compared the Capitol Tree to the White House tree and came up with the same conclusion as the Post did -- the Capitol Tree was by far the nicer of the two. Several visitors and residents, including children, were**

interviewed on the show and they all agreed that the
Capitol Tree was the most "spectacular" in the city.

*Dean Beaver of Newport has put together a very
nice two-hour VHS video tape of the various Capitol
Christmas Tree festivities. He's selling copies and
you can contact him at 473-2917.

*Did anyone find a pair of leather mittens at the tree
cutting ceremony on November 20? If so, they're
mine. They're brown leather, kind of like ski
mittens, lined, and oh, do they keep your hands
warm. I've missed them this past week during the
zero degree weather. If you found them, give me a
call at the office - 373-9055. Thanks.

*<u>Transport Topics,</u> a national trucking magazine,
recently featured a color cover photo of the Capitol
Tree being unloaded on November 30 in D.C.
There's also a short story inside the magazine about
the tree, mentioning R.O. Wetz Transportation and
Kenmack Lumber, Inc.

<u>Ohio Woodlands,</u> the quarterly magazine put out by
the Ohio Forestry Association, will soon be coming
out with photos and a story on the Capitol Tree.
<u>Ohio Woodlands</u> is sent to every high school library
in the state.

*Well, it's official! The Capitol Tree will be returning
to Washington County, Ohio. We hope to use the
tree in conjunction with 2 or 3 local high school
shop classes -- Frontier High and Washington
County Vocational School, in particular. Gil

**Courtney was primarily responsible for getting
permission to bring the tree back. He worked
closely with Congressman Douglas Applegate,
Capitol Architect George White, and Landscape
Architect Paul Pincus. Way to go, Gil! More on this
at a later date.**

January 11, 1988

*I received a nice note last week from Casimier Wojakowski,
who traveled here this past November to help us cut the
Capitol Christmas Tree.

I had sent Casimier some newspaper clippings and so had a
few other people. He really enjoyed them and said that he
and his wife held a warm spot in their hearts for all of their
Washington County friends. They really enjoyed their three-
day stay here.

Casimier has been in touch with R.O. Wetz and he also wrote
that he watched the December 9 tree lighting ceremony on
Cable News Network. The Escanaba (Michigan) Daily Press
has featured several articles on Casimier and our tree. He
wrote to say that he's received more press "than Gary Hart"
in his area. He said he told the Daily Press editor that they
had made him famous, but he'd rather they make him rich.

What a fine fellow. It was certainly a pleasure meeting and
working with him on the Capitol Tree project.

*Danny Thompson, of Carlton Oil Corporation, had some
beautiful Christmas cards made which showed his crew
standing in front of the Capitol Tree before it was cut. They
took a group photo right after that snowfall we had in early
November, and it was quite a shot. The cards were sent to

various customers and friends of Carlton Oil, and it should
be a very nice keepsake. Danny and his crew, of course, were
heavily involved in helping us cut and wrap the tree on
November 20.

*Harold Mueller of Marietta sent me a clipping from <u>Stars
and Stripes,</u> the newspaper published for U.S. servicemen in
Europe. It was an article about none other than our Capitol
Christmas Tree, which appears to be getting not only local,
state, and national coverage, but now worldwide coverage as
well! As that great orator Dizzy Dean once said, "Who'd a
thunk it?" Harold's son is currently serving with the U.S.
Army in Germany and sent the article home.

*Anyone who has photos (color or black and white), slides,
or videos of anything related to the Capitol Tree event is
asked to contact Wayne National Forest at 373-9055. We
would like to have as much pictorial documentation as
possible of the events. We can have copies made of your
slides and negatives if you'd just let us borrow them for a
short while. Thanks for your help with this.

*Carolyn Phipps, one of the granddaughters of Joseph and
Mary Holdren, loaned me a couple of old turn-of-the-century
photos from which I'm going to have copies made. They
show the Holdren family and will be displayed in a
prominent place in our office.

The Holdren's, of course, are the likely planters of the
Norway spruce which was selected as the Capitol Christmas
tree. Though the land at the mouth of Sheets Run is now part
of the Wayne National Forest, and has been since 1969, it
was in the Holdren family for many, many years throughout

the 1800's and the early part of the 1900's. The Capitol Tree was probably planted around 1910.

March 21, 1988
*We were all saddened by the recent death of Hugh Patterson, who lived out on State Route 26 near Sitka.

I grew to know Hugh over the past several years and he was quite a fellow – one of the most interesting outdoorsmen I've ever known. His love of bear hunting was known to all of his friends and it didn't take much to get him talking about tales of his many trips to Canada, where the black bears were thick and where Hugh had quite a time.

He also confided to me last Fall that he had seen three bears in Washington County over the past 25 years – one as recently as a couple of years ago. Hugh didn't tell that to very many people because most folks are skeptical of those kinds of claims. When that black bear was hit by a vehicle and killed near Marr in Monroe County last year, many people were surprised; but not Hugh, because he saw occasional tracks and bear sign in our area.

Hugh told me a lot of stories about coyotes, foxes, coon hunting, squirrels, and the local forests. He loved it all. We'll certainly miss Hugh Patterson, but will never forget his love for the outdoors.

***The Capitol Christmas Tree saga is about to close and here's a status report and thank you for recent help we've received.**

Many of you are aware that R.O. Wetz Transportation of Marietta was able to swing by the

U.S. Capitol in mid-January and bring back two 19-foot sections of the tree trunk. These were then unloaded and stored for a few days by the Forestry Class at the Washington County Career Center, where the logs were sawed down to shorter lengths.

Then the logs were divided up amongst the Career Center, Frontier High School Band Boosters, Swiss Hills Vocational School, and the Frontier Future Farmers of America. These groups were to use the wood to make souvenirs for fund raising events, and so on.

From the original 25-foot butt section of the Capitol tree (remember, we shortened it from 80 to 55-feet prior to shipping to D.C.), which had been stored by Kenmack Lumber of Newport, we were able to saw out a few hundred board feet of lumber. Kenmack Lumber did the sawing in February and Haessly Hardwood Lumber Company of Newport Pike dry kilned the boards for us. Haessly Hardwood also ran the boards through their planer and we picked them up in late February.

We've now begun the long process of edging the lumber here in our shop, culling out the bad stuff, and cutting out and finishing the many, many, many plaques, which will go to those who helped us throughout the entire project.

It's kind of like Prudential Insurance, except that instead of a piece of the rock people will get a "piece of the tree."

Zide's Sport Shop has agreed to donate metal tag plates for the plaques, so before long we should be distributing these mementos.

We want to thank all of those who have helped in this follow-up portion of the Capitol Christmas Tree project. Bringing things to a successful and memorable close is every bit as important as the earlier work.

Once again, thanks.

April 4, 1988

*In a recent column I forgot to mention the Tree Farm luncheon, which was held as part of the annual Ohio Forestry Association/Society of American Foresters meeting.

The luncheon was one of the treats of the meeting, honoring all the tree farmers, inspectors, and others who are involved in the program. The Tree Farm System is a national program, administered by the American Forest Council (AFC), which encourages private forest owners to manage and grow trees as a crop.

The luncheon was emceed by Cloyce Riddle - Ohio Division of Forestry and Clint Manns of Stone Container Corporation. Also on hand to give an overview of the tree farm program was John Herrington, AFC Regional Manager.

Herrington included a synopsis of Project Learning Tree in his presentation. PLT is another national program which is beginning to gain momentum. Its intent is to get forestry and conservation information into the hands, and minds, of educators and students across the United States.

Later on, I'll try to do a feature column on both the tree farm program and Project Learning Tree.

***Pat Murphy recently pointed out in one of her "Birds I View" columns that the proper name for the local geese we see (most of them, anyway) is Canada goose, not Canadian goose.**

It immediately reminded me of something which has been on my mind for quite awhile. The proper name for the tree species which served as this year's Capitol Christmas Tree is Norway spruce, not Norwegian spruce.

Many of my news releases and columns were incorrectly edited to read Norwegian spruce; and several broadcasts by various media from around the state ended up with the incorrect 'Norwegian' spruce, too.

So remember, not only are the birds Canada geese, but the trees are Norway spruce.

*We were pleased last fall to be able to contribute a small amount of money toward the reconstruction of the Reas Run Bridge. We've also been able to work with Frontier High School on some small cooperative projects, which will benefit their FFA program.

We're looking now at the possibility of a couple of small projects with Independence Township - Washington County and Washington Township - Monroe County. Nothing major, but just some slight financial help and some assistance related to roads and bridges.

We're glad whenever we're able to help out like this, but our budget is lean, too. We're pretty well committed for the rest of this year.

The Wayne National Forest is not a handout agency, nor do we award grants or anything like that. Our main responsibility is to manage the national forest and, goodness knows, we don't even get enough money to do that. The only way we can spend money on another agency's roads, bridges, or whatever else, is if it will be of some benefit to the users of the national forest. And then, only if we have some money available. So it's not a sure thing in any event.

We'll continue to help out and be a good neighbor as best we can. But we're not the answer to the financial problems that face not only our local areas, but all of rural America as well.

April 18, 1988
***Our Capitol Christmas Tree plaques are now finished and we'll soon be distributing them to all those people who assisted us with the project. They turned out very nice and since the plaques were sawn from the actual Capitol Tree itself, they will be keepsakes to be treasured for years to come.**

Gabe Zide and the folks at Zide's Sport Shop did a bang-up job on the metal tags which go on each plaque. We think everyone will be pleased with the final product.

***Speaking of the Capitol Tree project, one of the key members of our planning committee was Phyllis Richerson, of the Marietta Tourist and Convention**

Bureau. She was instrumental in helping out with several phases of the project.

Three areas I recall in particular were assistance with selling souvenir cards and jars; getting the ball rolling for the two tour buses which went from Marietta to Washington, D.C. for the lighting ceremony; and helping host Paul Pincus, the Capitol Landscape Architect, when he made his trip to Washington County in September 1986 to give final approval for our Norway spruce tree. At first Pincus wasn't real positive about approving our tree, but after Phyllis and a couple of others gave him the hard sell, we were "in like Flint."

Now I see where Phyllis will be leaving our area. She will be sorely missed and very difficult to replace as Director of the T&CB. Our best wishes go with her, as do our sincere thanks for all of her help with the 1987 Capitol Christmas Tree project.

*We are looking to hire someone for a position in our Senior Community Service Employment Program. This particular job will require someone to work in our Marietta Unit office, and we'd like to have some clerical or secretarial skills, if possible. There will be the usual typing, office cleaning, filing, answering phone calls, and so forth.

To qualify for this position you must be at least age 55, female, in good health, and unemployed at present. You must meet certain annual income requirements, too. Work will be approximately three days per week.

If you think you may be interested, please contact Connie Morris at 373-9055.

*I just saw a note which came through my office about the 55th anniversary of the start of the Civilian Conservation Corps program. Begun in April of 1933 by President Franklin D. Roosevelt, the CCC became one of the most successful government programs of all time.

Unemployed young people were put to work on a variety of forestry, flood control, and erosion control projects throughout the United States. Monthly allotment payments were sent back home to the families of the enrollees.

When the program ended in 1942, over 2.5 million young men had participated. The National Forests, including the Wayne, were the recipients of much of the work these young men did -- from building roads and trails, to firefighting, constructing campgrounds, planting trees on eroded ground, and building offices.

Many of the CCC structures still stand throughout the United States and are being evaluated through the Forest Service Cultural Resource Program for permanent preservation status.

April 25, 1988
*We had the opportunity last week to participate in a Management Review of the Wayne National Forest by a group of people from our Forest Service Regional Office in Milwaukee, Wisconsin.

It was an excellent chance for us to show some of the projects that we've been working on and also to get ideas from them as to how we might improve in certain areas.

The review team consisted of Deputy Regional Forester Jim Jordan, whose responsibilities cover resource management of 16 National Forests in the 20-state Eastern Region; Mike Wolfe, Director of Administrative Services, who is in charge of regional contracting, purchasing, etc.; Kathleen Burgers, who heads up the Employee Development Section in the Regional Personnel Office; Bob Van Aken, Director of Timber Management for the Eastern Region. All four of these folks are from Milwaukee.

Members of the review team also included Frank Voytas, Wayne Forest Supervisor from our Bedford, Indiana office and Sam Gehr, Deputy Forest Supervisor from the Mark Twain National Forest in Missouri.

The group spent one day on the Athens Unit with District Ranger Phil Barker, looking at a variety of projects including tree planting, reclamation, off-road vehicle trails and timber sales. They also had a chance to meet with some of the staff at Hocking Technical College and to travel to Columbus and meet with representatives of the Ohio Department of Natural Resources. The latter discussions included time spent with Anne Wickham, a native of Marietta, who is currently an ODNR Deputy Director.

The day following the Athens meeting the team members came to the Marietta Unit and spent the morning talking with our employees and getting an overview of what we're doing here locally.

In the afternoon we visited the Capitol Christmas Tree site and discussed plans for a picnic area to be built there. We were joined by Gil Courtney of New Matamoras, who gave special insight into the Capitol Tree project and also how we might build toward some cooperative recreation projects in the Frontier School District.

We also visited Leith Run Picnic Area, with a special emphasis placed upon converting the area into a developed campground. Plans are being prepared for this and we're hoping to complete the project within 3-5 years. Right now, money is the holdup, but we're hopeful we can receive budget consideration soon.

On the way back to town we drove down Jackson Run and looked at the road project which we completed with Independence and Grandview Townships a couple of years ago. We also discussed our Youth Conservation Corps summer program and how that fits in with construction of the North Country Trail.

On Saturday we took a four-hour canoe trip on the Little Muskingum River with a lunch stop at Myers' Store in Wingett Run. We talked about the canoe access developments along the river and how they fit into our overall recreation program.

We feel like the review was a good thing for us. We learned quite a bit from the folks who were here, got some new ideas, and at the same time had the opportunity to show off some of the good things we're doing locally.

We're constantly trying to improve the quality of our management here on the Wayne National Forest. If you have any ideas or suggestions, don't hesitate to stop by our office and let us know about them.

May 2, 1988
***The memory of our Capitol Christmas Tree project will live on in yet another way. Last week we finished building a picnic area on the site near Sheets Run. Actually, it's not completely finished yet, but it's certainly usable.**

We installed two picnic tables, fire rings, benches, and seats. You may have noticed the new signs on State Route 7 pointing to the area. We have some minor additions to make in the near future, but most things are now in place.

We received advice and assistance on the project from Pete Edgar, Jeff Edgar, Gil Courtney, Marilyn Ortt, Lewis Grimes, Calvin Martin, and several Frontier High School students. The Frontier FFA Club plans on helping out each year with maintenance at the site -- mowing, repair, litter patrol, and so on.

Dave Kissel, landscape architect from our main office, drew up the plans for the area and he did a fine job. We believe you'll enjoy the area. We hope that everyone can help us look after this recreation site and help us take care of it. The Capitol Tree project, after all, was shared by our entire communities and we wouldn't want anything to happen there -- like vandalism.

We've already had one minor incident occur. Judy Holdren Beaver planted a small Norway spruce right beside the stump of the Capitol Tree to honor and remember her grandparents, who had lived there around the turn of the century. Marie Holdren (Judy's mother), of New Matamoras, had been in touch with me about the new tree. They were extremely proud of it and so was I. It was a beautiful young tree and a fitting memorial.

It's a crying shame that someone slipped in there after dark one night and dug it up. We'll replace it and see what happens. Obviously, we can't go in there every week and plant another tree. So, we'll need everyone's assistance in helping us care for the area. Either that, or close down the site and chalk up another victory for the rowdies.

*Here's an ominous note which was recently reported on. The World Wildlife Fund and the World Health Organization announced at a recent conference that at the current rate of things, by the year 2050 over 60,000 plants with valuable medical properties are likely to become extinct.

That figure represents one in every four of the world's medicinal plants. Over 80 percent of the world's population depends upon these plants for their healing properties and their use in treating a variety of illnesses. These medicinal plants and herbs are widely used in modern countries, as well as the developing nations.

In fact, one research scientist noted that 25 percent of the prescription drugs being currently used in the United States are derived from plants. Shortages are beginning to occur in some instances and these medicine shortages are directly linked to the decline of forests and vegetation, primarily in South America and Africa.

May 16, 1988
Investment in our young people.

That's the type of investment which will surely pay dividends in the future. Our young people, of course, are our future and I'd like to tell you what some folks are doing to ensure that it is a bright one.

We'll go back to the beginning, which again was the Wayne National Forest's Capitol Christmas Tree project. Many worthwhile programs got their start because of the activities surrounding that event. I suspect that for years we will be tracing the beginnings of many additional programs to good will and public support that surrounded the Capitol Tree project.

When the tree was cut last November, among the 700-plus people in attendance were Roy Palmer -- from Hocking Technical College (HTC); Ron Cornell -- The Ohio Forestry Association; and Jack Haessly - Haessly Hardwood Lumber Co. These three men were very impressed with the entire ceremony and the coordination involved. They were especially impressed with the involvement of the young people who we had helping us out.

Those young people were none other than Calvin Martin's Frontier High School FFA group and Terry Schafer's Forestry Class from the Washington County Career Center. Several other young people, primarily Frontier students, helped out that day, also.

Roy, Jack, and Ron got to thinking that it would be great to take advantage of the Capitol Christmas Tree enthusiasm, do something positive for our youths, and somehow mesh that together with their interest and involvement in forestry and natural resources.

What they came up with was this: Hocking Tech put up $450 and Haessly Hardwood matched that amount. The money is to be used as scholarship funds for students entering Hocking Tech in any of the natural resource fields. The name associated with the awards will be:"Capitol Christmas Tree Scholarships."

Calvin Martin, who has been instrumental in urging his students to enter natural resource work, was able to chip-in $200 from the FFA toward the scholarship fund. The FFA earned that money, and more, from a couple of Wayne National Forest work projects this year.

What came out of this great idea was the awarding of scholarships to three high school seniors, who will be entering Hocking Tech next Fall -- Eric Wagner and Matt Farnsworth of Frontier High, who will be studying Parks and Recreation Management; and Bill Close of the Career Center, who will study Timber Harvesting at HTC.

On May 19 I went to the Capitol Tree site with Roy, Ron, Jack, and Judy Sinnott, who is the Information Director at HTC. There we were joined by Bob Forbes, Frontier High's principal, Calvin, Terry, and the three students, who were each presented with the very first Capitol Christmas Tree scholarships.

The feeling among all those involved is to try to make the scholarship awards an annual event. By so doing it will encourage local kids to further their education -- and further it in the natural resource fields which will be so important to us in this area of the state in future years.

It's another success story spawned by the Capitol Tree ceremony; and everyone who helped us out last fall played a role in making this come about. We thank you, and our young people thank you.

October 24, 1988
*Welcome back to Ohio, Al!

Al Wolter, known to many throughout the Buckeye State, is returning "home" to serve as the Director of Communications for the Wildlife Legislative Fund of America (WLFA), which is based in Columbus.

Wolter recently culminated 29 years of federal employment when he retired as the Deputy Director - Office of Information, U.S. Forest Service, Washington, D.C. He served stints on many of the national forests in the eastern region, including forests in Wisconsin, Minnesota, and Ohio. He also spent a few years working in both Oregon and Utah, among other places.

While in Ohio during the early to mid-1970's, Wolter served as the Ranger for the Wayne National Forest's Ironton District. He became well-known to many Ohioans through his active work in the Outdoor Writers Association, the Society of American Foresters, and other organizations.

Though born and raised in Minnesota, Wolter's roots extend into Ohio. His wife Ann is from Ironton and they have returned to the Buckeye State many times during the past decade to visit and to deer hunt, which is one of Al's passions.

Wolter's skills in communications combined with his lifelong interest in hunting, fishing, and trapping will bode well for his new employer. The WLFA is one of the nation's premier organizations working to defend the rights of outdoor sportsmen.

At every stop in his career Wolter has received awards, including a recent Distinguished Honor Award from the U.S. Secretary of Agriculture for his leadership in helping establish the popular "Take Pride in America" campaign.

I've worked for, and with, Al on several past projects and it's interesting to note that he was one of those on the other end of things when we were planning the Capitol Christmas Tree delivery to the nation's Capitol last year. He was very willing to help us out as much as he could, and he was there when they lit our tree on December 9.

I'm sure you'll come in contact with him if you're interested in Ohio's outdoors. I'm proud to call him my friend, and I certainly look forward to working with him in the future.

*Update on this year's gypsy moth trapping program in and around the Wayne National Forest. Sixty-nine traps were set out in mid-June and they were collected in August and September.

This year, 11 male moths were captured in the pheromone traps, compared with just two in 1987. While no moths were caught on the Ironton District, seven were caught at Athens and four at Marietta.

Those locations were:
Athens – Monday Creek, 1; Snake Ridge, 1; Murray City, 1; Utah Ridge, 2; Sand Run, 2.
Marietta – Fly, 2; Bell Ridge, 2.

This program is part of an ongoing effort to monitor the progress of the gypsy moth as it pushes west from Pennsylvania, Virginia, and West Virginia, where it has devastated acres of oak forests. Research scientists and forest pest management specialists are working at ways to slow down the spread of the destructive insect.

Dave Greenwood of our Marietta office and Art Martin of Athens work closely with those foresters and entomologists who are studying the gypsy moth.

October 31, 1988
*We've welcomed a new employee aboard.

His name is Morgan Beveridge and he comes to us most recently from a Forest Service job on the Shawnee National Forest in Illinois.

But that's not really his home country. Morgan was born and raised in our local area and is a graduate of Woodsfield High School. His wife, Teresa, is from Beallsville in Monroe County and they have one son, Brad, who will be attending Newport Junior High School. Another son, Pete, has graduated from high school and currently works in North Carolina.

Morgan's primary responsibilities will be working with oil and gas operators and special use permittees, those folks who have permits for a variety of things on Wayne National Forest land -- roads, pipelines, hay fields, electric lines, and so on.

Before working in Illinois, Morgan spent about 10 years working at various Forest Service locations in North Carolina, Idaho, and Arizona. He attended Hocking Technical College in Nelsonville, Ohio University, and the University of Arizona.

Morgan is very glad to be back home and we're very glad to have him. Stop and say hello if you get a chance.

*Notes from near and far -

- Guess what activity most people enjoy in a National Forest? Several surveys throughout the country indicate that driving through the forests looking at the scenery is the single, most popular activity. This surprises some people, but when you think about it, it's probably true.

- Talk about irony. The national record Ohio buckeye is located in Kentucky. However, to get even, the national record Kentucky coffeetree is located in, you guessed it, Ohio. Turnabout is fair play, I guess.

- The Superintendent of Yellowstone National Park recently reported that he has issued over 50 permits to various groups and individuals interested in taking photographs and making films since the fires of this past summer. Media inquiries have ranged from National Geographic to Readers

Digest. Good, accurate documentation of the recovery process seems assured.

- The support stand, which braced the butt of our Capitol Christmas tree last year during its shipping to Washington, D.C., is being put to good use once again. We recently loaned it to the Huron-Manistee National Forest in Michigan so they could use it to transport this year's Capitol Tree. After they're done, they'll return the stand.

In subsequent years we'll offer the stand to be used by other National Forests. Each year we'll have an engraved plate attached to the stand indicating which forest and state used it that year. The stand will become a rotating trophy of sorts.

We hope to have the stand put into some sort of permanent display, except for a month or two each winter when it's being used, at the Washington County Career Center. The Welding Class at the Career Center was the group that actually constructed the heavy-duty, adjustable stand, with materials and design coordinated by Roy Wetz - R.O. Wetz Transportation, Ray Johnson - Apache Tank, and Dave Archer - Pioneer Pipe.

It's another lasting memory of the great time we had with the Wayne National Forest's 1987 Capitol Christmas tree.

November 28, 1988
*Thanks for the notes and phone calls about recent columns. We try to keep the subject matter varied, so as to interest as

many of you as possible. Let me know if there are topics you'd like to see covered in the future.

One reader sent along a note about Christmas trees, as a follow-up to the column from a few weeks ago. Seems as though around these parts white pine is the favorite Christmas tree, followed by Scotch pine, Fraser fir, and Norway spruce.

I still favor the Fraser fir, myself, or perhaps a Douglas-fir, but I'll have to admit that the Kincaid family will have a Scotch pine in 1988.

I've never liked white pine for a Christmas tree, primarily because of the long needles (4-5 inches) and somewhat limp limbs. Limp limbs? You know what I mean: They bend easily! But many people love the white pine because of its pleasing scent, excellent needle retention, and soft-textured needles.

Fraser fir and Douglas-fir are sometimes sold interchangeably to the unknowing buyer, although it probably doesn't matter much. Fraser is a true fir and is somewhat uncommon, being native only to the higher elevations of the southern Appalachian Mountains. Douglas-fir is not a true fir species and is native to the Pacific Coast forests and parts of the Rocky Mountains.

The Fraser seems to have a more distinct evergreen aroma than the Douglas, but both keep their needles well. The needles on each species are short and somewhat spruce-like. The Fraser fir has a dark green tint to it, making it easy to identify once you're aware of what to look for.

Norway spruce, a native of Europe but widespread in the U.S. for many years, usually hangs in there at about the fourth or fifth most popular Christmas tree in our area. **This species, you'll recall, is the one which we sent to Washington, D.C. last year as the nation's Capitol Christmas Tree.** It has the short, dark needles that many people prefer, but its major drawback is that it drops needles rapidly. Those who prefer a Norway spruce tend to purchase a balled and burlapped tree, and then plant it in their yard following the holidays.

Which leaves the Scotch pine -- good needle retention, nice color (a blue-green tint), and normally with a full, attractive shape. The needles are stiff and sharp, which some people don't like, and they're about 2-3 inches long. Scotch, too, is an import from northern Europe.

***We've heard from several of you who fondly recalled the hoopla surrounding the 1987 Capitol Christmas tree festivities. Yes, it was a great time. And no, we're not ready to do it again! Not in my lifetime at least. I aged 10 years during 1987.**

Barb Anderson and the folks from the Huron-Manistee National Forest near Cadillac, Michigan have been in frequent contact, with questions about their tree and asking advice about certain things. They seem to be doing a great job up there with the 1988 tree, a balsam fir. Look for it on the national news.

Casimier Wojakowski has also been in touch. He is, once again, directing the cutting operations. He sends his best to all and hopes to visit the Marietta

area in 1989 -- this time as a tourist, not a lumberjack.

The New Matamoras Historical Society's 1989 calendars are very nice, featuring three photos related to the Capitol tree. We have about 15 or 20 of the calendars for sale here at our office on Route 7 in Reno (373-9055). Cost is $4.00 per calendar.

Also, it was very interesting to note the nice write-ups about the Capitol Tree event in the Frontier School District's annual report, which was published in November, 1988. In particular, the FFA, the band, and the chorus played major roles in the success of the overall project.

And one last thing -- John Carson tells me the Frontier Band Boosters are selling small ornaments, which were cut from the actual Capitol Tree itself. You'll recall the main stem of the tree was brought "home" in January specifically for that purpose. Credit Gil Courtney and Roy Wetz for that maneuver. Better contact the boosters for an ornament. They'll probably go like hot cakes.

March 20, 1989

It was just about this time two years ago that I first came to know Barb Hamilton.

The Wayne National Forest had been chosen to furnish the nation's Capitol Christmas Tree for 1987 and we formed a steering committee to help guide us through the project. Barb's name was one of the first recommended to us and she was very eager to assist in any way she could.

Along with her friend Iwana Simon, one of Barb's most important contributions to the Capitol Christmas tree effort was to involve city and county school children in the project. They contacted principals and teachers and before long it seemed as though everyone was doing something--making ornaments, Christmas cards, exhibits, putting on skits and plays, making posters. It was unbelievable. Everything was related to the Capitol tree through the Bicentennial theme.

When we delivered the main tree and several smaller ones to Washington, D.C., boxes of the homemade ornaments, cards, and posters were presented to Ohio's congressional delegation. They were certainly impressed. I remember especially the reactions of Senator Glenn and Congressmen Miller, Applegate, and DeWine.

Barb and Iwana got contests started among the school children and presented awards to the winners during the send-off ceremony at Marietta College. She did much more, too.

She helped arrange for the Marietta High School band to play during the sendoff. She helped make arrangements at the college and with the city. And on two separate Monday mornings she met me bright and early at the People's Bank on Second and Putnam streets to help set up window displays about the Wayne National Forest, the Capitol Christmas tree, and the Bicentennial.

Barb never missed many meetings either, and believe me, there were lots of them. It took the efforts of many people to pull things off and she did more than her share.

With me being a sports fan, especially West Virginia University (WVU) basketball, I obviously had to ask Barb about her husband Scotty's All-American basketball days at WVU. Being a West Virginia native (like Barb and Scotty), I knew that he had been WVU's first basketball All-American and had played high school ball in Grafton, WV. I also knew that Scotty had led WVU to a national (NIT) championship back in the 1940s, when that was the country's premier post-season tournament. Barb was pleased that I knew about those things and never seemed to tire of my questions. That made her even more special to me. I'll never forget those conversations we had.

All of us here were saddened when we heard of Barb's death. We felt we had lost a close friend.

But we are also glad that we had the chance to work with such a kind and caring lady. She helped make Marietta, Washington County, and the surrounding area a better place in which to live.

June 19, 1989
It's been exciting to see all the recent local support for, and interest in, the Wayne National Forest. Several groups and individuals are beginning to see what a positive factor the Wayne can be in many areas -- tourism, quality of life, economics, and recreation opportunities to name just a few.

Recent public meetings in both Monroe and Washington Counties have been generally favorable to the Wayne. Local groups are banding together to work with us on a variety of fronts.

While new projects are being discussed, the groups are also reminding us to not forget things such as providing a stable supply of timber and working to develop more federal oil and gas leases. These two areas generate the majority of our National Forest revenues, 25 percent of which we return to local counties for use on roads and schools. Therefore, timber and minerals projects are very important to the local economy, communities, and school districts. We certainly realize this.

We're also being reminded that in order to maintain local support for National Forest programs that we must continue to work with groups such as the farming community, the volunteer fire departments, and the Sheriff departments. We continually work with these groups trying to resolve as many problems as we can and trying to fulfill our role of being a "good neighbor."

Two groups we've worked with all along have been the county commissioners and township trustees. Their support is essential to our getting any major projects completed. We've worked with them in a variety of areas including road maintenance and reconstruction, sign locations, **the Capitol Christmas Tree project,** and bridge repairs.

A relatively new organization, the Little Muskingum Watershed Association, has formed to work with the Wayne National Forest in protecting the interests of the rural residents in and around the Little Muskingum River valley. Under the able leadership of Gale Eddy, Jack Clift, Calvin Mendenhall, Carl Heinrich, Bill Bowersock, Jim Fleeman, Cary Campbell, Darrell Cline, Gil Courtney, and others, the LMWA is taking an active role in promoting ideas which could be of benefit to local citizens. Many of those ideas revolve around the Wayne National Forest.

In Monroe County, Debbie Highman, Mike Lloyd, Pam Sloan and a host of other energetic people are working very hard on developing recreational, economic, and tourist oriented ideas.

It's all very interesting and worthwhile to be involved with these folks and to see the Wayne National Forest play a key role in helping things develop. I'm sure it won't happen overnight, but with everyone's persistence, I really feel we're on the verge of seeing some exciting things happen.

December 4, 1989

It was interesting to note that the U.S. Capitol Christmas Tree ran into some problems recently. Since the Wayne National Forest furnished the tree in 1987, many local people have followed the event through the newspapers and TV in 1988 and 1989.

In 1988 the Huron-Manistee National Forest in Michigan provided the tree for the nation's capitol. Casimier Wojakowski, the retired lumberjack from the Upper Peninsula of Michigan who traveled to Ohio to direct our cutting operation in 1987, supervised the felling and wrapping of the Michigan tree.

For those of you who remember Casimier and his knowledge, I'm sure it is no surprise that the Michigan event went off just like ours did -- without a hitch.

Another link to Ohio was present at the 1988 cutting, too. It was the heavy duty tree stand, which was built by the

Washington County Career Center's Welding Class, per specifications of Wojakowski and Roy Wetz of R.O. Wetz Transportation in Marietta. The tree stand is used to support the weight from the trunk of these heavy trees as they are shipped to Washington, D.C.

That tree stand is now back in our possession and will soon go back up to the Career Center where it will be displayed. Although it wasn't used for the 1989 tree in Montana, the folks running the 1990 event in Colorado have already contacted me about using the tree stand there.

Casimier will travel to Colorado for the 1990 cutting, also. Each year after the cutting and shipping operations, the tree stand will be returned to the Career Center for display. A label will be attached each year telling which National Forest used the stand. After a few years of traveling around the country, this stand should be quite a "trophy."

Now, back to the problems in 1989. This year's tree, an Engelmann spruce I believe, came from the Kootenai National Forest in Montana. In an unfortunate turn of events, the tree twisted and fell backwards during the cutting operation. Thank goodness no one was injured, but it scared a lot of people as they hurried for cover. Unfortunately, the top 16 feet of the tree broke off as it hit the ground.

The Montana folks, with thousands of back-up trees to choose from, simply went down the road a ways and cut another tree. We wouldn't have had that luxury with our local Norway spruce. That's one reason we were so extra careful with it. An oak or a tulip poplar wouldn't have made a very good back-up Christmas tree.

In retrospect, perhaps the Montana folks could have used Casimier and even our tree stand. Who knows? But his expertise was invaluable to us. And the Colorado folks, after hearing about the Montana debacle, are certainly looking forward to having both Wojakowski and our stand on hand for their 1990 cutting.

September 10, 1990
As the old saying goes, "All good things must end someday."

For me, a couple of good things will soon end. I'll be leaving my job with the Wayne National Forest and our family will be moving to a new area. Although we leave with mixed feelings, since we've grown to love the area so much, there are excellent opportunities ahead for the whole family.

I'll be taking a job with Westvaco Corporation near Paducah, Kentucky. Westvaco is one of the leading manufacturers of paper products in this country. My new position will be public affairs forester for their Timberlands Division in western Kentucky and three surrounding states. Westvaco manages over 230,000 acres of land in that area (Tennessee, Illinois, and Missouri, in addition to Kentucky), as well as operating a modern paper mill at Wickliffe, Kentucky.

Wickliffe is just below Cairo, Illinois, where the Ohio River joins the Mississippi River. We plan on living in Paducah, which is 20 or 30 miles upstream, where the Tennessee River flows into the Ohio. Having grown up in Huntington, West Virginia and living and working in the Marietta-Williamstown area for many years, my wife and I now move to another Ohio River town. There must be a subconscious attraction there somewhere.

As for leaving the U.S. Forest Service, that's not an easy decision to make. Working here on the Wayne National Forest has been an exciting and challenging job. The people of southeastern Ohio, especially Washington and Monroe counties, have been great to work with.

Some of the highlights have been:

-Increasing and adding to the recreation facilities on the forest.

-Working with local groups such as the Little Muskingum Watershed Association and the Southeastern Ohio Oil and Gas Association to ensure that local concerns were not overlooked when setting national forest policies.

-Adding more land to the national forest.

-Working with both counties on new tourism and forest recreation initiatives.

-Working with the media, schools, clubs, organizations, and other agencies to increase the public awareness and identity of the Wayne National Forest.

And, of course, the biggest highlight - for not only us here at the Wayne, but for many, many folks in our area - was the cutting of the U.S. Capitol Christmas Tree in 1987. That event, national in scope, will go down as one of the most remembered events in local history. We were proud to be the guiding force behind that.

We've tried to make the Marietta Unit of the Wayne a model national forest area, both in terms of management and in us being available to serve the public. I hope we've succeeded somewhat because the Marietta Unit has the chance to one day become the shining example of proper multiple-use management for public forest lands in Ohio.

It's been especially nice working with Dave Greenwood and Connie Morris, who have been here about as long as I have, and Lois Severin, Bill Engle, and Robert Florence who aren't far behind.

My family will miss the area, but we'll never forget it. As our emotions fluctuate during the coming days, we'll remember the good times and good friends we had here and know that it will strengthen us as we begin our new lives in Paducah.

So long, everyone.

PHOTOS

Capitol Christmas Tree as it stood in the woods in 1986, just off the banks of the Ohio River along Sheets Run

Dan Kincaid standing in front of the Capitol Christmas Tree a month prior to the cutting

Capitol Christmas Tree as it stood in the woods in the Fall of 1987 a week prior to cutting. Lynn Kantner of Wayne National Forest is seated at lower right pointing to the tree.

OHIO WOODLANDS

Cover of Ohio Forestry Association magazine, which went to all high school libraries in Ohio, Jan. 1988

Capitol Christmas Tree as it stood in front of the U.S. Capitol, December 1987

Capitol Christmas Tree Planning Committee – **Top photo**, L-R, Connie Morris, Marilyn Ortt, Barbara Lovely, Sandy Matthews **Bottom photo**, L-R, Gil Courtney, Iwana Simon, Barb Hamilton (Rear, filming,-Ray Beach)

Christmas cards sold as a fundraising effort. This is the front and inside of the card. On the back it read:
'Designed by Tim McKenzie and Lynn Murel'. Lynn was a Wayne National Forest Wildlife Biologist.

Part of the large crowd at the Cutting Ceremony on 11/20/87

Ceremonial first cut made by Holdren descendants. cousins
Judy Beaver (L) and Sandra Binegar (R), as Casimier
Wojakowski looks on

Crane being positioned prior to final cut

John Kerr examines location to cut off butt log.

Loading the wrapped tree at day's end on 11/20/87

Carlton Oil crew assists with the wrapping of limbs

Dave Greenwood and Art Martin of Wayne National Forest, near day's end on 11/20/87

Forest Service employees at cutting (L-R), Lynn Kantner, Frank Voytas, Connie Morris, Jim Apgar, Terry Hoffman, and Art Martin

Forest Service employees pose with Casimier Wojakowski, 2nd from left, after the loading. (L-R), Dale Newell, Casimier, Connie Morris, Dave Greenwood, Art Martin, Bill Engle, Bob Florence

Dan Kincaid and Casimier Wojakowski congratulate each other on a successful end to the cutting and loading operation

Dan Kincaid and Jean Pickering with one of the signs she painted to be placed on the side of the trailers hauling the Capitol Christmas Tree to Washington, D.C.

One of the signs made by Frontier High School students and faculty to accompany the Capitol Tree to Washington, D.C.

The crowd begins to gather in front of Marietta College's Hermann Fine Arts Center prior to the Send-Off Ceremony on 11/21/87

Marietta High School Band at the Send-Off Ceremony, 11/21/87

Smokey Bear at Send-Off Ceremony, with Ann Wickham, ODNR. front, and Marilyn Ortt, Christmas Tree Planning Committee, rear. Smokey was present at both the cutting and the send-off ceremonies and was a big hit with the many young children present.

Dan presenting Casimier Wojakowski with tokens of appreciation during the Send-Off Ceremony

One example of the many posters, cards, ornaments and other decorations made by school children as class projects in honor of the Capitol Christmas Tree and the Bicentennials of the Northwest Ordinance and the City of Marietta.

Some of the trees stored at the Ohio Division of Forestry Nursery in Reno and slated for Congressional offices and other locations in D.C. awaiting shipment on the Kenmack Lumber trailer on 11/29/87.

Tree arriving on the U.S. Capitol's west lawn on the R.O. Wetz Transportation trailer on 11/30/87.

The Capitol's Landscape Architect, Paul Pincus, arrives to take over responsibility for the tree. Hooray!

Tree arrives at the U.S. Capitol, 11/30/87. (L-R) Bob McElfresh, R.O. Wetz, Teena Sechler, Mack Haessly, U.S. Rep. Clarence Miller, Kenny Haessly, U.S. Rep. Mike DeWine, U.S. Rep. Ralph Regula, U.S. Rep. Doug Applegate and his wife Betty, Dan Kincaid, and Gil Courtney.

L-R, Teena Sechler, Gil Courtney, Dan Kincaid. I remember what Gil said to me in this photo. "Well, pardner, we made it."

L-R, Congressmen Applegate and Miller congratulate Dan Kincaid on the Capitol Christmas Tree project

Bob McElfresh (L), Senior Driver, and R.O. Wetz (R), Owner, R.O. Wetz Transportation in D.C. on 11/30/87

Gil Courtney and Rep. Applegate at lunch in the House Dining Room

Soon after we arrived on 11/30/87, the Capitol Grounds Crew
began unloading the tree.

L-R, Kincaid, Kantner, Sechler, delivering ornaments and office tree to Cong. Miller on 12/1/87

Delivering office tree 12/1/87 (L-R). Deputy USDA Sec'y Peter Myers, Sechler, Kantner, Kincaid, Assoc. Chief U.S. Forest Service, George Leonard

L-R, Lynn Kantner, Dan Kincaid, Teena Sechler, Senator John Glenn. Delivering ornaments and office trees on 12/1/87. Sen. Glenn was extremely pleased with the hand-made ornaments from Ohio school children. He sent me this photo a couple of weeks after the visit.

During a visit with Asst. USDA Sec'y Wilmer "Vinegar Bend" Mizell prior to the 12/9/87 Lighting Ceremony in D.C.

(Mizell was a former major league baseball pitcher for the St. Louis Cardinals and Pittsburgh Pirates. He was a two-time All-Star and pitched for the 1960 World Champion Pirates. Former Wayne National Forest Ironton District Ranger Al Wolter worked in the Washington Office of the Forest Service and pre-arranged this meeting so that Mizell could autograph an old baseball card that I had brought along with me.)

The Kincaid's: (L-R) wife, Vicki; daughter, Shannon; son, Brent; and myself on 12/9/87 in the office of the Secretary of Agriculture. (Oldest son Jeff was in college taking final exams and was unable to be with us on this trip.)

Senate or House Dining Room tree (unsure which) and supplied by either Mabel Howell of Athens or Norman Johnson of Monroe County.

In the far corner of the USDA Patio is a Norway spruce supplied by Diane and Luke Arnold of Oak Grove (Marietta)

USDA Office, Colorado blue spruce, supplied by Jess Latimer of Marietta

A Fraser fir in the office of the Chief, U.S. Forest Service.
It was supplied by the Ohio Christmas Tree Growers
Association and was one of about 30 trees transported
to D.C. on the Kenmack Lumber truck and trailer.

Mary Carson of New Matamoras singing the National Anthem during the Lighting Ceremony on 12/9/87.

Marietta Mayor Nancy Hollister delivering a short speech at the Lighting Ceremony on 12/9/87.

(L-R) Speaker of the House Jim Wright, who flipped the switch to light the tree; Marietta Mayor Nancy Hollister; and Ohio Governor Richard Celeste.

Forest Service employees at the Lighting Ceremony: L-R, Frank Voytas, Dan Kincaid, Teena Sechler, Terry Hoffman, and Jim Apgar.

The official photos of the lit tree were taken from the other side of the tree, looking back east toward the Capitol. I took this one from the Capitol steps looking west toward the Washington Monument. The photo may not be of the same quality as those of the official photographers, but it does offer a different vantage point.

We attended a reception in the office of Senator John Glenn
following the Lighting Ceremony. He told my daughter Shannon
that he would send a photo of himself during his astronaut days
to her and her two brothers. And he did!

When Wetz Transportation brought the butt logs back from
D.C. to Marietta, Mack Haessly sawed them into boards. Then,
Jack Haessly dried them in his kiln (above) and planed them
before we got several boards that we edged and made into
plaques to distribute to those who had assisted with the project.

Sample of one of the (horizontal) plaques that we gave to
volunteers who had helped us.

This was another one of the (vertical) plaques we distributed. Some were vertical and some were horizontal depending upon the various cuts that we made on the final boards. The labels were made for us by Zide's Sport Shop in Marietta. The tree outlines were branded into the wood by Art Nicholson of our office in Reno. Those who have these plaques have an actual piece of the original tree.

One of the few thousand ornaments made by school children in Washington County and other southeastern Ohio counties in honor of the 1987 Capitol Christmas Tree and the Bicentennial celebrations of both the Northwest Ordinance (1787-1987) and the City of Marietta (1788-1988).

A local elementary school student dropped this off for me at the office one day a few months after the cutting ceremony. I wasn't there that day, unfortunately, and they didn't leave their name; but I have kept this ever since.

Top photo, Certificate given to all who helped with the event.
Bottom photo, one of the 4" square glass ornaments made by Casto Glass (against a gray background)

One of the round ornaments made by Casto Glass and sold as part of the fundraising efforts surrounding the 1987 Capitol Christmas Tree event.

The three-piece set of glass canisters made by Fenton Glass and sold as one of the fundraising efforts for the event. The jars stood 6", 8", and 10" tall and sold for $20 a set. We also sold them individually for $7.50, $8.00, and $8.50 respectively.

Creighton Sports Center of New Matamoras sold several versions of both sweatshirts and T-shirts commemorating the events. This one read "Capitol Christmas Tree, 1987, New Matamoras, Ohio" and featured the tree in the forest prior to cutting. They could word it just about any way you wanted it, related to the cutting, send off, and lighting ceremonies.

This T-shirt, produced by Creighton Sports Center, featured the lighting ceremony in Washington, D.C. It read "Capitol Christmas Tree, I was there, Wayne National Forest, N.W. Territory Bicentennial, New Matamoras, Ohio." In small print just under the Capitol dome it listed the time and date of the tree lighting - 5:24 P.M., December 9, 1987.

<u>Photo Credits</u> – Author's Note: All of the photos in this section are courtesy of various government sources.
-I took the photos on pages 332, 334, and 335 (this last one was the January 1988 cover of Ohio Woodlands magazine.)
-Lynn Kantner took the photos on pages 333 and 337.
- The photo on p.336 was sent to me by the office of the Architect of the Capitol (AOC).
- Photos on pages 339-351 were taken by Dan Kincaid, Lynn Kantner, or Dale Newell of Wayne National Forest.
- Page 352 by AOC.
-Page 353 (top) by Cong. Miller's staff with my camera.
-Page 353 (bottom) and p. 355 by Al Wolter (USFS).
-Page 354 by Sen. Glenn's staff.
-Page 356 by USDA receptionist with my camera.
-Pages 357-359 by AOC.
-Pages 360-362 by Dan or Vicki Kincaid.
-Page 363 supplied by Senator Glenn's office.
-Pages 364-372 and p. 338 by Dan Kincaid.

<u>NOTE</u> – Walking around the various offices in D.C. we discovered that some of our trees were set up in different locations than we originally thought they would be. For instance, if we thought a local donated tree was going to go to the House Dining Room, it may have ended up in the Secretary of Agriculture's lobby. I never did find out if the Capitol grounds crew just delivered them to the wrong locations or whether the Landscape Architect changed locations based on species or size. I guess it didn't really matter; the trees were all still used and enjoyed by the various recipients in D.C.

REFERENCES

My applicable weekly newspaper columns written between 1979 and 1990.

Various websites of the U.S. Forest Service, the Architect of the Capitol, and the U.S. Department of Agriculture.

Articles, stories, and reports from a multitude of outlets, all referenced in the body of this book.

Conversations with Gil Courtney, Teena Sechler, Lynn Kantner, and others.

And to ensure that I had not left out anything important, I reviewed video tapes given to me by Brian Brooks and Dean Beaver. These primarily covered the cutting, send-off, and lighting ceremonies.

The video tape, **The Capitol Christmas Tree**. The script was written by Lynn Kantner – Wayne National Forest; video produced by her son, Ray Beach, with some film footage taken by her other son, Cullen Beach. I did the narration from Lynn's written script.

OTHER BOOKS BY DAN KINCAID

1-***The Penicillin Kids***, the 1966 West Virginia Class AA State Basketball Champions, copyright 2015.

2-***Your.....Wayne National Forest, Vol.I***, a historical collection of the author's weekly Ohio newspaper columns from 1981 and 1982, copyright 2016.

3-***Your.....Chattahoochee National Forest***, a historical collection of the author's weekly Georgia newspaper columns from December 1978 – June 1980, copyright 2016.

4-***Kade Holley, Forest Ranger, Vol.I***, fictional accounts of Kade's adventures on National Forests in Minnesota, Ohio, North Carolina, and Washington, copyright 2017.

5-***Your.....Wayne National Forest, Vol.II***, a historical collection of the author's weekly Ohio newspaper columns from 1983-1986, copyright 2017.

6-***Your.....Wayne National Forest, Vol.III***, a historical collection of the author's weekly Ohio newspaper columns from 1987-1990, copyright 2018.

7-***Kade Holley, Forest Ranger, Vol.II***, fictional accounts of Kade's adventures on National Forests in Georgia, West Virginia, Minnesota, Ohio, and Colorado, copyright 2018.

All books are available at Amazon.com, Booksamillion.com, and Barnesandnoble.com

Author Bio – Dan Kincaid

Dan Kincaid had a 31-year career with the U.S. Forest Service, working from 1981 – 1990 at the Marietta Unit on Ohio's Wayne National Forest (WNF), where he coordinated the effort to supply the U.S. Capitol Christmas Tree in 1987. Kincaid also worked at other national forest locations during his career - in West Virginia, Ohio, Minnesota, Georgia, and North Carolina, as well as temporary details, training and various other assignments in Colorado, Kentucky, California, Indiana, Michigan, Washington, Montana, and Tennessee. He also spent several years with the Forest Service's State & Private Forestry branch, working as federal liaison representative on cooperative projects with state forestry agencies in New Jersey, Delaware, Pennsylvania, Maryland, West Virginia, Ohio, and the District of Columbia.

After retirement in his final position as a District Ranger on WNF's Athens, Ohio District in 2006, Kincaid worked another six years for state forestry agencies in West Virginia and Ohio and two years as a contractor for the Wayne National Forest in Ohio. Earlier in his career he spent 2 ½ years in Wickliffe, Kentucky as Public Affairs Forester with Westvaco Corporation, a leading manufacturer of paper and paper products.

Kincaid received a Bachelors of Science degree in Forest Resource Management from West Virginia University, a

Masters degree in Forestry/Environmental Management from Duke University, and a Teaching Certification for Biology and General Science, Grades 7 – 12, from Marietta College in Ohio.

From 1978 to 1990 Kincaid wrote a weekly newspaper column about forestry and the Forest Service for various newspapers in Ohio and Georgia. In addition, for 5 ½ years (1985-90), he wrote a separate weekly hunting/fishing column for The Marietta Times daily newspaper in Ohio and served as a sportswriter/columnist for games, events and activities in a two-state, multi-county area. He has had over 1,000 columns and stories published under his by-line. This is his eighth published book.

Kincaid also served as a Public Information Officer for both federal and state agencies, a Fire Information Officer, and gave numerous presentations to natural resource professionals on public relations and the media. He has written hundreds of news releases, ads, speeches, text for pamphlets/brochures, and other related items.

Since 2014, Kincaid and his wife have lived in The Villages, Florida, where he enjoys playing softball, billiards, walking, writing, attending various club meetings; and, most of all, they enjoy the warm winter temperatures with no snow.